Investing Online For Du...

Cheat Sheet

Buying Investments

- **If possible, minimize fees.** See Invest-O-Rama (`www.investorama.com`) and Mutual Fund Interactive (`interactive.com`) for listings of no-load funds.
- **Buy shares directly from the company.** For a listing of companies that sell stock directly to the public, refer to `nt1.irin.com/sdi/offering.cfm`. For more information, see Net Stock Direct (`www.netstockdirect.com`).
- **Maximize your returns with Dividend Reinvestment Programs (DRIPs).** Online sources for information about DRIPs include DRIP Investor (`www.dripinvestor.com`) and Motley Fool (`www.fool.com/school/drips.htm`).
- **Pay the lowest brokerage fees available by trading online.** For a listing of electronic brokers and their services, see Cyberinvest (`www.cyberinvest.com`). For a quarterly ranking of online brokerages, see Gomez Advisors at Quote.Com (`www.quote.com`.)

Monitoring Investments

- **Use online portfolio management tools.** Check out Portfolio Tracker, at Reuter's Moneynet (`www.moneynet.com`), and the *Wall Street Journal* Interactive Edition (`www.wsj.com`).
- **Keep current.** Have the news sent to your e-mailbox from such online sources as InfoBeat (`www.infobeat.com`) and *The Economist* (`www.economist.com`), which sends you its free weekly wrap-up.
- **Watch for new investment opportunities.** Join a mailing list or an investment chat group, or search for new opportunities using Web sources such as Alert IPO! (`www.ostman.com/alert-ipo`) and IPO Interactive (`www.fedil.com/ipo/index.html`).

Selling Investments

- **Know when to hold and when to fold.** Beginning investors can gain valuable insights from such sources as Investorguide (`www.investorguide.com`) and Investor FAQ (`www.investor-faq.com`).
- **Minimize your trading.** If you can't resist trading online, join a free simulation such as Investment Club (`www.investmentclub.com`).

Cheat Sheet $2.95 value. Item 0336-7.

For more information about IDG Books, call 1-800-762-2974.

...For Dummies: #1 Computer Book Series for Beginners

Investing Online For Dummies®

Cheat Sheet

Getting Started

1. **Know your starting point.** Determine your net worth by using the online worksheets at E-Analytics (www.e-analytics.com) and Altamira-Resource Center (www.altamira.com.icat/toolbox/netcalc.html).

2. **Understand how much you can invest.** Use the online calculators at the Fountain (www.tmx.com/fountain/webwkpg1.htm) and FinanCenter (www.financenter.com).

3. **Determine your risk tolerance level.** Vanguard's online financial profile tool (majestic1.vanguard.com/RRC/DA/0.1.32) can help you decide how much risk you can take.

4. **Allocate your assets.** Bank of America Investment Services has a tool to help you determine how much of your personal wealth should be in cash, mutual funds, stocks, and bonds (www.bankamerica.com/tools/sri_assetall.html).

Investment Analysis

1. **Check out the economic landscape.** For economic data, use online sources such as GSA Government Information Locator Service (www.gsa.gov) and Federal Reserve Sites (www.cpcug.org/user/invest).

2. **Use mutual fund and stock screens.** Web sites such as Investor Square (www.investorsquare.com), Microsoft Investor (investor.msn.com/home.asp), and Quicken (www.quicken.com) offer online tools to help you screen investment candidates.

3. **Read the mutual fund's prospectus.** Internet sources for mutual fund prospectuses include EDGAR for Mutual Funds (edgar.stern.nyu.edu/mutual.html) and the Mutual Fund Resource Center (www.fundmaster.com).

4. **Analyze the company's annual report.** Online sources of company annual reports include EDGAR (www.sec.gov) and the Web sites of many firms. See Web 100 (www.web100) for links to the Internet's 100 most popular company sites.

5. **Do your homework.** For insights into a company's competitive environment, use such resources as Silicon Investor (www.techstocks.com) and Zacks Investment Research (www.zacks.com).

6. **Find out what the experts are saying about your investment selection.** Start with *Research Magazine* (www.researchmag.com), Standard & Poor's Enhanced Stock Report (www.stockinfo.standardpoor.com), and NRM Capital (www.nrmcapital.com).

7. **Understand the tax implications of your investment selections.** For information about tax-exempt mutual funds and municipal bonds, you can turn to many online sources, including Quote.Com Street Pricing (www.quote.com) and CBS MarketWatch — Super Star Funds (www.marketwatch.com/funds).

...For Dummies: #1 Computer Book Series for Beginners

INVESTING ONLINE
FOR
DUMMIES®

INVESTING ONLINE FOR DUMMIES®

by Kathleen Sindell

Foreword by Charles R. Schwab

IDG Books Worldwide, Inc.
An International Data Group Company

Foster City, CA ♦ Chicago, IL ♦ Indianapolis, IN ♦ Southlake, TX

Investing Online For Dummies®

Published by
IDG Books Worldwide, Inc.
An International Data Group Company
919 E. Hillsdale Blvd.
Suite 400
Foster City, CA 94404
www.idgbooks.com (IDG Books Worldwide Web site)
www.dummies.com (Dummies Press Web site)

Library of Congress Catalog Card No.: 98-70128

ISBN: 0-7645-0336-7

Printed in the United States of America

10 9 8 7 6 5 4 3 2 1

1B/QW/QT/ZY/IN

Distributed in the United States by IDG Books Worldwide, Inc.

Distributed by Macmillan Canada for Canada; by Transworld Publishers Limited in the United Kingdom; by IDG Norge Books for Norway; by IDG Sweden Books for Sweden; by Woodslane Pty. Ltd. for Australia; by Woodslane Enterprises Ltd. for New Zealand; by Longman Singapore Publishers Ltd. for Singapore, Malaysia, Thailand, and Indonesia; by Simron Pty. Ltd. for South Africa; by Toppan Company Ltd. for Japan; by Distribuidora Cuspide for Argentina; by Livraria Cultura for Brazil; by Ediciencia S.A. for Ecuador; by Addison-Wesley Publishing Company for Korea; by Ediciones ZETA S.C.R. Ltda. for Peru; by WS Computer Publishing Corporation, Inc., for the Philippines; by Unalis Corporation for Taiwan; by Contemporanea de Ediciones for Venezuela; by Computer Book & Magazine Store for Puerto Rico; by Express Computer Distributors for the Caribbean and West Indies. Authorized Sales Agent: Anthony Rudkin Associates for the Middle East and North Africa.

For general information on IDG Books Worldwide's books in the U.S., please call our Consumer Customer Service department at 800-762-2974. For reseller information, including discounts and premium sales, please call our Reseller Customer Service department at 800-434-3422.

For information on where to purchase IDG Books Worldwide's books outside the U.S., please contact our International Sales department at 650-655-3200 or fax 650-655-3295.

For information on foreign language translations, please contact our Foreign & Subsidiary Rights department at 650-655-3021 or fax 650-655-3281.

For sales inquiries and special prices for bulk quantities, please contact our Sales department at 650-655-3200 or write to the address above.

For information on using IDG Books Worldwide's books in the classroom or for ordering examination copies, please contact our Educational Sales department at 800-434-2086 or fax 817-251-8174.

For press review copies, author interviews, or other publicity information, please contact our Public Relations department at 650-655-3000 or fax 650-655-3299.

For authorization to photocopy items for corporate, personal, or educational use, please contact Copyright Clearance Center, 222 Rosewood Drive, Danvers, MA 01923, or fax 978-750-4470.

is a trademark under exclusive license to IDG Books Worldwide, Inc., from International Data Group, Inc.

About the Author

Kathleen Sindell has more than 20 years of financial services experience and is the founder of a firm that provides management consulting to the financial services industry. She is the former Associate Director of the Financial Management and Commercial Real Estate Programs for the University of Maryland, University College Graduate School of Management & Technology.

Dr. Sindell recently completed *A Hands-On Guide to Mortgage Banking Internet Sites,* a separate directory published by *Mortgage Banking* magazine (July 1997). She is the author of *The Handbook of Real Estate Lending* (Irwin Professional Publishing, 1996), and she edited a book titled the *Essentials of Financial Management Kit* (Dryden Press, 1993).

Dr. Sindell developed the *Lending Solutions Decision Support Program* to identify, assess, monitor, and mitigate the credit quality of real estate loans. This software application is based on her hands-on experience as a Real Estate Vice President for American Savings & Loan and as the Construction Lending Services Manager for Perpetual Federal Savings Bank.

Dr. Sindell has taught 19 graduate-level courses in financial management, she lectures for the New York Institute of Finance (owned by Prentice Hall), and she is a well-known speaker for regional and national conferences. Dr. Sindell is on the adjunct faculty of the Johns Hopkins University School of Continuing Studies, where she teaches graduate-level financial management courses. She has provided seminars to senior bank examiners from the Federal Reserve and various other regulatory agencies.

She received a B.A. in Business from Antioch University, an MBA with a concentration in finance from the California State University at San Jose, and a Ph.D. in Administration and Management from Walden University, Institute for Advanced Studies.

Dr. Sindell lives and writes in Alexandria, Virginia. She is interested in your comments about this book and can be contacted at
ksindell@ix.netcom.com.

ABOUT IDG BOOKS WORLDWIDE

Welcome to the world of IDG Books Worldwide.

IDG Books Worldwide, Inc., is a subsidiary of International Data Group, the world's largest publisher of computer-related information and the leading global provider of information services on information technology. IDG was founded more than 25 years ago and now employs more than 8,500 people worldwide. IDG publishes more than 275 computer publications in over 75 countries (see listing below). More than 60 million people read one or more IDG publications each month.

Launched in 1990, IDG Books Worldwide is today the #1 publisher of best-selling computer books in the United States. We are proud to have received eight awards from the Computer Press Association in recognition of editorial excellence and three from *Computer Currents'* First Annual Readers' Choice Awards. Our best-selling *...For Dummies*® series has more than 30 million copies in print with translations in 30 languages. IDG Books Worldwide, through a joint venture with IDG's Hi-Tech Beijing, became the first U.S. publisher to publish a computer book in the People's Republic of China. In record time, IDG Books Worldwide has become the first choice for millions of readers around the world who want to learn how to better manage their businesses.

Our mission is simple: Every one of our books is designed to bring extra value and skill-building instructions to the reader. Our books are written by experts who understand and care about our readers. The knowledge base of our editorial staff comes from years of experience in publishing, education, and journalism — experience we use to produce books for the '90s. In short, we care about books, so we attract the best people. We devote special attention to details such as audience, interior design, use of icons, and illustrations. And because we use an efficient process of authoring, editing, and desktop publishing our books electronically, we can spend more time ensuring superior content and spend less time on the technicalities of making books.

You can count on our commitment to deliver high-quality books at competitive prices on topics you want to read about. At IDG Books Worldwide, we continue in the IDG tradition of delivering quality for more than 25 years. You'll find no better book on a subject than one from IDG Books Worldwide.

IDG BOOKS WORLDWIDE

John Kilcullen
CEO
IDG Books Worldwide, Inc.

Steven Berkowitz
President and Publisher
IDG Books Worldwide, Inc.

*Eighth Annual
Computer Press
Awards ≥1992*

*Ninth Annual
Computer Press
Awards ≥1993*

*Tenth Annual
Computer Press
Awards ≥1994*

*Eleventh Annual
Computer Press
Awards ≥1995*

IDG Books Worldwide, Inc., is a subsidiary of International Data Group, the world's largest publisher of computer-related information and the leading global provider of information services on information technology. International Data Group publishes over 275 computer publications in over 75 countries. Sixty million people read one or more International Data Group publications each month. International Data Group's publications include: **ARGENTINA:** Buyer's Guide, Computerworld Argentina, PC World Argentina; **AUSTRALIA:** Australian Macworld, Australian PC World, Australian Reseller News, Computerworld, IT Casebook, Network World, Publish, Webmaster; **AUSTRIA:** Computerwelt Osterreich, Networks Austria, PC Tip Austria; **BANGLADESH:** PC World Bangladesh; **BELARUS:** PC World Belarus; **BELGIUM:** Data News; **BRAZIL:** Annuário de Informática, Computerworld, Connections, Macworld, PC Player, PC World, Publish, Reseller News, Supergamepower; **BULGARIA:** Computerworld Bulgaria, Network World Bulgaria, PC & MacWorld Bulgaria; **CANADA:** CIO Canada, Client/Server World, ComputerWorld Canada, InfoWorld Canada, NetworkWorld Canada, WebWorld; **CHILE:** Computerworld Chile, PC World Chile; **COLOMBIA:** Computerworld Colombia, PC World Colombia; **COSTA RICA:** PC World Centro America; **THE CZECH AND SLOVAK REPUBLICS:** Computerworld Czechoslovakia, Macworld Czech Republic, PC World Czechoslovakia; **DENMARK:** Communications World Danmark, Computerworld Danmark, Macworld Danmark, PC World Danmark, Techworld Denmark; **DOMINICAN REPUBLIC:** PC World Republica Dominicana; **ECUADOR:** PC World Ecuador; **EGYPT:** Computerworld Middle East, PC World Middle East; **EL SALVADOR:** PC World Centro America; **FINLAND:** MikroPC, Tietoverkko, Tietoviikko; **FRANCE:** Distributique, Hebdo, Info PC, Le Monde Informatique, Macworld, Reseaux & Telecoms, WebMaster France; **GERMANY:** Computer Partner, Computerwoche, Computerwoche Extra, Computerwoche FOCUS, Global Online, Macwelt, PC Welt; **GREECE:** Amiga Computing, GamePro Greece, Multimedia World; **GUATEMALA:** PC World Centro America; **HONDURAS:** PC World Centro America; **HONG KONG:** Computerworld Hong Kong, PC World Hong Kong, Publish in Asia; **HUNGARY:** ABCD CD-ROM, Computerworld Szamitastechnika, Internetto online Magazine, PC World Hungary, PC-X Magazin Hungary; **ICELAND:** Tolvuheimur PC World Island; **INDIA:** Information Communications World, Information Systems Computerworld; **INDONESIA:** InfoKomputer PC World, Komputek Computerworld, Publish in Asia; **IRELAND:** ComputerScope, PC Live!; **ISRAEL:** Macworld Israel, People & Computers/Computerworld; **ITALY:** Computerworld Italia, Macworld Italia, Networking Italia, PC World Italia; **JAPAN:** DTP World, Macworld Japan, Nikkei Personal Computing, OS/2 World Japan, SunWorld Japan, Windows NT World, Windows World Japan; **KENYA:** PC World East African; **KOREA:** Hi-Tech Information, Macworld Korea, PC World Korea; **MACEDONIA:** PC World Macedonia; **MALAYSIA:** Computerworld Malaysia, PC World Malaysia, Publish in Asia; **MALTA:** PC World Malta; **MEXICO:** Computerworld Mexico, PC World Mexico; **MYANMAR:** PC World Myanmar; **NETHERLANDS:** Computer! Totaal, LAN Internetworking Magazine, LAN World Buyers Guide, Macworld Netherlands, Net, WebWereld; **NEW ZEALAND:** Absolute Beginners Guide and Plain & Simple Series, Computer Buyer, Computer Industry Directory, Computerworld New Zealand, MTB, Network World, PC World New Zealand; **NICARAGUA:** PC World Centro America; **NORWAY:** Computerworld Norge, CW Rapport, Datamagasinet, Financial Rapport, Kursguide Norge, Macworld Norge, Multimediaworld Norge, PC World Ekspress Norge, PC World Nettverk, PC World Norge, PC World ProduktGuide Norge; **PAKISTAN:** Computerworld Pakistan; **PANAMA:** PC World Panama; **PEOPLE'S REPUBLIC OF CHINA:** China Computer Users, China Computerworld, China InfoWorld, China Telecom World Weekly, Computer & Communication, Electronic Design China, Electronics Today, Electronics Weekly, Game Software, PC World China, Popular Computer Week, Software Weekly, Software World, Telecom World; **PERU:** Computerworld Peru, PC World Profesional Peru, PC World SoHo Peru; **PHILIPPINES:** Click!, Computerworld Philippines, PC World Philippines, Publish in Asia; **POLAND:** Computerworld Poland, Computerworld Special Report Poland, Cyber, Macworld Poland, Networld Poland, PC World Komputer; **PORTUGAL:** Cerebro/PC World, Computerworld/Correio Informático, Dealer World Portugal, Mac*In/PC*In Portugal, Multimedia World; **PUERTO RICO:** PC World Puerto Rico; **ROMANIA:** Computerworld Romania, PC World Romania, Telecom Romania; **RUSSIA:** Computerworld Russia, Mir PK, Publish, Seti; **SINGAPORE:** Computerworld Singapore, PC World Singapore, Publish in Asia; **SLOVENIA:** Monitor; **SOUTH AFRICA:** Computing SA, Network World SA, Software World SA; **SPAIN:** Communicaciones World España, Computerworld España, Dealer World España, Macworld España, PC World España; **SRI LANKA:** Infolink PC World; **SWEDEN:** CAP&Design, Computer Sweden, Corporate Computing Sweden, Internetworld Sweden, it.branschen, Macworld Sweden, MaxiData Sweden, MikroDatorn, Natverk & Kommunikation, PC World Sweden, PCaktiv, Windows World Sweden; **SWITZERLAND:** Computerworld Schweiz, Macworld Schweiz, PCtip; **TAIWAN:** Computerworld Taiwan, Macworld Taiwan, NEW ViSiON/Publish, PC World Taiwan, Windows World Taiwan; **THAILAND:** Publish in Asia, Thai Computerworld; **TURKEY:** Computerworld Turkiye, Macworld Turkiye, Network World Turkiye, PC World Turkiye; **UKRAINE:** Computerworld Kiev, Multimedia World Ukraine, PC World Ukraine; **UNITED KINGDOM:** Acorn User UK, Amiga Action UK, Amiga Computing UK, Apple Talk UK, Computing, Macworld, Parents and Computers UK, PC Advisor, PC Home, PSX Pro, The WEB; **UNITED STATES:** Cable in the Classroom, CIO Magazine, Computerworld, DOS World, Federal Computer Week, GamePro Magazine, InfoWorld, I-Way, Macworld, Network World, PC Games, PC World, Publish, Video Event, THE WEB Magazine, and WebMaster; online webzines: JavaWorld, NetscapeWorld, and SunWorld Online; **URUGUAY:** InfoWorld Uruguay; **VENEZUELA:** Computerworld Venezuela, PC World Venezuela; and **VIETNAM:** PC World Vietnam.   3/24/97

Dedication

To my husband, Ivan Sindell. His enthusiasm added a lot to this work.

Author's Acknowledgments

My thanks to Ellen Camm, senior acquisitions editor, for recruiting me into the fold of IDG Books Worldwide. Thanks to my literary agent, Carole McClendon, and her staff for all the encouragement and support. My appreciation to John Pont for being a great coach and a wonderful project editor. His insights and attention to detail were a driving force in the creation of this book. Thanks also to Christy Beck for her fine editing. My appreciation to everyone who worked behind the scenes, especially all the people who are listed on the credits page. Thank you for making this book happen.

My thanks to son-in-law and research assistant, Richard Blegen. He helped round up all the copyright permissions and contributed to making the companion CD-ROM great (along with the hard work of Joell Smith, Heather Dismore, Joyce Pepple, and their colleagues in IDG's media development group).

And finally, my thanks to the folks who put investing information online for the public. They have changed the financial community forever.

Publisher's Acknowledgments

We're proud of this book; please register your comments through our IDG Books Worldwide Online Registration Form located at http://my2cents.dummies.com.

Some of the people who helped bring this book to market include the following:

Acquisitions, Development, and Editorial

Project Editor: John W. Pont

Acquisitions Editor: Ellen Camm

Media Development Manager: Joyce Pepple

Permissions Editor: Heather H. Dismore

Senior Copy Editor: Christine Meloy Beck

Technical Editor: Adam B. Bergman

Editorial Manager: Mary C. Corder

Editorial Assistants: Donna Love,
    Michael D. Sullivan

Production

Project Coordinators: Sherry Gomoll,
    Regina Snyder

Layout and Graphics: Lou Boudreau,
    Linda M. Boyer, J. Tyler Connor,
    Angela F. Hunckler, Todd Klemme, Anna
    Rohrer, Brent Savage, Janet Seib,
    M. Anne Sipahimalani, Deirdre Smith,
    Michael A. Sullivan

Proofreaders: Christine Berman, Kelli Botta,
    Michelle Croninger, Betty Kish, Nancy Price,
    Rebecca Senninger, Janet M. Withers

Indexer: Lynnzee Elze Spense

Special Help

Suzanne Thomas, Associate Editor;
Joell Smith, Associate Technical Editor;
Carmen Krikorian, Associate Permissions Editor

General and Administrative

IDG Books Worldwide, Inc.: John Kilcullen, CEO; Steven Berkowitz, President and Publisher

IDG Books Technology Publishing: Brenda McLaughlin, Senior Vice President and
    Group Publisher

Dummies Technology Press and Dummies Editorial: Diane Graves Steele, Vice President and
    Associate Publisher; Mary Bednarek, Director of Acquisitions and Product Development;
    Kristin A. Cocks, Editorial Director

Dummies Trade Press: Kathleen A. Welton, Vice President and Publisher; Kevin Thornton,
    Acquisitions Manager

IDG Books Production for Dummies Press: Beth Jenkins Roberts, Production Director;
    Cindy L. Phipps, Manager of Project Coordination, Production Proofreading, and
    Indexing; Kathie S. Schutte, Supervisor of Page Layout; Shelley Lea, Supervisor of Graphics
    and Design; Debbie J. Gates, Production Systems Specialist; Robert Springer, Supervisor
    of Proofreading; Debbie Stailey, Special Projects Coordinator; Tony Augsburger,
    Supervisor of Reprints and Bluelines; Leslie Popplewell, Media Archive Coordinator

Dummies Packaging and Book Design: Patti Crane, Packaging Specialist; Kavish + Kavish,
    Cover Design

♦

The publisher would like to give special thanks to Patrick J. McGovern,
without whom this book would not have been possible.

♦

Contents at a Glance

Cartoons at a Glance

By Rich Tennant

page 9

page D-1

page 155

page 71

page 231

page 269

Fax: 978-546-7747 • E-mail: the5wave@tiac.net

Table of Contents

Foreword

- -

Smart, forward-thinking investors have a new partner — the Internet. Along with delivering travel information, sports scores, breaking news, and online shopping, the Internet provides some of the best financial tools and resources available. Such Internet resources can assist you in determining your investment objectives, deciding how to allocate your personal wealth, and obtaining high-level performance data for mutual funds, stocks, and bonds. In addition to providing online trading and tracking of your investments, the Internet allows you to do all this rationally, effectively, and faster than ever before.

Internet resources can provide the knowledge you need for getting the edge on investors who rely on paper-based publications. As an online investor, you have the time to plan intelligently, get the facts you need quickly, and make high-level investment decisions.

Although you can find lots of investing information out there on the Internet, not all of it is trustworthy. You may need some direction on using the Internet. What's required is more than a directory (although this book shows you some of the best Internet investment tools, links, and resources). You may need expert guidance as you apply Internet tools to your personal financial problem-solving efforts. And that's just what you can find in *Investing Online For Dummies*.

Investing Online For Dummies provides clear instructions and ample illustrations so that you don't get lost in cyberspace. The author, Dr. Kathleen Sindell, draws on her considerable experience as the Financial Management Program director for the University of Maryland, University College Graduate School of Management & Technology. She also draws from her experience from her lectures for the New York Institute of Finance and from the graduate-level financial management courses she teaches for the Johns Hopkins University, School of Continuing Studies. She has organized this book to be a comprehensive guide to online investing that explains the basics and shows how to build wealth for investors of all ages and income levels.

While you're gathering the tools you require for becoming a successful online investor, please visit Schwab's Web site at www.schwab.com or one of our 270 branch offices throughout the United States. At Schwab, our goal is to bring you the latest in interactive computer technology and information delivery systems to meet the specialized needs of online investors. We can assist you in managing your trading and account services online. You'll enjoy the security and reliability that comes with trading with the acknowledged leader in electronic brokerage.

Whether you access your account in person, over the telephone, through the Web, or through our StreetSmart software, Schwab gives you everything you need to manage your investments online — including real-time quotes, news and research, interactive planning tools, and trading at some of Schwab's lowest commission rates.

Charles R. Schwab
Chairman of the Board
The Charles Schwab Corporation

Introduction

*W*elcome to *Investing Online For Dummies.* The Internet offers an astounding amount of financial information, and *Investing Online For Dummies* provides clear instructions and ample illustrations so that you don't get lost in cyberspace. With the assistance of this book, you can develop personalized investment strategies and start investing online.

Plenty of books are available about online investing, but most assume that you are a practiced investor who enjoys talking in "Wall Street-speak." This book is different; it doesn't include statements like "Our goal is to maximize after-tax returns at a controlled risk level" or "Even though the stock has done well, it remains cheap at midyear, trading at 40 cents on the dollar of net worth and a third of the market's P/E." In other words, this book is a comprehensive guide to online investing that explains the basics and shows how to build wealth for beginning investors of all ages and income levels.

Investing Online For Dummies shows you how to get started, what you really need to know, and where to go on the Internet for additional information. You don't need to memorize complex commands or formulas. I describe everything in plain English, and I leave the Wall Street-speak out in the street.

Who Are You?

In writing this book, I assumed that

- You would like to take advantage of all the timely investment information available on the Internet.
- You want to get some work done with the Internet. (Online selecting, evaluating, and monitoring of investments can be time-consuming — online investing really is work.)
- You are not interested in becoming the next Warren Buffett — at least not this week.

About This Book

Many online investing books are written by individuals who maintain Web sites, and these books often promote their authors' investment systems, products, and services. Other investment books are written by professional money managers to promote their newsletters or mutual funds. This book, however, has no hidden agenda. It focuses on commonsense ways to create and build wealth with the Internet.

I've designed *Investing Online For Dummies* for beginning online investors, but it can also benefit so-called financial professionals and planners. Each chapter stands alone and provides all the instructions and information you need for solving an investment problem or making an investment decision.

Most online investors will read this book in chunks, diving in long enough to solve a particular investment problem ("Hmmm, I thought I knew how to contact an electronic brokerage, but I don't seem to remember . . .") and then putting it aside. However, the book is structured in such a way that if you want to read it through from beginning to end (even though the book's primary function is as a reference tool), you can do so. I discuss online investment topics in a logical way, from checking your bank balance online through bond transactions to trading stocks online.

Here's a quick rundown on some of the topics I cover in *Investing Online For Dummies:*

- ✔ Using the Internet to help you make money
- ✔ Getting up-to-the-minute quotes and company data 24 hours a day
- ✔ Finding the best savings rates and treasury securities data on the Internet
- ✔ Locating Internet resources for the selection of mutual funds
- ✔ Working with Internet tools for analyzing and selecting stocks and bonds
- ✔ Trading online and paying the lowest commissions possible
- ✔ Keeping track of your portfolio
- ✔ Discovering down-to-earth strategies that can build wealth with small investments

Additionally, I offer warnings to help you avoid dangerous or costly traps, and I point out excellent online investment resources. *Investing Online For Dummies* is your road map to cyberspace. It provides the Internet knowledge that you need to get the edge on investors who rely on newspapers and magazines.

How to Use This Book

If you have a question about an online investing topic, just look up that topic in the table of contents at the beginning of the book or in the index at the end of the book. You can get the help you're seeking immediately or find out where to look for expert advice.

Investing has evolved into a specialized field and isn't particularly easy for normal people. Don't feel bad if you have to use the table of contents and the index quite a bit. Luckily, the Internet offers plenty of sites that let you practice before you buy or trade.

If you want to experience electronic trading and are concerned that a mistake may cost you money, try practicing at Edustock (tqd.advanced.org/3088/welcome/welcomenf.html). Edustock isn't associated with any electronic brokerage and is designed to help you get started with online trading.

If you're new to investing on the Internet, read the first three chapters in Part I. They give you an overview of the Internet and some important investor tips. To get yourself more familiar with the Internet, try some of the activities that I detail in these chapters.

If you are new to the Internet, I recommend getting a copy of *The Internet For Dummies,* 5th Edition, by John R. Levine, Carol Baroudi, and Margaret Levine Young. This book is great for anyone who needs help getting started with the Internet. *The Internet For Dummies* can assist you in hooking up with local Internet providers, surfing the Net, downloading free software, and joining mailing lists or user groups.

If you're a new investor, read Chapter 4, which offers warnings about online frauds, schemes, and deceptions. When you start subscribing to investor newsgroups, mailing lists, or online publications, you're likely to receive e-mail stock tips and investment offers. Treat these messages like you would any telephone "cold call." Thoroughly examine the investment and get a second opinion from an independent investment expert you respect before you purchase.

Part II covers "Finding the Right Investments." This part of the book discusses online banking, mutual funds, stocks, and bonds on the Internet. You can start anywhere, but I suggest beginning with the type of investment that intrigues you the most.

Part III covers online trading and portfolio management. This part of the book includes instructions on how to open a cash account with an electronic broker.

Part IV provides extra support for online investment initiatives, how to get your financial house in order before you start investing, retirement planning, and online money-saving tax tips.

How This Book Is Organized

This book has five parts. Each part stands alone — that is, you can begin reading anywhere and get the information you need for investment decision-making. Or you can read the entire book from cover to cover. If you do, you find that the simplest financial transactions come first, and I cover the more difficult transactions later.

Here are the parts of the book and what they contain.

Part I: Online Investing Fundamentals

In Part I, you find out what investor tools are available on the Internet. The chapters in Part I discuss important investor uses of the Internet: searches for financial topics, electronic mail, newsgroups, and access to databases that until recently were only available to large financial institutions. You also find out how to download interesting and useful stuff. Part I also offers warnings about online frauds, schemes, and deceptions.

Part II: Finding the Right Investments

The chapters in Part II show you how to cut through the jargon and get to the heart of what investments are (and what they're not). These chapters help you understand rates of return and what mutual funds, stocks, and bonds are all about. You clearly see how online investing can fit into your personal financial aspirations.

Part III: Paying the Right Price

Part III includes chapters that detail how to evaluate a mutual fund's performance and buy or sell a mutual fund online. I also discuss how to research and analyze stocks and bonds online. I point you to many online sources for annual reports, economic data, analyst recommendations, industry standards, and more.

Part IV: Making More Money on the Internet

Part IV shows how you can pay the lowest commission rates possible and track your portfolio online. No more guessing about what to hold and when to fold. Figure I-1 shows a good example of an online portfolio management tool at Thomson Investors Network, located at www.thomsoninvest.net.

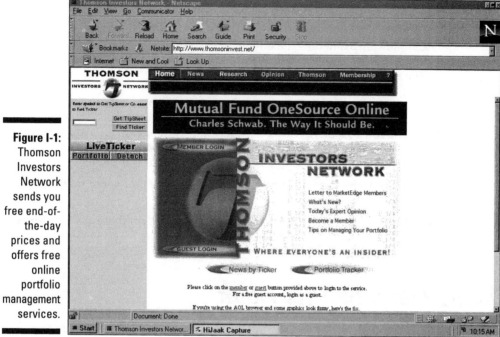

Figure I-1:
Thomson
Investors
Network
sends you
free end-of-
the-day
prices and
offers free
online
portfolio
management
services.

(Copyright © 1997 Thompson Investors Network.)

Part V: The Part of Tens

Part V provides handy top-ten lists packed full of ready online references. The chapters in this part cover such essentials as getting ready for online investing, planning for a comfortable retirement, and finding tax help online.

Special features

Check out this book's Internet Directory, which includes the latest and greatest investor sites on the Internet. The focus of this directory is on the sites you are most likely to use when you try to allocate your capital among mutual funds, stocks, and bonds.

The companion CD-ROM packaged with this book contains a selection of the finest Internet investment software tools available for investors. You also get Microsoft Internet Explorer 4.0, and a complete Web version of the book's Internet Directory. You don't have to type in the Web addresses of sites you want to visit; just launch your browser program, access the Internet Directory on this book's companion CD-ROM, connect to the Internet, and click on a site's name.

Technical Requirements

The following list details the minimum system requirements for connecting to the Internet. This list describes all the computer hardware and software you need:

- ✔ An IBM PC-compatible computer with a minimum of 8MB of RAM, 6MB available hard disk space, a 486 or faster processor, and Windows 3.*x*, Windows 95, or Windows NT operating systems. Or . . . a Macintosh or Mac clone with a minimum of 8MB of RAM, 5MB available hard disk space, a 68030 or faster processor, and System 7 or higher.
- ✔ Any Internet browser (such as Netscape Navigator 4.0 or Internet Explorer 4.0).
- ✔ A SLIP or PPP Internet connection, with a modem that runs 14.4 Kbps (28.8 Kbps is preferred), or a direct connection.

Icons Used in This Book

Throughout *Investing Online For Dummies*, I use icons to help guide you through all the suggestions, solutions, cautions, and World Wide Web sites. I hope you find that the following icons make your journey through online investment strategies smoother.

This icon indicates an explanation for a nifty little shortcut or time-saver.

Arrghhh! Don't let this happen to you!

This icon points out a resource on the World Wide Web that you can access with Netscape Navigator, Microsoft Internet Explorer, or other Web software.

The Technical Stuff icon lets you know that some particularly nerdy, technoid information is coming up so that you can skip it if you want. (On the other hand, you may want to read it.)

Feedback, Please

If you have any comments, suggestions, or questions, I'd love to hear from you. Please feel free to contact me in care of IDG Books Worldwide, 7260 Shadeland Station, Suite 100, Indianapolis, IN 46256. Better yet, send me an e-mail message at `ksindell@ix.netcom.com`.

Part I

Online Investing Fundamentals

The 5th Wave By Rich Tennant

"The first thing you should know about investing online is that when you see the exploding bomb icon appear, it's just your browser crashing— not your portfolio."

In this part . . .

The chapters in this part help you discover why the Internet should be your starting point for researching investments. These chapters point you to a variety of online investor resources and data. The chapters in this part also detail the Internet tools you need for successful online investing, and they offer timely advice about how you can tell a good deal from a scam.

Chapter 1

Why Look to the Internet for Investment Information?

In This Chapter

▶ Taking advantage of Internet investment opportunities

▶ Picking winning investments online

▶ Visiting an Internet investor supersite

▶ Getting started with the Internet

*T*imely, high-quality information has always made the difference between making money and not making money. In the past, big-time investors had ticker tape machines in their offices tapping out the latest Wall Street stock prices. Now you can have a ticker automatically run on your desktop computer. You even have the option of running a ticker that shows just the stocks in your personal portfolio.

In this chapter, I help you get started with investing online by showing a short example of how the Internet can help you with each step in the investing process:

1. Selecting assets that meet your financial objectives.

2. Analyzing investment candidates.

3. Buying securities online.

4. Monitoring your investments.

5. Selling your investments to harvest your profits.

To help you get started, I point you toward some helpful online investment resources, and I offer examples of the types of investment information you can find on the Internet. (I assume that you're already connected to the Internet at work, at school, or at home.)

If you need help getting started on the Internet, pick up a copy of *The Internet For Dummies,* 5th Edition, by John R. Levine, Carol Baroudi, and Margaret Levine Young (IDG Books Worldwide, Inc.). *The Internet For Dummies* shows what the Internet is (and what it is not), introduces you to Internet terminology and concepts, explains different Internet services, shows you how to navigate the Web, and provides details about how to download software and other types of files from sites on the Internet.

Can You Earn Big Bucks by Investing on the Internet?

Imagine that it's Monday around 7:00 a.m. You have more than enough time to read the newspaper and check your e-mail before you head out to work. With your cup of coffee in hand, you go to your computer and read your morning e-mail newspapers: *The New York Times* interactive edition (www.nyt.com), Individual Newspage (www.newspage.com), and *Money Magazine*'s daily Internet newspaper (www.infobeat.com).

You're interested in the banking industry and have watched the large banks consolidate over the last five years. You notice that XYZ Bank's stock has taken a tumble. You find news about disappointing earnings at XYZ Bank but no speculation about additional problems. The share price has declined from $30 per share to $21, and it's now in your price range. Is XYZ Bank's declining stock price an investment opportunity for you?

If you're an online investor, here's what you do:

1. **Go to the Dow Jones News Retrieval Service and The Wall Street Journal Interactive Edition (at** bis.downjones.com **and** www.wsj.com, **respectively) and get more information about XYZ Bank.**

   You find more news about the disappointing earnings but no speculation about additional problems.

2. **Go to Hoover's Online (**www.hoovers.com**) and get an in-depth company report.**

   The report indicates that the company hasn't experienced any recent management or financial problems.

3. **Go to XYZ Bank's home page and get a copy of the bank's most recent annual report.**

   You look over the ten-year summary of financial figures, stock prices, and dividends.

4. **Compare XYZ Bank's performance to the industry average at**
   `www.researchmag.com`.

   The company's return on equity (ROE) is 19 percent. That's better than most banks.

   Note: ROE is the shareholder's bottom line. It measures an investor's gain or loss for a particular stock.

5. **Check what Value Line has to say about XYZ Bank at**
   `www.valueline.com`.

   Value Line indicates that XYZ Bank's growth in profits and operating income has consistently improved.

6. **Check what the experts have to say at Zack's (`www.ultra.zacks.com`).**

   They recommend buying the stock and expect earnings to jump ahead early next year.

7. **Crunch a few numbers, perform your fundamental analysis (as I discuss in Chapter 12), and decide that future returns will pay for the risk you're taking now.**

8. **Contact your online brokerage and place your order.**

   When the market opens, you want to purchase 100 shares of XYZ Bank stock. Your online broker will e-mail you notification later in the day that your trade was executed. You can check on it at lunch.

It's now 8:15 a.m. — time to drive to work, confident that the stock you just bought for your Individual Retirement Account (IRA) will bring you the returns you are seeking.

So does online investing sound complicated? It's not, and thousands of people invest online every day — men and women in all walks of life. If you have a computer and Internet access, you can do it, too. This book shows you how.

Picking a Winning Investment Online

You may be a beginning investor who is unsure about how to leap into the finance world, or you may be an experienced investor looking for an extra edge or something new. Whatever category you fall into, the Internet can provide you with the tools and resources you need.

You don't have to be a technical genius to access all the available Internet tools, research sources, and financial data. You don't even have to be an experienced investor. This book can help you pick winning investments that match your financial objectives. Here are just a few of the many ways the Internet can assist you in picking winning investments:

- ✔ You can use the Internet to find investment opportunities in the news, user groups, and mailing lists you subscribe to.

- ✔ *Push technology* can send you the information you want each day by using such services as BackWeb (www.backweb.com) and PointCast (www.pointcast.com). (I explain push technology in Chapter 2.)

- ✔ You can use Internet *updatebots* (small programs) to monitor the Internet for Web site revisions that may indicate changes in investment conditions. (See Chapter 2 for more information about updatebots.)

- ✔ You can subscribe to investor supersites to study specific industries and general conditions of the market and to watch what professionals say and do. (I offer examples of these supersites later in this chapter. For even more information, see Chapters 11 and 12.)

- ✔ You can study the past-performance data and review earnings estimates of investment candidates online (see Chapter 13).

- ✔ You can create your own analyses and make decisions based on your own online research (see Chapter 8).

- ✔ You can take advantage of opportunities that you didn't even know about before you became an online investor. (For example, you can find information about reinvestment and direct stock purchase plans, as I detail in Chapter 15.)

Untangling the Internet

Just what is the Internet and how do investors use it? The Internet is a collection of computers connected in different ways. The World Wide Web (the *Web*) lives on top of the Internet. The Web contains tens of millions of pages that are connected by *hyperlinks,* sometimes called *links.* When you click on a link, your *browser* (a program that talks to the Web) gets the Web page you want.

A second way to reach a Web site is to enter the Web page's address in your browser. A Web page's address is called a *URL* (Uniform Resource Locator). Enter the URL in the appropriate space in your browser's main window, and your browser fetches the Web page you want. Web pages can include real-time stock quotes, breaking news, audio or video clips, spreadsheets and software that you can download to your computer, animation, text, graphics, and more.

What Can Investors Find on the Net?

I believe that the Internet is the greatest single source ever placed in the hands of the individual investor. With the Internet, you don't need to be a Wall Street insider to build your small savings into a solid investment portfolio. All you need is to be online. Here are a few examples of what you can find:

- ✔ Company annual reports, 24-hour access to SEC filings, other in-depth industry and company data, earnings estimates, and broker recommendations for companies you're considering as candidates for investment.
- ✔ Alerts for when the prices of your chosen stocks reach predetermined buy or sell targets.
- ✔ All the information you need for buying and selling Treasury securities and government, agency, and corporate bonds.
- ✔ Internet programs that sort through thousands of mutual funds so that you can find those few special mutual funds that meet your investment criteria.
- ✔ Internet screening tools to sift through thousands of stocks to find the ones that meet your predefined needs and financial goals.
- ✔ Online portfolio management programs that automatically update your portfolio each evening.
- ✔ Real-time and delayed stock quotes displayed on your desktop.
- ✔ The lowest commission fees anywhere for your online trades.

A word of caution

Some Internet investments may sound too good to be true. Well, they are. Just like any other place, the Internet has its share of frauds, schemes, and deceptions. Investments in stocks, mutual funds, and bonds are not guaranteed to $100,000 like Federal Deposit Insurance Corporation (FDIC) savings deposits. If your legitimate investment loses money or if someone deceives you in some type of "get rich quick" scheme, no FDIC insurance payments exist to cover your losses. However, the Securities Industry Protection Corporation (SIPC) insures your money should your brokerage go out of business.

Don't invest until you determine your personal financial goals and figure out how much risk you can take. (Chapter 18 describes ten prerequisites for online investing.) You should also give some consideration to spreading your investments around to diversify your risk. After you complete these tasks, online investing allows you to take control of your finances and start building wealth.

Where Should You Start?

Picking your first investor resources is an important task. You can get a good feel for what's available on the Internet at compilation sites called investment *supersites*. Here are a few examples:

- ✔ **Invest-O-Rama** (www.investorama.com) is a collection of links to online sources such as electronic brokers, mutual funds, financial reports, and related investor sources.

- ✔ **InvestorGuide** (www.investorguide.com), shown in Figure 1-1, features newsletters, articles, stock analyses, and links to thousands of investment sites.

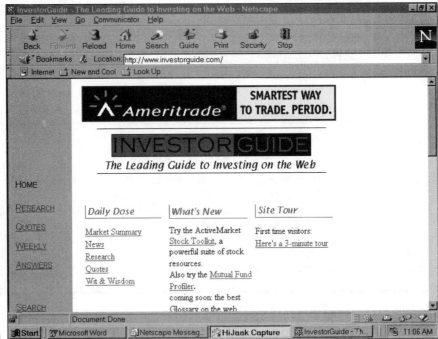

Figure 1-1: Connect to thousands of investor sites at Investor-Guide.

✔ **InvestorWeb** (www.investorweb.com) can assist you in finding
information about private and publicly traded companies.

✔ **Networth and the Internet Investors Network** (networth.quicken.com)
is a comprehensive compilation site that includes mutual fund and
stock investment information and resources.

✔ **PAWWS Financial Services** (www.pawws.com) provides individuals with
portfolio tracking, securities and market analysis tools, quotes, and
online trading.

✔ **Wall Street Directory** (www.wsdinc.com), shown in Figure 1-2, includes
2,500 pages of investment information for traders and investors (market reports, mutual funds, news services, data services, educational
services, and so on).

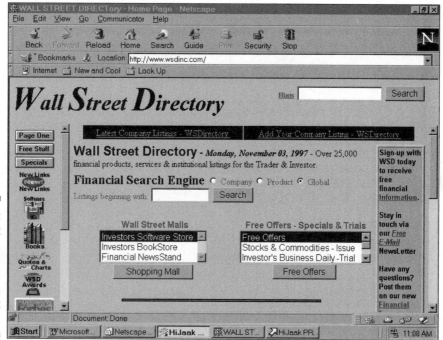

Figure 1-2:
Get market
reports,
mutual fund
news, and
more at the
Wall Street
Directory.

Chapter 2

Internet, Here I Come

● ●

In This Chapter

▶ Understanding why so much cool stuff is available for free

▶ Getting started with some of the best investment sites

▶ Downloading and uploading files (and not catching a virus)

▶ Opening one of those zipped files you downloaded

▶ Staying on top of cyberspace

● ●

*T*he Internet is expanding at a rate of a million Web pages per month. When you connect to the Internet, the power of your computer increases dramatically, and you suddenly have access to vast amounts of high-quality investment data, including economic forecasts, industry studies, company profiles, and historical stock prices. In the past, only large financial institutions had this type of data. Investment bankers used this information to make analyses and then charged their clients hefty fees for their recommendations. Much of this high-grade information is now available to the online investor.

Knowing how to use the Internet can help you avoid pricey investor services and allows you to make your own analyses and financial decisions. This chapter assists you in locating high-quality Internet information, downloading and unzipping free investment software programs, and taking advantage of investment opportunities by showing you how to discover what's new on the Internet.

Online Investor Starting Points

You may have heard that some people waste their time on the Internet, become less productive at work, neglect their families, forget to bathe, and so on. Although that story may be true for a very few people, it's not true for most Internet users.

Connecting to the Internet gives you access to millions of documents, a vast variety of software programs, and high-caliber information that in the not-too-distant past only large financial institutions could access. The World Wide Web provides an easy-to-use interface that allows you to access the Internet's many financial resources. Smart investors can often avoid costly services and conduct their own high-grade online research.

Getting online with the best investment sites

You can find many investor news organizations and large investment banking groups on the Internet. Competition is high, so they're willing to give away a large amount of high-quality resources for free. Many of these organizations hope that you become a fan of their great services. They want to acquire you as a steady paying customer for their products.

Here are a few examples of investor Web sites that provide good content that is free:

- ✔ **Smith Barney Wall Street Watch** (www.smithbarney.com): This Web site includes online portfolio tracking, an online newspaper for late-breaking financial news, and financial planning calculators. Online news includes stock market summaries and glimpses of research that is usually reserved for high-paying clients. This site's daily Stock Hit List rates the ten most requested stocks on Wall Street.

- ✔ **Briefing.com** (www.briefing.com/schwab): Stocks on the move, news summaries, stocks making the news, live market analysis, ratings changes, daily stock commentary, technical stock analysis, hourly stock market statistics, upcoming economic data, and earning estimates are just a few of the things this site offers. This site also provides reviews of 75 stocks and expert opinions.

- ✔ **Motley Fool** (www.fool.com): Figure 2-1 shows Motley Fool, a punning online investment magazine with the motto "The best person to manage your money is you." This site provides investor education, investing suggestions, and news. Motley Fool supports a 13-step investment program and suggests investing in *small cap* stocks — that is, companies that are financed by stockholders' investments of $50 million to $500 million. In contrast, large cap companies are capitalized by more than $5 billion. (For more information about small cap stocks, see Chapter 9.) As proof of the program, they report the performance of their portfolio daily.

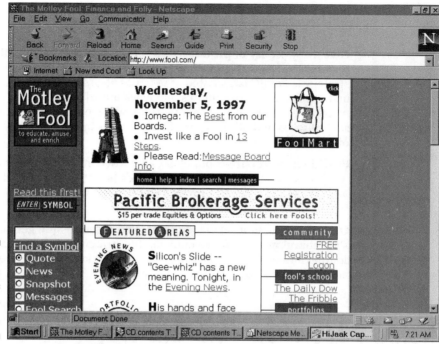

Figure 2-1:
Motley Fool
is loads of
"pun" for
investors.

✔ **Silicon Investor** (www.techstocks.com): Before you spend a dime (or invest your fortune), visit Silicon Investor, which ranks as one of the best free investor sites on the Internet. Silicon Investor provides 100 weeks of stock data and charts for all the leading technology companies. You can track industries and product lines to forecast stock trends. By joining the discussion groups at this site, you can share ideas and insights with other nonprofessional, but savvy, investors.

Is all this cool Internet stuff really free?

The Internet grew out of government agencies and academics sharing tools, knowledge, and software. Consequently, the notion that no one should be charged for anything on the Internet is part and parcel of the Internet's culture.

Additionally, no one ever developed a payment methodology to charge for the distribution of high-quality information. As a general rule, Internet users expect to get something for nothing. This expectation makes commercialization of the Internet difficult. Most Internet users won't use the resources of a Web site unless the provider is willing to give something away for free.

Internet businesses have developed three strategies to make money on the Net:

- ✔ **Give away plenty of products and services, prove to advertisers how popular the site is, and sell advertising.** A good example of this strategy is PointCast, located at www.pointcast.com. PointCast has up-to-the minute stock quotes and news but what some folks call a *high noise-to-content ratio.* (In other words, you have to wade through lots of sales pitches and other types of meaningless information to get that bit of needed investor data.)

- ✔ **Provide free resources but charge for a second level of information.** A good example of this strategy is Zack's Investment Research, at www.zacks.com. Zack's provides all the basic information you want, but for more details, you need to subscribe.

- ✔ **Offer an important service for free, and when people get hooked, start charging a fee.** An example of this strategy is The Wall Street Journal Interactive Edition (www.wsj.com). It started as a free Internet newspaper, but now you have to pay for it.

Using FTP: They Put 'Em Up; You Take 'Em Down

As you surf the Net, you may notice enticing ads that say *Free Software; Download Now!* If you click on the download icon, your browser program automatically transfers — or *downloads* — that software from the Web site to your computer. The reverse process — transferring a file from your computer to another site — is called uploading.

Internet Service Providers (ISPs) provide you with the capability to upload and download files. The most popular method for moving files is by using the File Transfer Protocol (FTP). Most Internet browsers have built-in FTP capabilities.

An FTP server is simply a computer on the Internet that permits access to files for downloading and uploading. FTP servers that allow public access are easy to use and let you to download stuff. However, some Internet FTP servers are private. To download information from a private FTP server, you need to ask permission from the system administrator. Here's how you download a file from a remote site to your computer by using FTP:

1. **Locate the FTP server that has the shareware, freeware, product updates, patches, press releases, technical data, or other media you want.**

2. **Enter the FTP server's address in the appropriate space in your Web browser.**

   Usually, you enter the FTP server's address in the same area you use for entering a Web site's URL.

3. **If you're asked for a login name, type** anonymous **in lowercase letters. (The program expects you to use all lowercase letters; it is sensitive about this.)**

   You are now in the root directory of the FTP server.

4. **Move your cursor down to the appropriate directory and find the file you desire.**

5. **Click on the icon next to the short text description of the file.**

   A dialog box opens, asking whether you want to save the file or open it.

6. **Save the file to a disk that you select, or open the file.**

   If you open the file, you can always save it later.

To upload a file to an FTP server:

1. **Locate the FTP server to which you want to send your file, and enter the FTP server's address in the appropriate space in your Web browser.**

2. **Enter your password (if required).**

   For most FTP servers with public access, the password is anonymous.

3. **Click on your browser's File icon.**

4. **In the dialog box that appears, find the directory of your computer that has the file you want to upload.**

5. **Highlight the appropriate file and click on Open.**

   A small box appears, showing what percentage of the file has been uploaded. You're finished when 100 percent of the file is uploaded.

If the FTP server doesn't accept your anonymous password, you aren't at a publicly accessible FTP server. In this case, you must contact the systems administrator for a password and permission to access the FTP server.

Who Ya Gonna Call?

Now that you know all about downloading and uploading, where are the FTP servers? Table 2-1 lists several locations from which you can download shareware, freeware, product demonstrations, and other media. It's not a complete list, but a good starting place to find investment tools that can help you track your investments or monitor your stocks. You reach these sites by using the World Wide Web. After you get to the right location, select the file you want and follow the steps I describe in the preceding section to download the file. The selected file is downloaded from an FTP server.

Table 2-1	Download Free Software from These Sites
Download Site Name	*URL*
Windows95.com (32-bit shareware)	www.windows95.com/apps
Shareware.com	www.shareware.com
Download.com	www.download.com
Free Software Shack	www.softwareshak.com
Internet Goodies	www.ensta.fr/internet
Jumbo!	www.jumbo.com

Zipped Out? Compressing and Uncompressing Files

Many of the files that you download from the Internet are compressed to save time in transferring the file. Quite simply, a smaller file downloads faster than a large file. Consequently, any online investor needs to know how to *zip* and *unzip* — that is, compress and uncompress — files. Zip files are also handy for transferring multiple files at the same time. With all the desired files compressed into one zip file, you need to download only the one zip file.

You can use WinZip or any other zip program to create a zip file. Complete these steps to zip a file:

1. Create a zip file, using the filename extension .ZIP.

This file holds all the graphics, text, or other media that you want to send.

2. Select the file (or files) you want to compress.

3. Save the new zip file.

The zip program makes a copy of the media you want to send and places it in the zip file. The entire file is then compressed.

Other formats you may encounter

Zip files are the most common compression format for PC users, but the Internet links computers of all types. Folks on UNIX workstations, Macs, and other platforms don't always rely on zip compression. Other common formats that you may encounter when downloading files from the Internet include StuffIt (.sit), Arj (.arj), Arc (.arc), gzip (.gz, .z), uuencode (.uu, .uue), and BinHex (.hqx). You may also find Arj self-extracting archives (.exe, .sea) and Macintosh files in MacBinary (.bin) format.

To open a zipped file, you extract or execute the file, as I detail in the following steps:

1. **Launch your zip program.**

2. **Click on the open (extract or execute) icon.**

   The zip program opens a dialog box.

3. **In the dialog box, click on the name of the zip file you want to open.**

   The zip program lists the contents of the zip file. In other words, if the zip file contains several files, each file is listed. You now have the option of either saving each file to your disk or opening the file.

4. **Just click on the filename and make your selection.**

   Opened zip files are larger than the zipped files, so make certain that you have enough disk space to accommodate all the information in the zip file.

Sometimes zip files contain instructions, or *Read Me* files, that tell you more about the software you've downloaded. Read these instructions before performing any other task.

Figure 2-2 shows the home page for WinZip at `www.winzip.com`. WinZip is a compression program that allows you to zip and unzip files that you have downloaded from the Internet. You can download a free evaluation copy of this software for Windows 3.1 or Windows 95. The program includes a wizard program, WinZip Wizard, which is designed for individuals who have never worked with zipped files. It simplifies the process of unzipping and installing software distributed in zip files.

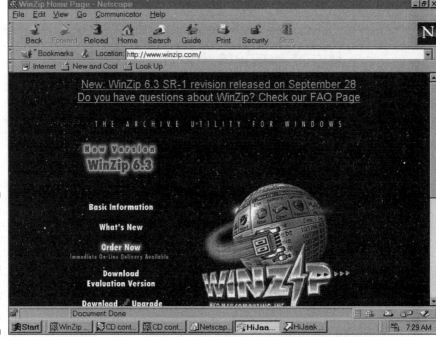

Figure 2-2:
Download
a free
evaluation
copy of
WinZip, a
zip file
utility.

(Copyright © 1991-1997 Nico Mac Computing, Inc.)

How can I download zip files and not get a nasty virus?

Anytime you download a file from the Internet, you run the risk of infecting your computer with a virus. Internet browsers such as Netscape Communicator and Internet Explorer have deluxe editions, *plug-in* products, or helper applications that include antiviral scanners. (Plug-ins are browser extensions that you can add to your browser. They play or show you a document from within your browser.)

The antivirus scanner launches automatically every time you download a file or receive an e-mail attachment. The scanner is invisible until it discovers a virus. Then it steps you through the process of disinfecting the file before actually saving it to disk. The manufacturers guarantee that these programs allow you to safely download programs, documents, and compressed files.

Staying Ahead of the Game

Whatever your financial goals — accumulating vast wealth, sending the kids to college, or having a comfortable retirement — you need to watch for new opportunities and new ways to invest. Financial change is often the only way to wealth building.

The Internet provides a vast amount of information, but how do you find out what's new? How can you get breaking business and investment news? Can new information be delivered directly to you? In the following sections, I provide answers to these questions.

Manually browsing for new sources

The Internet has many compilation sites that provide links to what's new this day, week, month, and so on. Table 2-2 lists examples of these Web sites.

Table 2-2   Some General Guides to What's New on the Internet

Title	*Internet Address*	*Description*
Big Kahuna What's New	www.QuantumLeap. net/SURF/NEW.htm	A listing of more than 150 interesting "what's new" and "cool" sites
Linkmonster	www.linkmonster.com	A new, well-organized Web directory and announcement site
Search Internet — What's New	www.isleuth.com	Metasearch for new Web sites that accesses six databases at once
Starting Point	www.stpt.com	Provides a listing of new sites and an Internet search engine. New sites are divided into categories (business, computing, entertainment, health, investing, magazines, personal, news, reference, sports, travel, and weather)
Staying Current	www.cybergate.com	Index of links for daily Internet and worldwide news, general information, e-zines (electronic magazines), and "best of the Web" lists

(continued)

Table 2-2 (continued)

Title	Internet Address	Description
What's New	www.whatsnew.com	An announcement site for new places to visit on the Web
What's New on the Internet	www.whatsnu.com	A continuously updated directory of new sites on the Internet
What's New Too	www.nu2.com	Announcements of new Web sites
Yahoo! New Listings	www.yahoo.com	Sites listed on Yahoo! within the last day, three days, or week

News you can use: Online sources for breaking business and investment news

Table 2-3 shows the types of business and investment news that are available on the Net. No more soggy newspapers when it rains or hunting for the newspaper in thorny bushes. Even better, most of these online newspapers are free. Just subscribe to them, and they're delivered to your e-mailbox.

Table 2-3	Get Up-to-the-Minute News with Online Newspapers Sent Directly to You	
Title	Internet Address	Description
CNET Digital Dispatch	www.cnet.com	Free information about computer software and hardware
Data Broadcasting Corporation	www.dbc.com	A full range of market and investment information. Includes the "clueless investor" with tales of misadventure in the land of stocks
The Economist	www.economist.com	Free weekly summaries of business and political news from the front pages of *The Economist* magazine
Edupage	www.educom.edu	A free information technology summary sent to your e-mailbox three times a week. Designed for educators and researchers

Title	Internet Address	Description
Infobeat	www.money.com	Free daily financial news from the *San Jose Mercury News*
NewsPage Direct	www.newspage.com	Free daily news summaries you can tailor to your specific interests or needs

Keeping smart with push technology

Some online investors complain about information overload. They may rely on *pull technology* (search engines, metasearches, mailing lists, newsgroups, and so on) to mine for specific facts to help investment decision making. With pull technology, you may spend excessive amounts of time and effort in getting the information that really matters.

Using push technology, you can select the type of information you desire and have it pushed to your desktop computer. For example, you can have CNN news and real-time stock quotes automatically *sent* (pushed) directly to your computer. You receive only the information you are interested in, at the times you want it. In this way, you can cut down on information overload.

You can get just the information you want in either of two ways: with push technology that's built into your Internet browser, or with a stand-alone program that runs on your desktop computer and doesn't need a browser.

Push technology in browsers

Both Internet Explorer 4.0 and Netscape Communicator have built-in push technology. Internet Explorer uses Active Desktop, and Netscape Communicator uses NetCaster. You can program these browsers to bring business and investor news directly to you.

Both Active Desktop and NetCaster allow you to select the content you want by choosing a *channel*. These channels come to your computer at scheduled intervals that you select. This information can be saved to your computer's hard disk for offline viewing. Channels include ABC News, CNNfn (finance news), and CNET. More channels are added each day.

For additional information, go to the Web site at www.cnet.com, select Reviews, and click on Netscape NetCaster.

Stand-alone products

At this time, several stand-alone push technology products exist. The following are three popular programs:

✔ **PointCast** (www.pointcast.com), shown in Figure 2-3, delivers the information you select to your computer. The company's *smart screen* acts like a screen saver. You can customize the program so the latest prices of your investments scroll across the screen. The PointCast program has more than 200 information channels; about 40 are money and investment topics. The program is free and downloadable.

✔ **BackWeb** (www.backweb.com) flashes the news that you select across your screen when you're not using your computer for another task. The program downloads data only when your computer isn't in use, so it doesn't disturb you. BackWeb has 50 channels to select from. It is free and downloadable.

✔ **Marimba** (www.marimba.com) can distribute software updates and information directly to your computer. To set up the program, you initially install all the channels. Then it tunes in only the channels you select. When it detects new or updated information, it retrieves and saves the new information on your hard disk, and then you can see it at your leisure. Marimba offers content from more than 100 channels that are maintained by different companies. Material ranges from serious financial information to a ridiculous interactive Rubik's cube and a '70s disco Trivia Quiz. You have to click through the channels (Java programs) to see what's useful. The program is free and downloadable.

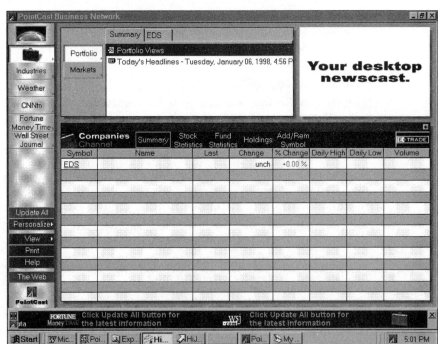

Figure 2-3:
PointCast
brings the
investment
news you
select
to your
desktop.

Using agents, spiders, and bots to stay on top of cyberspace

Over the last several years, smart Internet developers have designed special programs to assist you in updating Web addresses and informing you of new Internet sources:

- ✔ **Agents:** Like virtual administrative assistants, agents scour the Internet for the specific information you want.
- ✔ **Spiders:** These programs wander throughout the Internet and are often used by search engines to index new Web pages.
- ✔ **Bots:** These special small programs are designed to perform different tasks. For example, *updatebots* check for changes in your favorite Web sites and find new Web sites that concern a topic you preselect; *shoppingbots* seek the lowest price of a product; *stockbots* check the real-time stock price of a stock you're interested in; and *newsbots* find news about specific investment topics or companies.

About those new Internet agents

Internet Explorer and Netscape Navigator now use agents to make your research time smarter and quicker. The programs allow you to download documents for offline browsing. The programs manage and track your favorite Web sites, and download documents with new information so that you can read them at your convenience. The programs work even when you aren't connected to the Internet.

This agent technology can also assist you in organizing your hundreds of bookmarks into folders so that you can keep track of important Web sites. The programs also save and monitor frequently used searches and notify you of new results. For additional information, see `search.netscape.com/comprod/power_pack.html`.

Spiders

Nearly 200 search engines exist on the Internet, so checking each search engine would take hours of time online. To assist you in making your research time more efficient, you can use a *search robot* to find the data you desire. Search robots are small programs that go out over the Internet and seek the data you want. One example of a search robot is Subject Search Spider (SSSpider). The program submits your search criteria to eight search robots simultaneously and as results come in, additional search robots are automatically queried.

Subject Search Spider sorts the responses, eliminates duplicates, and lists the most relevant responses first. You can store the results in a library for later review. Subject Search Spider lets you know which search engine provided you with the best results. Figure 2-4 shows the home page of the company that developed Subject Search Spider. The PKWare Web site at `www.pkware.com/ssspider` shows how you can download a copy of SSSpider. The firm offers free evaluation copies of its software at this site.

Updatebots help you stay current

The BotSpot at `botspot.com` provides information about the latest bots on the Internet. You can search the Web site for special types of bots for specific functions. (How about a shoppingbot? Or a guardbot? Maybe a knowledgebot?) The Web site provides links to each bot's home page and downloadable software.

Updatebots go out and seek specialized data. You choose the topic that you are interested in and the updatebot will notify you if a Web page has changed, and search for new Web sites that include your search topic. Figure 2-5 shows the Informant (`informant.dartmouth.edu`), an updatebot. The Informant is free to individuals.

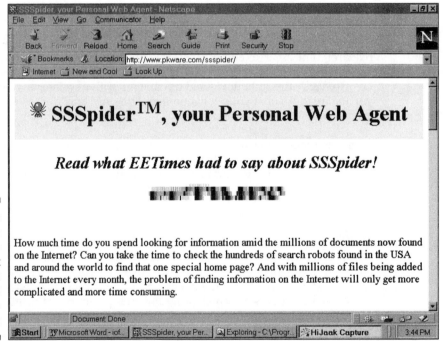

Figure 2-4:
Now you can have Subject Search Spider find that elusive home page.

(Reprinted with permission of Kryloff Technologies.)

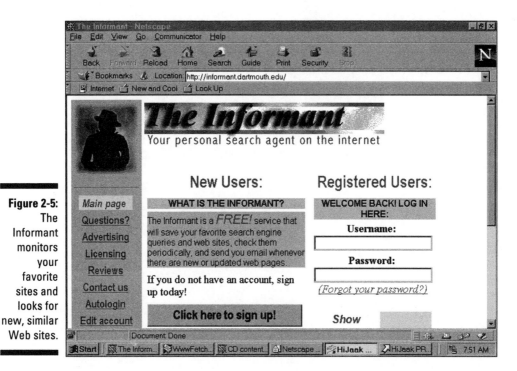

Figure 2-5:
The
Informant
monitors
your
favorite
sites and
looks for
new, similar
Web sites.

The program notifies you (by e-mail) of any new or updated Web pages. You can specify how often you want to be advised (3, 7, 14, 30, or 60 days). After you receive your e-mail notification, you may want more details. Go to the Informant's home page, sign in, and see what's new.

Chapter 3

Finding Investor Stuff on the Net

*T*he Internet has more than a million Web pages and is still growing. This information overload has sent some timid investors to full-service brokers, where they pay high commission fees for brokerage services and investment advice. Smart online investors can avoid information overload by developing their own information systems.

This chapter shows how you can take maximum advantage of the Internet's many investment tools, links, and resources. The chapter discusses Internet basics such as using search engines, locating company profiles, finding newsgroups, subscribing to mailing lists, and accessing online databases to maximize your personal wealth.

Building Your Own Online Information System

Investments provide opportunities to make money in both a *bull* market (that is, an up market) and a *bear* (down) market. No one ever knows for certain whether the market will go up or down, which means that investors need to develop an information system to watch indicators for potential price changes and investment opportunities. Your personal information system may be complex or simple. This chapter shows how you can build your own online information system.

Investment indicators often signal future market trends. For example, changes in bond prices and interest rates are frequently good indicators of market trends that may affect stock prices. That is, if bond yields decline, investors often rush to purchase stocks, causing stock prices to increase. Investors need this information to decide whether they should buy, sell, or hold. Gathering, organizing, and saving this information can be time-consuming. However, using your own online information system can make the process more efficient.

Successful investing involves five basic steps:

1. **Identifying new investments**

2. **Analyzing investment candidates**

3. **Purchasing investments**

4. **Monitoring investments**

5. **Selling investments — to reap your rewards**

The following sections summarize the online sources for the information you need for each step. Knowing what type of information you need and where to get it online can help you build your personalized online information system.

Identifying new investments

Before investing, you need to clearly state your financial objectives and know your risk-tolerance level. This information can help you determine your required rate of return. By doing this type of homework, you can determine which categories of financial assets you may want to consider investing in. For example, if you're selecting investments for your Individual Retirement Account (IRA), you don't want to invest in tax-exempt municipal bonds (because being tax-exempt twice doesn't make sense).

Here are some examples of online sources for identifying investment opportunities:

✔ Company profiles describe a firm's organization, products, financial position, chief competitors, and executive management. (See Chapter 13 for details.)

✔ Direct purchase plans show how to purchase stock in a company without paying a broker's commission (see Chapter 15).

✔ Directories of investor sources provide hard-to-find information that is necessary for investment decision making. (See this book's Internet Directory for a listing of sources.)

✔ Dividend reinvestment plans describe how to join dividend reinvestment programs to purchase company stock at a discount and without a broker. (Chapter 15 shows you how to get started.)

✔ Initial public offerings are new opportunities for investor profits (see Chapter 15).

✔ Investing *e-zines* (electronic magazines) provide educational articles and pertinent facts for beginning and experienced investors.

✔ Mailing lists provide opinions and investors' insights about investment candidates. (I discuss mailing lists later in this chapter, in the section "Getting Investor Information from Mailing Lists.")

✔ News reports on the Net can provide information about new investment opportunities (see Chapter 13).

✔ Newsgroups are informal, online groups of individuals who share ideas about a common interest. You can find dozens of investment-related newsgroups with topics ranging from specific types of investments to investor strategies. (See "How Newsgroups Can Help You," later in this chapter.)

✔ Online databases (free and fee-based repositories of information) provide historical stock prices, economic forecasts, and more. (See the section "Free and Fee-Based Online Investor Databases," later in this chapter, for examples of what's available.)

✔ Search engines (specialized Internet programs that seek the data you desire) provide you with links to the Web pages that have the investor information you desire. (I discuss search engines later in this chapter, in the section, "Your Basic Investment Search Strategy.")

✔ Stock recommendations from professionals enable you to find out what brokers and analysts are saying about your investment selections (see Chapter 13).

✔ Mutual fund and stock screens for selecting specific securities enable you to sort through thousands of investment candidates in seconds to find not only the right investment but also the best investment available. (I discuss Internet-based stock screens in Chapter 9.)

Analyzing investment prospects

The process of analyzing investment prospects includes examining groups of investments or individual securities. For this task, you need information to forecast the timing and amount of future cash flows of investment candidates. That is, the price you pay today is based on the future income of the asset. To figure out what the asset will be worth in the future requires some homework, analysis, and good luck. Here are a few examples of online sources for this type of information:

- ✔ Company profiles and annual reports often forecast the company's future revenues and earnings. (For more information, see Chapter 12.)

- ✔ Databases (free and fee-based online sources) provide news, market commentary, historical stock prices, economic forecasts, industry standards, and competitor information. (See this book's Internet Directory for a good overview of what's available for investors.)

- ✔ Earnings estimates from brokers and analysts give you forecasts of a company's future earnings (see Chapter 13).

- ✔ Industry or business-sector news can frequently indicate whether an industry is in a downward cycle. (See this book's Internet Directory for a listing of online investor news, news services, and newsletters.)

- ✔ National and economic data can point you toward a particular investment strategy. For example, if the country is going into a recession, you may want to select stocks that provide you with some defense.

- ✔ News databases offer breaking news that can help you judge whether your stock purchase is a winner or a loser. (See this book's Internet Directory for a good overview of online news sources.)

- ✔ Securities and Exchange Commission (SEC) filings provide you with financial statements from publicly traded companies. These companies are required to file financial statements every 90 days and more often if big events are happening within the firm. More than 7,000 of these filings are now online. (For details, see Chapter 12.)

Purchasing investments

After you decide which investments you want to purchase, you have to decide how you want to purchase them. For example, you must decide whether you want a full-service broker, a deep-discount broker, or an electronic broker. Usually, deep-discount, online brokerages can execute your trades but do not offer any recommendations or advice. (See Chapter 16 for details about how to open an account with an online brokerage.)

You may participate in an automatic investment plan (AIP). With your approval, this type of plan deducts a certain amount from your checking account to purchase mutual funds, savings bonds, or other investments. (Chapter 6 provides step-by-step directions for opening an AIP account.)

Monitoring investments

If you have more than one investment, you will likely want a way to monitor and compare their performances to the market and similar investments. Here are a few examples of the information and the software you need to accomplish this objective (see Chapter 17 for more details about online portfolio management):

✔ Market monitoring tools are often alerts that you determine. For example, if your stock increases by 25 percent, you may want to consider selling it. You can set up an alert that sends you an e-mail message notifying you that your stock has reached this target.

✔ The Internet provides many portfolio management programs that let you know when your investments are in the news.

✔ Online portfolio management tools can automatically send you an e-mail message at the end of the day letting you know whether your investments gained or lost value.

✔ PC-based portfolio management tools are downloadable software programs that assist you in tracking your investments and record keeping.

✔ Your online broker may track your portfolio for you and keep records of your profits and losses.

Selling investments

You need to decide what proportion of your personal wealth you want to invest in specific assets, how long you want to hold those assets, and whether now is a good time to sell those assets to harvest your rewards. To that end, you need information about the following topics:

✔ **Asset allocation methodologies:** You need to determine what portion of your portfolio should be invested in mutual funds, stocks, and bonds. (See Chapter 11 to find a strategy that's right for you.)

✔ **Capital gains and tax issues:** You must understand how tax issues impact your profits. (See Chapter 20 for more information.)

✔ **Selling strategies:** Determining when you should harvest your investments requires using specific order execution strategies, mutual fund redemption plans, and analyses. (Chapters 11 and 16 explore these topics in more detail.)

Your Basic Investment Search Strategy

Search engines are commercial enterprises that collect and index Web pages or Web page titles. Some of these enterprises review the sites they collect and others provide site information unfiltered and unedited. Some search engines are hierarchical indexes (like Yahoo!) and use subject listings that are similar to the card catalog in a library. Often hierarchical indexes allow you to search by *keyword* (a word that sums up or describes the item or concept you are seeking) and by topic.

Knowing how to use a search engine is a basic Internet skill. Currently, more than 200 different search engines exist on the Net. These Internet tools can be divided into two categories: metasearch engines and search engines.

Metasearch engines have the capability of searching multiple search sites at one time, so you can query several search engines with a single search term. Metasearch engines allow you to enter a single search term to query many individual search engines. This kind of all-in-one shopping is used to match your inquiry to the millions of Web pages on the Internet.

Metasearch engines delete duplicates and collate the results. Some meta-search engines even provide update reports for search progress. Figure 3-1 shows MetaCrawler, located at `www.metacrawler.com`. MetaCrawler is probably the greatest metasearch engine on the Internet; its program even eliminates invalid Web addresses — a real time-saver.

Metasearches generate quite a bit of debate. The disadvantages include having more results to examine and poorly constructed queries taking a very long time to finish. For example, one poorly stated query can take as long as 45 minutes to complete.

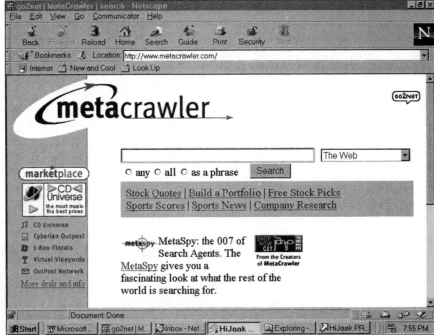

Figure 3-1:
MetaCrawler
can assist
you in
finding
exactly
what you're
looking for.

(Reprinted with express permission from go2net, Inc.)

Selecting the best search engine

Search engines are likely to become your starting point to investor information. They use keywords, quotes, phrases, or questions.

Commercial search engines are competitive and are always adding new features. This means that not all search engines are equal. Some search engine databases include Usenet, mailing lists, news sources, indexes, directories, Web sites, company profiles, and other information. Other search engines only include a portion of this data.

Everyone has a favorite search engine. The search engine that is best is the one that works the best for you. However, as new search engines and new search technologies become available, you should give them a trial run.

Search engines often bring more results than you're looking for. Here's some helpful advice for getting better results:

- ✔ Don't use just one word for your search. The more words you use to describe what you're looking for, the better.

- ✔ If the search engine has a prepackaged subject database, start your search there. Using one of the prepackaged subject databases can reduce your search time. For example, Lycos has a Stock Find category. Click on Stock Find and you see links to mutual funds, an IPO (Initial Public Offering) Corner, money market fund information, and more investor-related links.

- ✔ Use synonyms of the topic you want — for example, Treasury securities, U.S. bonds, savings bonds, and EE bonds.

- ✔ Find out how to use Boolean operators to fine-tune your searches.

A Boolean what?

Boolean operators allow you to combine words to increase the relevancy of your search results and limit the number of *hits,* or responses, you receive. At first, Boolean operators may seem complicated, but you can master this skill after a little practice.

To get a handle on the use of Booleans, assume that you want some information about an initial public offering. You can't remember the company's name, but you know the IPO is scheduled for March. If you search for the term IPO, you get thousands of responses. A search for IPO AND calendar is more usable and reduces the number of responses.

More advanced Boolean searches

Using combinations of Boolean operators can really target your search. The following Boolean searches are for more advanced search engine users:

✔ AND narrows your search. You can limit words like **(cats or felines) and dogs**. The records retrieved by this search contain the original search set and the new subject. For example, this search set provides you with information only about cat's relationships to dogs. Notice the parentheses. If you forget the parentheses, you end up with a large set of useless records.

✔ NOT narrows your search, but use caution. Search engines only compare words and don't take their context into consideration. They also evaluate the search from left to right. NOT is most useful when you want to limit something by language or date — for example, **dogs and (cats or not felines)**. This search is evaluated from left to right, although the operation in parentheses is evaluated as a whole first. Another example is **not (cats or felines) and dogs**. The phrase *cats or felines* is evaluated first, a NOT operation is performed on that, and then everything is "anded" with *dog*.

Boolean operators use three basic concepts: OR, AND, and NOT. The software written for search engines varies, so how each search engine treats each Boolean operator varies. However, the general rules are as follows:

✔ OR allows you to expand your search. You can link words such as **cats or felines**. The records retrieved by this search contain either the word *cat* or the word *feline* or both words. Each record contains at least one word. The results don't have to contain both words.

✔ AND allows you to expand your search. You can link words such as **cats and dogs.** The records retrieved by this search contain both the words *cat* and *dog.* Each record contains at least both words.

✔ NOT allows you to limit your search. You can link words such as **cats not kittens**. The records retrieved by this search contain only grown cats. The results are often more manageable because the search is more specific.

To simplify the process of creating a search phrase , some search engines let you use a plus sign (+) for AND and a minus sign (–) for NOT.

A few of my favorite things: Search engines

Search engines are trustworthy Internet programs that match the words in your query to words on the Internet. Each search engine is a competitive, commercial enterprise with different databases, search programs, and features. Here are a few of the most popular search engines on the Net:

- **AltaVista** (altavista.digital.com) may be the best search engine on the Web. AltaVista has the largest database on the Internet — twice the size of Infoseek. AltaVista and Infoseek have more features than their competitors.

- **Excite** (www.excite.com) allows you to browse many subject categories. It uses a combination of concept (a general idea) and keyword (a specific word in the Web page) searches, so the results are usually pretty good. Excite also offers helpful reviews (editor evaluations of Web sites) and Boolean advanced searches.

- **Infoseek** (www.infoseek.com), shown in Figure 3-2, is easy to use and results are fast. It also has company profiles, stock prices, and other investor information for one-stop shopping. My favorite feature is the capability to search the search results. After several iterations, you can reduce the number of responses to the several that you can effortlessly check. For example, if you are beginning your general research on retirement planning. you may search for **Retirement Planning** in your first search. This search results in 19,534 responses. You can refine your search by entering **Online** and clicking on Search These Results. This search produces 224 responses. If you add **Women** to the query and click on Search These Results, you get 11 responses. You can then print a copy of the search results and begin visiting Web sites.

- **Lycos** (www.lycos.com) searches its subject categories and provides editor reviews and a listing of its top 5% of the search results.

- **Open Text Index** (www.opentext.com) is a handy search engine that provides relevance scores (how likely the record matches your search requirements), file sizes, site abstracts, and links to similar pages.

- **WebCrawler** (webcrawler.com), owned and sponsored by America Online, is a good all-purpose search engine.

- **Yahoo!** (www.yahoo.com) is a popular starting point. This search engine includes a vast array of subject directories and special services such as people search, weekly picks, and What's New This Week.

Although all this information about search engines is interesting, you may be wondering how they compare. Table 3-1 shows how these search engines stack up against each other.

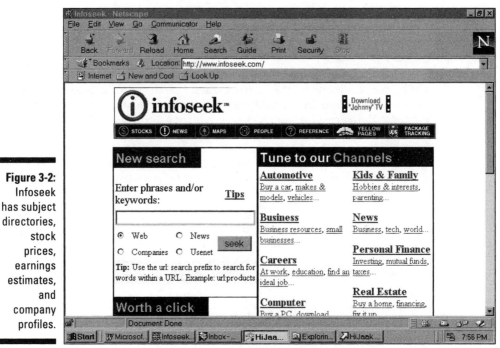

Figure 3-2:
Infoseek has subject directories, stock prices, earnings estimates, and company profiles.

Table 3-1   Comparison of a Few Popular Internet Search Engines

Search Engine	Pages in Database	Searchable Subject Directories	Results Ranking	Web	Usenet	URL	Summary	Boolean
AltaVista	100 million	N	Y	Y	Y	Y	Y	Y
Excite	50 million	Y	Y	Y	Y	N	Y	N
Infoseek	50 million	Y	Y	Y	Y	Y	Y	Y
Lycos	70 million	Y	Y	Y	N	Y	Y	Y
Open Text	5 million	N	Y	Y	N	Y	Y	Y
WebCrawler	2 million	Y	Y	Y	N	N	N	Y
Yahoo!	½ million	Y	N	Y	N	Y	Y	Y

Here's an overview of the criteria I used to make the comparisons in Table 3-1:

✔ **Web Pages in Database:** How many Web pages does the search engine consider to find your results?

TIP

Personalized search engines

With more than 100 million Web pages, your search for investment information is likely to dredge up many articles that are outdated or simply not relevant. One way to increase your treasure-to-trash ratio is to use a personalized search engine. My Yahoo! (my.yahoo.com) allows users to set up profiles for (among other things) specific news topics and a stock portfolio.

The My Excite Channel (my.excite.com) — known as Excite Live in a previous life — includes much of the same personalization features as My Yahoo! The Wall Street Journal Interactive Edition (www.wsj.com), the granddaddy of all investor information, lets readers build a personalized profile that monitors your news interests, favorite *Wall Street Journal* features, and stock portfolio.

- ✔ **Subject Directory:** Does the search engine enable you to limit searches to specific subject areas? Searches are quicker if the search engine offers a subject directory because the search engine searches only in the topic area that you specify.

- ✔ **Results Ranking:** Does the search engine rate your search results so that you know how likely you are to find what you're looking for? (For example, listings with relevancy ratings of less than 90 percent are usually worthless.)

- ✔ **Web:** Does the search engine look through the World Wide Web for your results?

- ✔ **Usenet:** Does the search engine look through newsgroups for your results?

- ✔ **URL:** Does the search engine provide the Internet addresses for your search results? Getting the address can be very helpful; you can save or print the results of your search and then later you can backtrack and get to those difficult-to-find Web sites.

- ✔ **Summary:** Does the search engine provide a short text description of the search results?

- ✔ **Boolean Searches:** Does the search engine allow you to conduct more targeted searches?

Finding Those Elusive Company Profiles

Before you start researching an investment candidate, you need to define exactly what you are looking for. When searching for company information, you need the following data:

✔ **Company name:** Many company names are similar; make certain you have the correct name.

✔ **Ticker symbol:** You can't purchase the stock without the ticker symbol.

✔ **Company overview:** What are the company's goals and aspirations?

✔ **History:** Was this firm part of another company five years ago?

✔ **News:** Can you find any company events that are newsworthy, such as higher or lower earnings?

✔ **Executive management and employees:** Who's the CEO? Is this person new to the company, or is the firm looking for someone new?

✔ **Location:** Regional economics often affect national companies.

✔ **Products and services:** Is the product an up-and-comer or an old standby?

✔ **Competitors:** Who are the chief competitors?

✔ **Financials:** How are sales and profits?

These questions may lead to more in-depth questions about specific firms. The Internet provides many sources to answer these questions. For starters, you may want to consider using Infoseek's (www.infoseek.com) Company Profile feature. For example, if you're looking up a subsidiary, Infoseek can point you to the headquarters home page, and it offers links to stock information and news releases. Excite provides similar features and is also good at finding company information.

Here are a few of my favorite sites that may provide just the company information you're looking for:

✔ **EDGAR** (www.sec.gov) is a searchable database of 15,000 publicly traded companies. Publicly traded firms must file at least every 90 days, so information is always current. Data includes income statements, balance sheets, and good industry summaries in the narratives. New York University also provides access to EDGAR documents at edgar.stern.nyu.edu.

✔ **Hoovers Online** (www.hoovers.com) includes free information about 8,500 companies. You can search for ticker symbol, location, and sales at this Web site. Company profiles include the firm's address, phone numbers, executive names, recent sales figures, and company status. Companies are also ranked. Links are provided to stock quotes and SEC financial data. Basic service is free. For $9.95 per month or $99.95 per year, in-depth information is provided on more than 2,700 companies.

> ✔ **The Global Network of the Chambers of Commerce and Industry**
> (www1.usal.com/~ibnet.champshp.html) provides links to 640
> U.S. Chamber of Commerce home pages. The site also includes the
> _International Business Monitor,_ a weekly news service.
>
> ✔ **Web 100** (www.web100.com) provides links to the company home
> pages of the Internet's 100 most popular sites.

How Newsgroups Can Help You

Newsgroups are discussion forums (or electronic bulletin boards) where
individuals post messages for others to read and answer. New newsgroups
appear — and old, unused newsgroups disappear — almost daily.

The advantage of these groups is that the opinions of authors are disparate
and come from around the world. More than 5,000 publicly accessible
newsgroups exist, ranging from serious to silly. Newsgroups support almost
all religious ideologies, political points of view, and philosophical beliefs. If
you want to know what investors think about a particular investment, a
newsgroup is a good place to start. Newsgroup participants aren't investment professionals but many of them are savvy investors.

Knowing how newsgroups are named can help you determine whether a
certain newsgroup may interest you. Newsgroup names typically have two
or more parts. The first section of a newsgroup's name is the most general
grouping or topic. Examples of different first names are as follows:

Section	Description
Alt	Alternative subjects, ranging from the serious (investing and finance) to the weird (occult and alternative life styles)
Biz	Business subjects, including commercials
Misc	Miscellaneous topics, from items for sale to finance

Newsgroup names with two sections — for example, alt.finance — don't
have any subgroups under that major topic. Groups such as
alt.invest.funds branch into other newsgroups. That is, each component
of the name represents a different level in the newsgroup. The last named
component is the actual theme of the group. For example,
alt.invest.funds is about investing in mutual funds.

Subscribing to a newsgroup is very easy. With most browsers, you simply
click on the name of the newsgroup you want to subscribe to. For details,
use your Web browser to check out Beginners Central (Chapter 5) at
www.northernwebs.com/bc/begin04.html.

Tired of the same old newsgroups? Find out what's new at netINS's List of Recently Created Newsgroups, located at `www.netins.net/usenet/hyperactive/recent-newsgroups.html`.

Finding the perfect newsgroup

The Internet provides various sources for finding Usenet newsgroups. Here are a few examples:

- ✔ **Usenet Info Center Launch Pad** (`sunsite.unc.edu/usenet-i`) uses an excellent search engine that can help you find the right newsgroup. Additional information includes statistics about the number of messages posted per month and the percentage of Usenet sites that carry the group.

- ✔ **Infinite Ink Finding News Group** (`www.ii.com/internet`) is a user-friendly site that can assist you in finding the perfect newsgroup.

- ✔ **Robot Wisdom Newsgroup Finder** (`www.mcs.net/~jorn/html/finder/finder.html`) allows you to search by historical period, numbers of articles, and country or state locations. This site uses clickable maps of the U.S. and the world. Responses include the newsgroup name, address, description, charter, and sometimes Frequently Asked Questions (FAQs) if available.

Note: Frequently Asked Questions (FAQs) are lists of the most frequently asked questions about specific topics. Some newsgroups have one or more FAQs. FAQs can have a table of contents and several sections.

Finally, some newsreading

My favorite newsgroup site is Deja News (`www.dejanews.com`), shown in Figure 3-3. This site lists thousands of Usenet newsgroups and provides a sophisticated search engine. You can search categories such as Business/Money and then search subcategories such as Investments. Web pages indicate the name of the newsgroup and the number of articles available.

The best feature of this site is that it allows you to post your questions directly to the newsgroup without a great deal of fuss. You can also search newsgroup articles for keywords. For example, if you're researching Delta Airlines, you can see what (and when) newsgroup members had something to say about the airline.

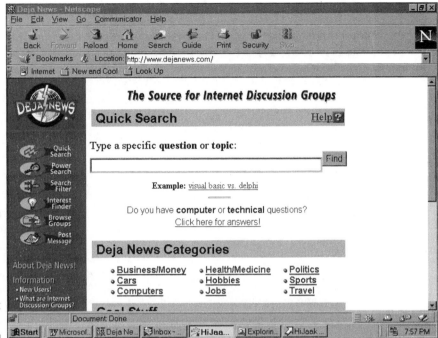

Figure 3-3:
Deja News
allows you
to post your
questions to
the right
newsgroups.

Another great feature is that you can research the author of the newsgroup article. Deja News shows how many articles the author has posted and which newsgroup he or she is posting to. This data can indicate which newsgroups regularly carry the type of information you're seeking.

Posting the matchless question

Newsgroups give you an opportunity to read the opinions of other people who are interested in the same topics as you. Before you ask a question, read the newsgroup's Frequently Asked Questions (FAQs) section to see whether someone has already answered your question. Checking out the FAQs is likely to save you from being *flamed* (receiving a hot, angry message from an experienced newsgroup user) by an old hand who is tired of seeing the same question over and over again. Another good reason to read this file is that FAQs are often the real pearls of newsgroups. Narratives vary from insipid to brilliant.

If you still want to ask a question, you can use your browser's newsreader or the Deja News Web site. Deja News provides you with instructions, and *The Internet For Dummies,* 5th Edition, by John R. Levine, Carol Baroudi, and Margaret Levine Young (published by IDG Books Worldwide, Inc.) can show you how to configure your Internet browser's newsreader.

Getting Investor Information from Mailing Lists

Mailing lists are e-mail groups that are started by organizations or individuals who purchase mailing list programs. Then they advertise to others who may be interested in joining a topic-specific discussion group. The advertisement usually provides precise instructions for subscribing to the mailing list. (To find the right mailing list, see the next section in this chapter.)

You subscribe to a particular mailing list by sending an e-mail message to the list's moderator. In return, you receive an e-mail message confirming your enrollment. This message typically includes the address you use for posting messages to the mailing list, the rules of the discussion group, and instructions for removing your name — that is, *unsubscribing* — from the mailing list.

To answer questions or make comments, subscribers send an e-mail message to the mailing list address (which differs from the mailing list program's address), and everyone gets a copy of the message. Unlike newsgroups, most lists are moderated so that inappropriate messages aren't sent to the group.

Finding the right mailing lists

You may find a mailing list while surfing the Net, but they tend to be private. The best source for finding investor-related mailing list is Liszt, at www.liszt.com. Liszt has more than 71,000 mailing lists and is growing. Don't despair; the site is searchable. However, the amount of information available about each group varies. Here are some other directories of mailing lists:

- **CataList** (www.lsoft.com/lists/listref.html) has only 14,000 mailing lists but is searchable by site, country, and number of list subscribers. (Sometimes knowing how many subscribers will receive your investment question is a good idea.)

- **PAML — Publicly Accessible Mailing Lists** (www.neosoft.com/internet/paml) is a small mailing list of 2,000 or so.

- **Listserv Home Page** (www.liszt.com) is an index of listservers (mailing list programs) arranged alphabetically, by description, name, and subject. The site is searchable.

Subscribing, using, and contributing

Mailing lists are generally groups of individuals with the same interests. Participants exchange e-mail about issues in their subject areas. If someone starts a *thread,* or topic, that you want to comment on, you post your comments to the list, using the instructions you received when you subscribed. Each mailing list is different, so reading the instructions is important.

Three primary types of list servers exist:

- ✔ **Listserv:** Named for a list server program that was created by Eric Thomas (L-Soft International). Listserv is a generic term used for any program that automates list operations.

- ✔ **Majordomo:** A centralized system for managing e-mail distributions that use a single list for multiple computing systems.

- ✔ **Listproc:** A system list processor that routes mail to particular mailing lists and services user-defined requirements.

In the following sections, I show you how to subscribe and unsubscribe to each type of list.

Listserv

A Listserv mailing list usually has an address such as `listserv@` `fictionalexample.com`. To subscribe, you send an e-mail message to the Listserv's address. In the body of the message, type **subscribe *name of list first name last name,*** as in the following example:

```
subscribe exampleinvestment_issues-l john doe
```

Of course, you should enter your name in place of `john doe` in the body of your message.

To unsubscribe, you send an e-mail message that says **unsubscribe *name of list*,** as in the following example:

```
unsubscribe exampleinvestment_issues-l
```

Majordomo

A Majordomo mailing list usually has an address such as `majordomo@` `fictionalexample.com`. To subscribe, you send an e-mail message to the Majordomo's address. In the body of the message, type **subscribe *name of list e-mail address*,** as in the following example:

```
subscribe exampleinvestment-costs johndoe@ix.netcom.com
```

Again, you enter your e-mail address (not John Doe's) in this message.

To unsubscribe, send an e-mail message that says **unsubscribe *name of list***, as in the following example:

```
unsubscribe exampleinvestment-costs
```

Listproc

A Listproc mailing list usually has an address such as `listproc@fictionalexample.com`. To subscribe, you send an e-mail message to the Listproc's address. In the body of the message, type **subscribe *name of list first name last name***, as in the following example:

```
subscribe exampleinvestment-brokers John Doe
```

Use your name (not John Doe's) in this message.

To unsubscribe, you send an e-mail message that says **unsubscribe *name of list first name last name***, as in the following example:

```
unsubscribe exampleinvestment-brokers John Doe
```

Mailing lists sometimes have *archives* of Frequently Asked Questions (FAQs) and past messages. (An archive is a repository of all the past mailing list messages.) Using keywords, you can search the archives. A mailing list's archive locations are usually in the new member's introductory message. However, Majordomo mailing programs don't support archive searches.

The fastest way to search a mailing list archive is to access Reference.com (`www.reference.com`), shown in Figure 3-4. This service allows you to research all the messages for one specific mailing list or conduct a keyword search for all mailing lists.

Mailing lists members receive an average of 30 messages per day. If you just signed up for four mailing lists, you may have more than a hundred messages tomorrow.

Free and Fee-Based Online Investor Databases

Online investors have their choice of searching free or fee-based online databases. One advantage of both types of databases is that they are constantly open. That is, you can access them 24 hours a day, 7 days a week.

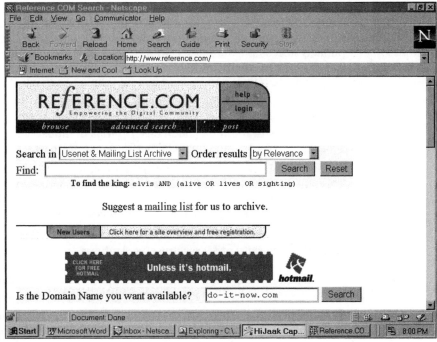

Figure 3-4:
Reference
.com can be
easily
searched
for FAQs
and past
messages.

It's a no-brainer that savvy online investors should start with the free databases. If the information you desire isn't available in the free databases, then try fee-based databases. If you carefully select a fee-based database for your well-constructed query, you can often get the information you want without paying big bucks.

Totally free databases

Colleges and universities played a large part in the development of the Internet. These organizations never charge for the knowledge they create. Consequently, many free databases exist online. Here are a few examples of free online databases:

✔ **Internet Federal Reserve Sites** (www.stls.frb.org/other/websites.html) provides links to all the Federal Reserve home pages. Publications include high-quality statistics, analyses, and forecasts of regional, national, and international economic and financial conditions. For example, the Cleveland Federal Reserve publishes *Economic Trends,* a monthly report on the Gross Domestic Product (GDP), consumer income, housing starts, and consumer price index. *U.S. Financial Data* is a weekly publication of the St. Louis Federal Reserve and includes statistics on the money supply, interest rates, and Treasury securities yields. Regional economic indicators are published in the *Fed Flash.*

✔ **Government Information Locator Service** (www.gsa.gov) includes many U.S. government agency reports in both full text and abstract forms. Government agencies are now required to provide and maintain publicly accessible databases. To meet this requirement, most federal agencies are using the Internet. Sources are cataloged and searchable. This GSA site allows you to search more than one agency at a time.

✔ **American Society of Association Executives** (asaenet.org) provides links to Web sites for different industries. The sites offer helpful industry overviews that often include descriptions of industry trends, geographic profiles, and financial performance statistics.

✔ **FINWEB** (www.finweb.com) is from the University of Texas at Austin. This site offers links to many finance and economic departments of universities, commercial sources, and financial institutions. This financial supersite includes high-quality recommendations, and all links are screened for content.

✔ **Govbot, University of Massachusetts, Amherst** (ciir.cs.umas.edu/ciirdemo/Govbot/index.html) is sponsored by the Center for Intelligent Information Retrieval (CIIR). The free database allows you to search more than 200,000 government and military Web pages.

✔ **STAT-USA** (www.stat-usa.gov) is sponsored by the U.S. Department of Commerce. This site includes economic indicators, statistics, and news. It also offers data about state and local bond rates, foreign exchange rates, and daily economic news. Statistics include interest rates, employment, income, prices, productivity, new construction, and home sales. For an annual fee of $150, you can receive the *National Trade Data Bank*. A free trial offer is available for new database users.

When all else fails — fee-based databases

For specialized investor topics, the only information available may be in an online database that you have to pay for. How each organization charges for database access varies from company to company. Charges can be by query, month, hour, or document. Most firms were designed for large corporate use, and they tend to flounder at their attempts to find equitable ways of charging individuals for private use.

Fee-based databases have several limitations. Often they use their own search methodologies that require some getting used to, and they can be costly. The fee structure may be geared for corporations and too expensive for individual use. Databases tend to be traditional and may not have that bit of unique information you're seeking.

Here are a few examples of fee-based databases (all price quotes are as of this writing and subject to change, just like everything else on the Internet):

✔ **IBM Info Market** (www.infomarket.ibm.com) includes a database that has 75 newswires, 300 newspapers, 819 newsletters, 6,882 journals, and 11 million companies. The site charges by the document.

✔ **Lexis-Nexis** (www.lexis-nexis.com) recently added a new database of 20 market summaries of industry sectors or demographic markets. Among other things, their databases include *Market Share Reports* (from 1991 to present) and *Computer Industry Forecasts.* Pricing can be by month, hourly, or by transaction. Charges vary depending on the database you use. If you need to know the exact price of a piece of research, contact Lexis-Nexis. The least expensive service is Lexis-Nexis Tracker Pricing, which begins at $4.99 per month. The service follows the progress of a 100-employee (or greater) firm and sends you monthly results by e-mail.

✔ **The Electric Library** (www.elibrary.com) has, among other things, many newspapers, periodicals, and journals. Searches can be by keyword. The Electric Library is a good source for background or academic financial research. Pricing is for unlimited access. Charges for individuals are $39.95 for 6 months and $59.95 for 12 months.

Chapter 4

Warnings about Online Frauds, Schemes, and Deceptions

● ●

In This Chapter

▶ Recognizing potential online investment scams

▶ Identifying pyramid schemes

▶ Requiring real financial disclosures

▶ Unmasking dishonest brokers by asking the right questions

▶ Knowing where to complain online if you receive an unscrupulous investment offer

▶ Evaluating the security of Internet transactions

● ●

*D*on't get taken for a ride on the Information Superhighway. The North American Securities Administrators Association, an association of state investment watchdogs, estimates that more than $10 billion a year is lost in investment fraud. That's about $1.1 million every hour.

In the past, swindlers used the U.S. mail and telemarketing boiler rooms to exploit unsuspecting investors. Fraudsters have now invaded cyberspace. The Federal Trade Commission database shows that in 1996 individuals reported losses due to online investment schemes ranging from $2,900 to as much as $400,000. Some organizations estimate that the average loss per investment victim is $15,000.

Investigating investments is difficult. The terms of the deal may be hard to understand, and the investment literature and salespeople may omit key facts. However, you can observe warning signs of potential scams, schemes, and deceptions. Doing so involves a little effort, homework, and investigating, but isn't that what investing is all about?

In this chapter, I provide warnings about online investment information and offers that may be too good to be true. I provide guidelines for checking out brokers and investments, and tips for identifying a pyramid scheme. I show you how to read financial disclosures to get the facts, and I explain how to complain online. I also offer a few thoughts about the online security of your personal and financial information.

Don't Believe Everything You Read

Every investor dreams of being an early stockowner in a Microsoft or Intel Corp. Dishonest brokers and stock promoters prey upon this greed and offer unsuspecting investors low-priced stocks in companies with new products or technologies (like the self-chilling soda can). Often these companies have a lot of sizzle and no steak.

Most folks believe that they can't be swindled. However, swindlers target investors with deep pockets as well as small investors who are counting on large returns. (For small investor schemes, you just have to get more investors.) To swindlers, everyone's money is the same.

The Internet allows swindlers to inexpensively reach millions of potential victims. Currently more than 40 million Americans are online. In contrast, *The Wall Street Journal* has a mere 1.8 million subscribers. One online posting designed to fleece unsuspecting investors can easily reach thousands of people. According to one regulatory agency, one of the major national online services in the U.S. had 5,600 new messages with investment topics posted to 969 different topic areas in a two-week period. (The company processes about 75,000 new messages per day.)

Online frauds mirror the types of frauds that are perpetrated over the phone or through the mail. Many Internet messages are about general stock-picking advice or mention other investment possibilities. However, some messages tout specific stocks, moneymaking ventures, and service providers. Investment chat rooms now have sales pitches that offer more details by private e-mail and toll-free telephone numbers.

Investment swindlers can work anywhere, from dingy telemarketing offices to expensive hotel suites to cyberspace. They may be friends of friends, and they may wear natty suits or hard hats. They may be so-called "recognized experts" or have no connection to the investment community. However, they all have one goal — to get your money into their pocket.

If an Offer Seems Too Good to Be True, It Usually Is

As the popularity of the Internet grows, millions of people flock to the new Global Village. Inevitably, individuals with criminal intent are following the crowd. They seek to deceive the innocent, the hopeful, the naive, the poor, and the greedy.

Online investor fraud often starts when you receive an e-mail message describing an appealing offer. Offers that seem too good to be true usually are. Here are a few of the warning signs to help you identify potential scams:

- ✔ **Exceptional profits:** Usually the profits are large enough to get your interest but not large enough to make you suspicious.

- ✔ **Low risk — high return:** All investments involve some risk. If a fraudster advertises "no-risk," this should be an immediate red flag that something is wrong. Don't invest if you don't know exactly what the risks are. (Remember, fraudsters don't honor money-back guarantees.)

- ✔ **Urgency:** Fraudsters usually offer a reason why you must invest as quickly as possible. They may tell you that delays may mean losses of big profits or that they're limiting the offer to just a few individuals. Confidence artists often play on new technological advances that create a brief market that you must get into right away. However, if you feel that the posting is valid, wait before you respond. Others won't be shy about posting their opinions.

- ✔ **High pressure tactics:** Fraudsters often act like they're doing you a favor by letting you get in on the investment opportunity. Don't be afraid to ask questions publicly. Post a follow-up message. If the original post is valid, the person who sent it will be happy to post a public response.

Although you can find plenty of helpful investment-related postings online (after all, that's what this book is all about), the Internet, like other places, has its share of fraudsters. Figure 4-1 shows the National Association of Securities Dealers Web site at `www.investor.nasd.com/ni5d.html`. This site provides investor education about different types of investment scams, including Ponzi schemes, precious metal frauds, and stock swindles.

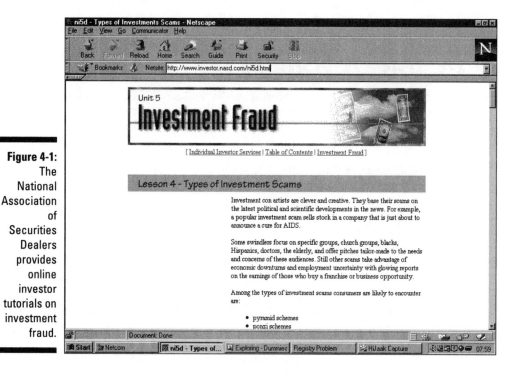

Figure 4-1:
The
National
Association
of
Securities
Dealers
provides
online
investor
tutorials on
investment
fraud.

Checking It Out Before You Put Your Money Down

The explosion of the Internet has created new opportunities and new dangers for investors. If you're an online investment victim, the chances of getting your money back are slim. Even in cases where government agencies recover money, the consumer usually gets back less than 10 cents on the dollar. The best defense is to thoroughly investigate an online investment *before* you put your money down. Here are some suggestions about how to investigate that "once in a lifetime offer":

✔ Check with your city or state consumer protection agency; it may have information about the firm you're considering investing in. Additionally, a consumer protection agency can direct you to other organizations that may have information about the investment.

  ✔ Contact regulators. Organizations that you can contact include the Federal Trade Commission, the Securities and Exchange Commission, and the National Association of Securities Dealers.

  ✔ Write or telephone law enforcement agencies. Fraud is illegal in every state in the nation. You can contact the local public prosecutor, the state attorney general, and the state securities administrator.

Figure 4-2 shows the About the Better Business Bureau Web page at `www.bbb.org/about/index.html`. Their reports on firms can be helpful to you before making a purchase. Their reliability reports on firms indicate how long the firm has been in business, how long the Better Business Bureau has known about the company, complaint patterns (if any), and whether any government agencies — for example, the Federal Trade Commission (FTC) or the State Attorney General — have taken any enforcement actions in the last three years.

Figure 4-2:
Check with
the Better
Business
Bureau to
discover
whether the
firm has
received
any
complaints
or is subject
to any
government
enforcement
actions.

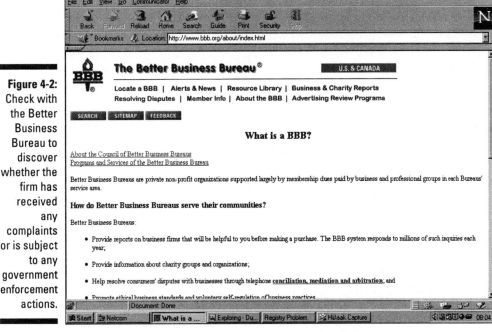

Determining Whether an Investment Is a Pyramid Scheme

Pyramid schemes, sometimes called *multilevel marketing plans,* are sure ways to lose money. One person recruits six friends; those six people recruit six more friends — and so on, in a relentless search for new recruits. If everyone cooperates, then by level 15, the scheme needs 7.6 billion participants — more than the Earth's population. See Table 4-1 for details.

Table 4-1	New Recruits Needed for a Pyramid Scheme	
Level	*New Recruits*	*Total Participants*
1	1	1
2	5	6
3	25	31
4	125	156
5	625	781
6	3,125	3,906
7	15,625	19,531
8	78,125	97,656
9	390,625	488,281
10	1,953,125	2,441,406
11	9,765,625	12,207,031
12	48,828,125	61,035,156
13	244,140,625	305,175,781
14	1,220,703,125	1,525,878,906
15	6,103,515,625	7,629,394,531

Profits from these schemes don't come from selling products or distributorships but from recruiting new participants. The endless recruiting of more participants eventually leads to an oversupply of sellers. Investors are left with garages full of products and the loss of their investment.

Three elements characterize pyramid schemes:

 ✔ A reliance on funds from new investors (recruits) to pay returns, commissions, or bonuses to old investors.

> ✔ The need for an inexhaustible supply of new recruits.
>
> ✔ The promise of earning profits without providing goods or services.

The Securities and Exchange Commission estimates that the American public has lost $400 million to fraudulent pyramid schemes. States such as New Mexico require all sales companies to register with the Attorney General so that fraudulent companies can be identified.

Figure 4-3 shows a Web page from the Computer Incident Advisory Capability group (CIAC) of the U.S. Department of Energy (`ciac.llnl.gov/ciac/CIACChainLetters.html`). This page offers warnings and shows how you can recognize an e-mailed chain letter (pyramid scheme). Established in 1989, CIAC provides computer security services to employees and contractors of the United States Department of Energy. CIAC is an element of the Computer Security Technology Center (CSTC) and is located at the Lawrence Livermore National Laboratory.

In September 1996, the FTC charged several defendants from Fortuna Alliance with fraud. The Fortuna Alliance induced consumers to invest $250 to $1,750 and promised $5,000 per month in "profits" as others joined the pyramid. Fortuna used its Web site to increase its credibility and to facilitate communications between the firm and its team leaders. After six months, the firm had taken $13 million from more than 25,000 investors. About half the victims live outside the U.S.

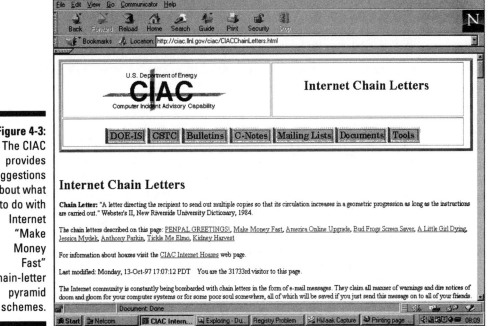

Figure 4-3: The CIAC provides suggestions about what to do with Internet "Make Money Fast" chain-letter pyramid schemes.

What Real Financial Disclosures Include

If you're considering investing in a company, you may want to download and print a copy of the investment offer. If the sales literature doesn't include a prospectus with financial statements, ask for one.

If you're told that the company doesn't have a prospectus, request a written financial disclosure about the company. All in all, you should have the following information:

  ✔ **Offering circular:** Sales literature that presents the investment.

  ✔ **Prospectus:** A formal written statement that discloses the terms of a public offering of a security or a mutual fund. The prospectus is required to divulge both positive and negative information to investors about the proposed offering.

  ✔ **Annual report:** A written report that includes a statement by the chief executive officer, a narrative about last year's performance, and a forecast for next year's performance. Financial statements include a balance sheet, income statements, a statement of cash flows, and retained earnings.

  ✔ **Audited financial statements:** Financial statements audited by a certified public accounting firm.

Figure 4-4 shows the Web site for the Securities and Exchange Commission (SEC), located at www.sec.gov. The SEC doesn't require companies that are seeking less than $1 million to be "registered," but it does require these firms to file a *Form D*. Form D doesn't include an audited financial statement but it does state the names and addresses of the owners and promoters of the firm. Other information is limited. If a Form D isn't available, the SEC suggests that you call its Investor Education and Assistance Department at 202-942-7040.

Tell-Tale Signs of Dishonest Brokers

Dishonest brokers often ask their victims a steady stream of questions designed to derail honest investors from asking the right questions. Dishonest brokers don't want curious customers. In contrast, honest brokers encourage you to ask questions, provide you with additional educational materials, and make certain that you understand the risks involved in your investment decision. And if you decide not to spend your money, they are untroubled by your investment decision.

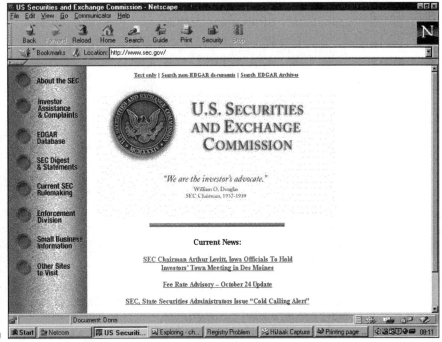

Figure 4-4:
The
Securities
and
Exchange
Commission
has all the
financial
data you
need for
registered
securities.

The National Futures Association has collected 16 questions that are turn-offs for dishonest brokers (www.pueblo.gsa.gov/cic_text/money/swindles.txt). In the following list, I've tailored those questions to meet the needs of online investors:

- **Where did you get my name?** The dishonest broker may say "a select list of investors," but your name was probably obtained from a Usenet newsgroup question you asked, a bulk e-mail response, or from a mailing list subscription list. Individuals who have been duped in the past may be on the "select list." They were conned before and probably can be conned again.

- **What risks are involved in the investment?** All investments except U.S. Treasury securities have some risk. Some investments have more risk than others do. A salesperson that really has a sure thing won't be on the telephone talking with you.

- **Can you send me a written explanation of the investment, so I can consider it at my leisure?** This question provides two turn-offs to dishonest brokers. First, swindlers are reluctant to put in writing anything that may become evidence in a fraud trial. Second, swindlers are impatient; they want your money right now.

✔ **Would you explain your investment proposal to my attorney, financial planner or investment advisor, or banker?** You know the investment is a scam if the salesperson says something like "Normally, I would be glad to, but . . ." or "Unfortunately, we don't have enough time," or "Can't you make you own decisions?"

✔ **Can you give me references and the names of your principal investors and officers?** Swindlers often change their names so you can't check their histories. Make certain that the reference list contains the names of well-known banks and reputable brokerage firms that you can easily contact. Figure 4-5 shows a Web page titled Checking Out Your Financial Professional. This page, located at www.investorprotection.org/checkout.html, includes links to various resources you can use to check out a broker or other financial professional.

✔ **Which exchanges are the securities traded on? Can I have copies of the prospectus, the risk disclosure statement, or the audited financial statements?** For legitimate, registered investments, these documents are normal. A legitimate investment may or may not be traded on an exchange. However, fraudulent investments never are. Exchanges have extensive rules for competitive pricing and fair dealing. Those that don't follow the rules are subject to severe sanctions.

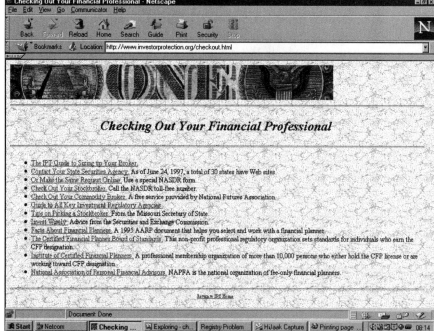

Figure 4-5:
Use the links at Investor Protection to check out your broker or financial professional before you invest.

✔ **What regulatory agency is the investment subject to?** Tell the broker that you want to check the investment's good standing with its regulatory agency before going forward. The possibility of having to talk to a representative of a regulatory agency is a real turn-off to a swindler.

✔ **How long has your company been in business, and what is your track record? Can I meet another representative of your firm?** If the broker or the investment doesn't seem to have a past, the deal may be a scam. Many swindlers have been running scams for years and aren't anxious to talk about it.

Legitimate brokers can tell you how much of a return investors have enjoyed in the past. Even if you do get this information in writing, keep in mind that past performance doesn't indicate future performance. However, dishonest brokers often won't take the time to meet with you, and they don't want you in their place of business.

✔ **Where will my money be? What type of accounting can I expect?** Often, funds for certain investments are required to stay in separate accounts, at all times. Find out which accounting firm does the firm's auditing and what type of external audits the firm is subject to. (Make certain that the well-known accounting firm is actually the auditor.)

✔ **How much of my money will go to management fees, commissions, and similar expenses?** Legitimate investments often have restrictions on the amount of management fees the firm can charge. Getting what the firm charges in writing is important. Compare the firm's fees to charges for similar investments.

✔ **How can I get my money if I want to liquidate my investment?** You may discover that your investment can't be sold or that selling your investment involves substantial costs. If you're unable to get a solid answer in writing, the investment may be a scam.

✔ **If a dispute arises, how will it be resolved?** No one wants to go to court and sue. The investment should be subject to a regulatory agency's guidelines so that disputes are resolved inexpensively through arbitration, mediation, or a reparation procedure.

 Is your broker dishonest or just incompetent? The Stock Detective at www.stockdetective.com/states.html can help. This Web site provides a list of state investment watchdog agencies. It includes the name of each state's securities commission, addresses, telephone numbers, names of directors, and contact people.

Where to Complain Online

The Internet provides many ways to complain about online investor fraud. Here are three good resources:

- ✔ **Better Business Bureau** (`www.bbb.org`) has an online complaint form and promises to follow up within two weeks of your complaint.

- ✔ **Securities and Exchange Commission** (`www.sec.gov`) has an excellent online complaint process.

- ✔ **National Fraud Information Center** (`www.fraud.org`), shown in Figure 4-6, forwards your complaint to the appropriate organizations and includes it in their Internet fraud statistics (which may not help you get your money back but may be helpful to other online investors).

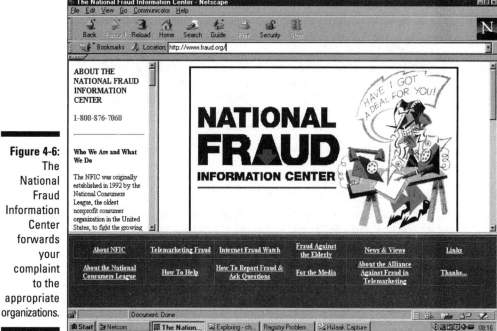

Figure 4-6: The National Fraud Information Center forwards your complaint to the appropriate organizations.

Your Bank Account Number, Security, and the Internet

Just as you take various precautions to protect your home and its contents, you must prevent online thieves from accessing your personal and financial assets via the Internet. Locked doors, alarm systems, and nosy neighbors can help you safeguard your home. Precautions on the Internet take such forms as firewalls, passwords, and encryption of important information.

An informal (and absolutely unscientific) survey of 2,200 Internet computing systems was completed in December 1996. The survey results indicate that approximately 66 percent of Web sites have potential security vulnerabilities (see `www.trouble.org/survey`).

For example, in December 1996 several catalog companies incorrectly installed an Internet shopping program. Consequently, hackers were able to get the credit card numbers of the catalogs' customers.

In contrast, online banks use a distributed security system. Security is on your computer during the transmission of information and in the bank's own computer system. Online banks use several types of security systems simultaneously:

- ✔ **Encryption:** *Encryption* is a high-tech word for encoding and is used by more people than spies. It is used so that your banking information is gibberish to unauthorized individuals.

- ✔ **Passwords:** Personal passwords are necessary to access your account information.

- ✔ **Automatic sign-off protection:** When you sign off, your session terminates so that no one can continue in your absence.

- ✔ **Browser security:** Your browser isn't allowed to save any of your bank information.

- ✔ **Monitoring:** The system constantly scans for unauthorized intrusions.

At banks, your money is insured by the Federal Deposit Insurance Corporation (FDIC), but online securities firms don't have similar insurance for consumers. To date, electronic theft has been slight, but as more money flows over the Internet, the need for insurance is certain to change.

Part II
Finding the Right Investments

The 5th Wave   By Rich Tennant

"I'm not sure — I like the mutual funds with rotating dollar signs, although the dancing stocks and bonds look good, too."

In this part . . .

The chapters in this part of the book show you how to use the Internet to select investments that match your financial objectives. See how to manage your checking account electronically. Identify the best savings rates and certificate of deposit rates online. Find out why everyone is talking about mutual funds and how the Internet can help you select the fund that's right for you. Check out the different types of stocks and bonds and see how online stock and mutual fund screens can help you whittle down investment candidates to a manageable number.

Chapter 5

Getting the Most Out of Online Banking

· ·

In This Chapter

▶ Getting in tune with online banking

▶ Combining your online banking with online investing

▶ Shopping the Internet for the best rates and online banking deals

· ·

*O*nline banking is booming. About one-third of the largest banks in the U.S. offer online banking, and nearly 2.5 million Americans use it. Forecasts indicate that by the year 2002, more than 18 million U.S. households will bank online. Although concerns about security, privacy, and fraud prevention currently hold back the widespread use of online banking, these issues should be resolved within a few years.

MECCA Software now offers its Managing Your Money, a personal finance program with online banking, directly to banks. Banks can offer this program to customers at no cost. Bank customers who are connected to Marimba (a push technology product; see Chapter 2 for details) can access their bank accounts and check out investment news without logging on to the Internet.

Software that uses intelligent agents is also getting into the act. Vertigo Development Group uses a knowledgebot to let consumers receive personalized messages like Your three-year CD is coming due next month. Click here to examine investment options. (See Chapter 2 for more information about knowledgebots and other intelligent agent software.)

Online investors don't have a great deal of time to access different accounts. They want to see their checking accounts and their brokerage accounts at one-stop-shopping sites. In response to this demand, online brokerages are beginning to offer online banking services that customers can access by using the Quicken Deluxe and Microsoft Money 98 personal finance software packages.

This chapter offers information about how you can combine your online banking with your online investing. For example, approximately 100 financial institutions — such as Citibank Direct Access (www.citibank.com) — enable you to buy or sell stocks and mutual funds and then pay for your purchases from your online checking account.

This chapter describes what you can expect with online banking, and the strengths and limitations of Internet banks. I cover such important details as smart questions to ask your online banker, what gear you need, and the kind of troubles you may expect at the beginning. I also discuss how to use the Internet to find the best rates for various types of accounts.

What You Can Expect with Online Banking

To start banking online, you need some software and a computer. Your bank usually provides the software, but you have to provide your own computer gear (I outline the requirements later in this chapter). After you start online banking, you'll quickly notice that it takes many of the tasks you used to perform manually and does them electronically.

With most online banking software, when you access your account, you see a display of all your current balances with the bank, including your checking account, savings account, money market account, CDs, and credit card balances. By double-clicking on one of your accounts, you open another screen that shows the transaction details for that account.

The online transaction register looks like your usual check register. You can enter transactions or wait for the bank to automatically update your account when the checks and deposits clear. ATM transactions are also automatically entered into your register.

At the end of the month, you can reconcile your checkbook by just clicking on a few buttons. What may have taken up to an hour now takes less than five minutes.

If you need to make a one-time payment to someone, complete the payment information form and click on the appropriate button. The bank creates an electronic check and mails it to your creditor.

For the bills you pay each month, use the program to set up who you want to pay, how much, and when. Online banking automatically pays those bills each month.

If your checking account needs a refill so that you can pay your monthly bills, you can automatically move money from your money market or similar account to your checking account.

If you have your credit card account with your bank, you can view current charges, see what's due next month, and review past statements. To see more details, just click on the account.

If you're interested in a demonstration of how online banking works, see Security First Network Bank (SFNB) at `www.sfnb.com`, shown in Figure 5-1. SFNB has two demonstrations: a quick view of SFNB's online banking services and a longer and more detailed presentation of online banking. Each online tutorial steps you through the types of transactions you may encounter if you bank online.

Advantages of online banking

Online banking is generally safe, convenient, and less time-consuming than other types of banking. You can simplify your life by performing the following banking tasks online:

Figure 5-1:
The demonstrations at Security First Network Bank show what you can expect with online banking.

> ✔ **Transfer money from one account to another.** You can wear your bathrobe while you transfer money from your savings account to your checking account. No more running to the bank before the 2:00 p.m. cut-off time.
>
> ✔ **Determine which checks and deposits have cleared the bank.** For example, many households write checks from two different check-books. You can easily track purchases and deposits (as often as you like) from the two checkbooks by using online banking.
>
> ✔ **Pay your bills online.** Setting up payment for monthly recurring bills takes about an hour, but when you're done, the bills get paid automatically, and you don't have to worry about due dates.
>
> ✔ **Make stop-payment requests.** You may use this feature only once a year, but when you need it, you really need it. Online stop-payment requests are especially useful for folks who travel and can't get to the bank.

Limitations of online banking

One limitation of online banking is that many of the major banks don't describe their fees and minimum balance requirements at their Web sites. *The Wall Street Journal* recently stated that a search of the Web sites for NationsBank (`www.nationsbank.com`), Citibank (`www.citibank.com`), and First Union (`www.firstunion.com`) showed that each bank had online enrollment forms for online banking but didn't describe their fees and minimum balance requirements.

A second limitation of online banking is the out-of-state problem. For example, how can you make a quick deposit to Security First Network Bank in Atlanta when you live in San Francisco? After all, SFNB is an electronic bank and doesn't have any branches. Using an expensive overnight express mail service is likely to wipe out any financial gains you enjoy with online banking.

Local merchants who don't honor out-of-state checks may be another problem. However, one possible solution is an ATM card. In addition to cash withdrawals, ATM cards can now be used for many purchases.

Is online banking right for you?

Online banking may not be for everyone. If you have concerns about online security, don't want to deal with anything new, and are leery of electronic bill paying, you may be wise to wait for better and more convenient online banking software. However, online banking may be just your ticket if you

✔ Frequently transfer money from one account to another.

✔ Keep careful records of checks and deposits.

✔ Mail more than ten checks per month to creditors.

✔ Don't require canceled checks for your records.

Smart questions to ask your online banker

As you probably have discovered, things on the Internet vary a great deal. Specifically, not all online banking services are the same. As you investigate different banks, ask some very pointed questions, like the following examples:

✔ How long does it take for each transaction to be posted?

✔ Are transferred funds available immediately?

✔ What about your institution's online banking security? Have you experienced an online security failure?

✔ What steps does the bank take to correct errors?

✔ If I pay a bill twice, how can I correct the error?

✔ How difficult is closing an online account?

✔ What fees are associated with the online account?

Table 5-1 compares the three leading online banks: Bank of America, Security First Network Bank, and Wells Fargo Bank. To protect your money, each bank uses software encryption and Federal Deposit Insurance Corporation (FDIC) insurance, which insures your deposits (of up to $100,000). Additionally, Security First Network Bank has a separate insurance policy that insures your assets from any hacker thefts. Each bank's Web site has an online enrollment form.

Table 5-1	Comparison of the Three Leading Internet Banks		
	Bank of America	**Security First Network Bank**	**Wells Fargo Bank**
URL	www.bofa.com	www.sfnb.com	www.wellsfargo.com
Interface	Simple	Somewhat complex	Easy to use
Fees	$6.50 monthly	None	$5.00 monthly bill paying (first two months free)

(continued)

Table 5-1 *(continued)*

	Bank of America	Security First Network Bank	Wells Fargo Bank
	$4.50 checking	All services free	All other services free with $100 minimum checking account balance
	(First three months free)	All services free if you have direct deposit of your paycheck into your checking account	
	All services free if you have direct deposit of your pay-check into your checking account	No direct deposit requirements	
Minimum to Open an Account	None	$100	$100
Browsers	Netscape Navigator	Internet Explorer, Netscape Navigator	Internet Explorer, Netscape Navigator
Software Supported	Quicken, Microsoft Money, Managing Your Money	Quicken, Microsoft Money, Managing Your Money	Quicken, Microsoft Money

NationsBank and online banking

If you are curious about personal financial software, NationsBank can help you. NationsBank offers a free customized version of Managing Your Money, which you can download from the NationsBank Web site at www.nationsbank.com. If you have a 28.8 Kbps modem, the download time is estimated to be between 25 and 40 minutes. (NationsBank launched online banking in June of 1996. In the next year, more than 350,000 customers enrolled in its program.)

Online banking extras you may desire

Different banks have different fees for account access and bill payment services. Some banks offer online trading in addition to online banking. You may use your Internet browser, Money 98, Quicken, or your bank's proprietary software to access your account. Your online banker may also have some additional features that you consider indispensable.

The following list describes 12 features that you may want for your online banking account. One of these features may be critical to your selection of an online bank:

- **Security:** What sort of insurance does the bank offer in addition to FDIC?

- **Online banking statements:** Besides knowing your debits and credits, can you get an online banking statement?

- **Type of online payment:** When you pay bills online, does the bank transfer money electronically or create an electronic check and send it by U.S. mail? For example, does your mortgage company accept electronic payments from this online bank?

- **Account transfers:** Can you transfer funds between accounts? For example, if you have a checking and a savings account at your bank, can you transfer funds from one account to the other?

- **Bank contact person:** Who can you contact if the bank doesn't credit an electronic deposit?

- **Investment information:** Does the bank offer delayed stock quotes, investment updates, economic reports, and other investor-oriented services?

- **Popular ATM or debit cards:** Does the bank offer a debit card that is a member of ATM networks such as Star or Cirrus?

- **Bank software:** Does the bank use Quicken, Money 98, or some other finance package? How do these software programs work with the bank's online services?

- **Access to previous statements:** Can you call up last month's bank statement? Do you have access to all your account information since you opened your account?

- **Access to all your bank accounts:** Can you check your other accounts at the bank (credit cards, mortgages, mutual funds, and so on)?

- **Online trading:** Can you buy and sell stocks and mutual funds online? Can you pay for your purchases from your checking account?

- **Online transfers to different banks:** Can you transfer money to a different bank?

After you have a good idea of what services are available, you may wonder what they cost. BanxQuote (`www.banxquote.com/banx/online/usonline.htm`), shown in Figure 5-2, provides an excellent list of online banks, their fees for account access and bill payment, and other features.

What gear do you need for online banking?

To get started with online banking, you need a few items. First, you may need online banking software. Depending on your bank, you may use a personal finance software package or the bank's proprietary software.

Online banking uses one of four interfaces:

- ✔ Microsoft Money 98
- ✔ Quicken
- ✔ Manage Your Money
- ✔ The bank's own software, such as Citibank's Smart One

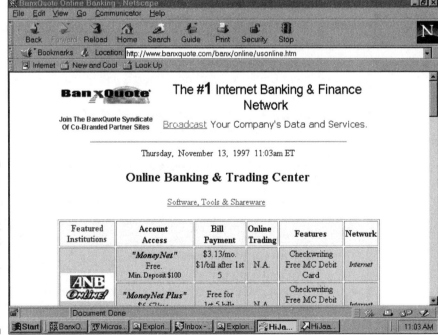

Figure 5-2: BanxQuote Online lists the current fees that banks charge for online banking services.

(Copyright © 1998 BanxQuote.)

You can usually download any of these software programs from the bank's Web site or purchase them from the bank for the cost of shipping (about $5 to $10).

You may have a problem transferring data to a spreadsheet or your personal financial software from the bank's proprietary software, so check out the programs' compatibility before you sign up.

For some online banking, you may not need a personal finance software package. In some cases, the online banking interface may take the form of an Internet browser such as Internet Explorer or Netscape Navigator. These programs cost around $60 and can be downloaded from the Internet.

These programs *encrypt* your bank data, which means that if anyone tries to spy on your bank session, all that person receives is gibberish. (The need for encryption is one reason why online banks don't allow you to use the beta version of an Internet browser.)

Online banking that doesn't require Microsoft Money, Quicken, or the bank's proprietary software is considered the wave of the future. Called *second generation* Web sites, they allow you to access account information directly through your Internet browser.

Regardless of which software you use, online banking requires a computer and a modem. Many banks can't handle high-speed modems, but don't use a modem that transmits less than 14.4 Kbps. Your computer should have at least 8MB of RAM and 20MB of free space on your hard disk. The average cost of an adequate computer system for online banking is about $500.

Personal computers aren't the only delivery medium for online banking. Cable companies are working hard to make television truly interactive. These companies hope to offer online banking within the next ten years.

You and online banking: Trouble at the beginning

Most people find that online banking is a big hassle in the beginning. Even experienced PC users have some troubles or traumas setting it up, but almost everyone who sticks with the program says that it's worth the effort. In other words, after you get started, you probably won't return to manually reconciling your bank statement. However, the troubles at the beginning are real. Here are some examples of what you may encounter:

✔ **Connectivity problems:** Your online banking software says you can't connect because of the bank. The bank says the problem is with your software. For example, when I enrolled for online banking, my bank entered my social security number incorrectly. When my Microsoft Money program asked for my social security number and compared it to the bank's records, the numbers didn't match. No match, no connection, much frustration. Straightening out the problem took about two weeks, but online banking has been smooth sailing ever since.

✔ **Missed electronic payments:** If your electronic bill payment isn't sent, you may not have any paper records of your attempt. The results can include late-payment fees, negative credit record entries, and other problems. Some online customers report that straightening out errors takes about two months.

✔ **Paying the same bill twice:** Can the bank get the second payment back? Results vary from bank to bank.

The solution to these problems is patience. You just have to work with your bank to straighten out any errors or misunderstandings. After you correct these start-up problems, you'll soon wonder how you got along without online banking. For example, I monitor one personal checking account and two business checking accounts. These accounts are tied to automatic bill paying, ATM cards, and six active checkbooks. With online banking, I know the exact status of each account. I can get a bigger bang for my buck because I don't have to keep a high minimum balance in each account. In other words, online banking allows me to invest my excess cash in something more profitable.

Which Is Best — Quicken or Money 98?

The leaders in personal financial software are Microsoft Money and Quicken Deluxe. The Microsoft Money 98 Financial Suite sells for around $55, and the Quicken Deluxe package is about $60. Table 5-2 compares the features of the two products.

Table 5-2	Comparing Microsoft Money 98 Financial Suite and Quicken Deluxe	
Feature	*Money 98*	*Quicken Deluxe*
Internet Explorer software	X	X
Download brokerage statements (from financial institutions that use Open Financial Exchange)	X	X

Feature	Money 98	Quicken Deluxe
Budgeting and loan tracking	X	X
Tax planning	X	X
Reports and graphs	X	X
Online banking and bill payments	X	X
Home inventory		X
Mutual fund finder	X (see note)	X
Online stock information, quotes, research, and news	X	X
Debt reduction planner	X	X
Tax deduction finder	X	X
Assists in finding mortgages and insurance quotes		X
Credit report		X
Program speed		X
User friendliness and easier to use		X
Address book		X
FYI Advisor offers personalized financial tips	X	

Note: Data on 8,000 equities and mutual funds, analyst recommendations, earnings estimates, and e-mail market alerts cost $9.95 per month.

Like previous versions of the program, Microsoft Money 98 Financial Suite is slow and not very user friendly. One of its better features is access to more than 8,000 equities and mutual funds, earnings estimates, professional recommendations, and e-mail alerts. However, to get this service, you must subscribe to Internet Investor for $9.95 per month.

The program includes personalized financial advice from the FYI Advisor. The best feature is that Microsoft has signed up more than 100 financial institutions (banks, brokers, and credit card issuers). You can access your online broker (if your broker is one of the 100 who participate in the Open Financial Exchange program) and your online banker without having to switch programs.

Quicken provides more free investment information through www.Quicken .com, which assists users in shopping for insurance and mortgages via the Internet. The 401(k) planner is much improved and is easier to use than Money 98. Quicken has about 50 financial institutions signed up, so you can access your online broker (if your broker is one of the 50 who participate in the Open Financial Exchange program) and your online banker without having to switch programs.

If you want to know more about the Microsoft Money 98 Financial Suite program, you can download a trial version at www.microsoft.com/money/nav_side.htm.

Checking Out the Best Online Banking Deals on the Internet

My favorite place for evaluating the best online banking deals is Bank Rate Monitor (www.bankrate.com). Bank Rate Monitor has 1,600 pages of timely bank fees and rates. It's a free nationwide consumer source for credit card rates, auto loan rates, checking account fees, ATM fees, home equity loan rates, personal loan rates, and online banking fees.

Figure 5-3 shows Bank Rate Monitor's Web page for online banking fees. This page indicates each bank's name, whether the bank offers a free trial period for online banking services, the monthly online banking fee, and the availability of any free bill-paying sessions per month. This Web page also shows how you can access the bank (Internet, online service such as AOL, or dial-up network with Microsoft Money, Quicken, or a proprietary program).

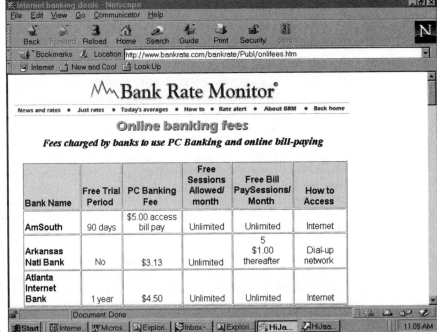

Figure 5-3: Check out online banking fees at Bank Rate Monitor.

You may be surprised to discover that because so many banks operate on the Internet, some organizations have developed listings of the Internet leaders. Figure 5-4 shows The Money Page's Top Ten Banks in Cyberspace, located at www.moneypage.com. You also may be interested in NETbanker, located at www.netbanker.com. NETbanker has listings of the top 100 banks and true Internet banks.

How Much Can Your Savings Earn?

Savings accounts are the most familiar type of fixed income investment. These accounts provide substantial safety of the principal balance, a low probability of failure to receive earned interest, and high liquidity.

The one drawback to a savings account is that the *return* (the amount of money you earn for giving up the immediate use of your money) is often the lowest available. Savings accounts are a classic example of low risk and low return.

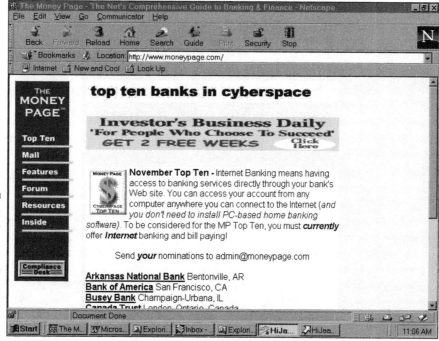

Figure 5-4: Discover the top ten banks in cyberspace at The Money Page.

The FinanCenter Web site (www.financenter.com) has an online calculator that can assist you in determining how much your money can earn. In other words, you can use this calculator to figure out how much money you'll have at some future date, or how long it will take to reach a predetermined savings goal, or how much you need to set aside each month to reach a predetermined savings goal. After you reach this Web site, click on the savings icon and then click on "What will it take to become a millionaire?" All you have to do is enter four of the five values and then click to calculate the remaining value.

When to Choose a Money Market Deposit Account (MMDA)

Your online banking program can provide you with information about your Money Market Deposit Account. A Money Market Deposit Account (MMDA) is a good place to keep your emergency fund and to park funds temporarily. (*Emergency funds* may range anywhere from 10 percent of your annual salary to three months of take-home pay.) An MMDA is a savings account with several unique features. You can withdraw the money whenever you like and you can write up to three checks per month.

TIP

Choosing between money funds and money market accounts

Your bank may have money market deposit accounts and money fund accounts. The two types of accounts are easily confused, but big differences exist between them.

Money market deposit accounts (MMDAs) are Federal Deposit Insurance Corporation (FDIC) insured up to $100,000. *Money funds* are mutual funds offered by an investment trust company in short-term (no more than 90 days), safe investment opportunities such as bonds. These funds are *not* FDIC insured.

Three types of money funds are available:

✔ **General-purpose funds** invest in short-term debt instruments such as certificates

of deposit, Treasury securities, and short-term corporate IOUs.

✔ **Government funds** usually invest in U.S. Treasury securities.

✔ **Tax-exempt funds** invest in short-term municipal bonds (which are federally tax-exempt and sometimes state tax-exempt).

BanxQuote (www.quote.com) is a good online source for the best rates for money market deposit accounts. BanxQuote shows rates and allows searches by location or terms. Data include the financial institution's name and contact information and the money market account's rate of return.

Most banks have a minimum balance for this type of account. As long as you maintain the minimum balance, you earn the money market rate of interest (currently, about 5 percent). If the balance falls below the required minimum balance, you earn the current NOW account interest rate, and you may incur a service charge (usually about $5). All in all, an MMDA is the perfect place for your emergency fund.

Bank Rate Monitor (www.bankrate.com) includes a listing of financial institutions that offer special deals on MMDAs. Some of the offers are available only to Internet shoppers, so read the instructions at each Web site carefully. One example of a special Internet deal is a free Motorola cellular phone, a $10 credit, and free checks when you open an account on the Internet. Some institutions even offer more than one special deal.

Finding the Best Rates with the Internet's CD Scanner

In the past, doing all your banking at one bank was common practice. The consolidation of the banking industry and deregulation has changed all that. Banks are now very competitive. One bank may have the best checking account, another may have the best rates on CDs, and so on. Tracking down the best rates can be a full-time job, but the Internet simplifies the task.

To find the banks that offer competitive rates on CDs, check out Bank Rate Monitor at www.bankrate.com and Bank-CD Rate Scanner at www.bankcd.com. As of this writing, Bank-CD Rate Scanner, shown in Figure 5-5, charges $9.95 for its services. However, its literature suggests that you can get such a great rate on your CD to make the service worth the price. You can sign up right away for Bank-CD Rate Scanner. The firm sends you an invoice in 15 days. The firm guarantees its service; if you can find a higher rate at an FDIC-insured institution that accepts nationwide deposits, your invoice is voided.

Opening a High-Yielding Deposit Account

After you find a great MMDA or CD account rate, how do you open an account? Don't worry; it's easy. Just follow these simple instructions:

1. **Call the bank's toll-free number to open an account.**

2. **Ask for the person who supervises personal accounts.**

   Some banks have a "national desk" for out-of-town customers like you.

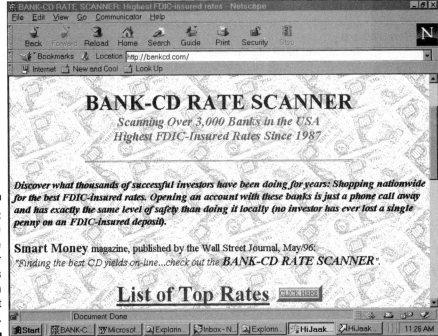

Figure 5-5:
Bank-CD
Rate
Scanner
guarantees
that it can
find the best
deal for you.

3. Tell the contact person how much you have to invest and the type of account you're interested in.

4. Ask for the latest interest rate and annual percentage yield (your return).

5. Find out when you will begin earning interest and when you can first withdraw funds.

6. Ask for an application to open an account.

7. Complete the application forms and signature cards; make copies for your records.

8. Send the completed bank forms and your check by U.S. mail.

The bank confirms your deposit by return mail.

Chapter 6

What's So Great about Mutual Funds?

*W*ant to participate in spectacular stock market profits but you're scared of the risks? Want to start investing but you don't have $1,000 to $2,500 for an initial minimum balance? Don't want to pay high brokerage commissions and fees? Well, a *mutual fund* (a managed investment company, with an unlimited life, that stands ready to purchase shares from its owners and sell shares to the public) may be for you.

Mutual fund mania is rampant. Everyone is talking about mutual funds. Mutual funds are rapidly becoming the most popular way for Americans to invest — which is remarkable, considering that before the 1920s mutual funds didn't even exist. In the 1940s, only 68 funds existed, with $400 million in assets. Today more than 7,000 mutual funds exist, with assets of $2.8 trillion. About 25 percent of all U.S. households are invested in mutual funds. In the nation, individuals are collectively investing about $20 billion per month.

In this chapter, I explain how you use the Internet to select mutual funds, and I list the latest Internet tools and resources. I also provide step-by-step instructions for opening a mutual fund account online, and I show you how to use the Internet to start a mutual fund account for as little as $50. I also explain how you can join an online investment club.

Mutual Fund Mania

Mutual funds offer a good solution for individuals who don't have the time and the technical knowledge to track individual stocks. Mutual funds are a convenient way of investing in stocks, bonds, cash, gold, commodities, and so on. In a mutual fund, professional managers pool the money of small investors. The shareholders (the small investors) own the fund. The goal of the investment company is to make more money for the small investors. In return for handling the investments, the fund managers receive a management fee of approximately 2 percent of the value of the total investment.

Often, the portfolio manager and technical analysts invest in a collection of about 35 securities. The portfolio manager expects these investments to earn interest from bonds, dividends from stocks, capital gains from buying and selling stocks at opportune times, and any other spin-off profits that can increase the value of the mutual fund. The mutual fund doesn't pay any taxes because all the profits are distributed as dividends to the small investors (the shareholders).

The shareholder pays the management fee, registration fees, expenses for annual meetings, custodial bank and transfer agent fees, interest and taxes, brokerage commissions, marketing costs, and sometimes expenses related to the distribution of fund materials (prospectus, annual statement, and so on). These fees and expenses are usually deducted from the dividends paid to shareholders.

Mutual funds are a good investment choice because funds offer individual investors several benefits that they don't ordinarily receive:

✔ **Diversification:** You spread your risk by purchasing several types of investments. A mutual fund can hold anywhere from 20 to 200 or more securities. No single stock or bond investment is greater than 3 percent of the total fund. If one stock loses half its value in one day, the effect on the entire fund is small. On the other hand, if one stock skyrockets, you still won't be able to buy that yacht you wanted.

✔ **No broker required:** If you're confident about your investment choices, you're likely to purchase no-load mutual funds directly from the mutual fund company, instead of paying a *load* (a broker's commission). For more information about no-load funds, see Chapter 7.

✔ **No investor homework:** The mutual fund does the tracking and record-keeping for you.

✔ **Professional management:** The professional managers, employed by the fund, search for fast-growing investments on your behalf. To have these professionals working for you full-time provides you with competitive advantages over other investors.

For more information about mutual funds, see Mutual Funds Interactive at `www.fundsinteractive.com/newbie.html`. This Web site offers tutorials for beginners interested in mutual fund investing. For example, Figure 6-1 shows "Funds 101 — Mutual Funds for the New Investor." Also, check out *Investing For Dummies* by Eric Tyson, MBA (published by IDG Books Worldwide, Inc.).

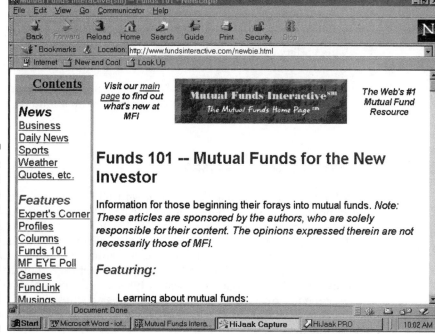

Figure 6-1: Mutual Funds Interactive has a mutual fund tutorial designed for beginning investors.

(copyright © 1995-1997 Brill Editorial Services, Inc.)

Finding Mutual Fund Information on the Internet

The Internet provides many mutual fund supersites that are timely, interesting, and best of all, useful. Here are a few examples of these all-purpose sites:

- ✔ **Mutual Funds Interactive** (www.fundsinteractive.com/ profiles.html) has fund manager profiles and strategies for using funds to meet your investment goals.

- ✔ **Mutual Funds INVESTOR'S CENTER** (www.mfea.com) provides a news center, information about the new tax rules, links to mutual funds, and a research center that allows you to track from a list of more than 1,000 funds.

- ✔ **CBS MarketWatch — Super Star Funds** (cbs.marketwatch.com/news/ newsroom.htx) provides articles, news, market data, fund research, links to fund sites, mutual fund tutorials for new investors, market data, portfolios, and a stock chat room.

- ✔ **Mutual Fund Magazine** (www.mfmag.com) requires your free registration, but the site is worth registering for. This online magazine has a wide variety of features, departments, screens, reports, online calculators, and tools to assist you in making your mutual fund selections.

- ✔ **Nestegg Interactive** (nesteggiddis.com/mutfund) includes a mutual funds center and listings of top and bottom mutual fund performers.

Buying Mutual Funds

Mutual funds can give you a much better return than savings accounts, money market deposit accounts, or certificates of deposit. However, the Federal Deposit Insurance Corporation (FDIC) doesn't insure mutual funds. The FDIC doesn't even insure the mutual funds sold by your bank. Even mutual fund portfolios consisting only of guaranteed U.S. government bonds contain some element of risk. On the other hand, returns from stock mutual funds average about 12 percent a year, while savings accounts may earn only 4 percent. However, although your savings account pays 4 percent year after year, your mutual fund may be up 35 percent this year and down 10 percent the next.

Over the years, the stock market has outperformed any other investment. Unlike a mutual fund, however, individual investors frequently can't purchase a large number of different securities to diversify their investment risk. Buying shares in a mutual fund solves this problem. When you invest in a mutual fund, the diversity of the portfolio reduces the risk of losing your total investment. Selecting the right fund may be difficult, but you can find plenty of online help.

Assume that you have $1,000 to invest in a mutual fund. With your investment, you're purchasing a share of the total assets in the fund. If the share price of the fund is $10 per share, you can purchase 100 shares. The price of each share is the Net Asset Value (NAV). You calculate the NAV of the mutual fund by adding up the value of the securities in the fund and dividing by the number of outstanding shares.

The NAV increases and decreases as the market fluctuates. The Securities and Exchange Commission (SEC) requires that the NAV of each mutual fund is calculated and published for investors at the end of business each day. Here are a few examples of online quote servers that provide mutual fund NAV information:

- ✔ **Briefing.com** (www.briefing.com) provides a free introductory service that includes market commentaries, mutual fund and stock quotes, charts, portfolio tracking, sector ratings, and an economic calendar. They have two levels of premium service. The first level, called Stock Analysis, is $6.95 per month (with a free trial) and includes stocks on the move, technical stock analysis, earnings calendar, splits calendar, stock ratings, upgrade and downgrade reports, company reports, and more. The highest level of service, called Professional, is $25 per month (with a free trial) and includes stock analysis, constant bond analysis, economic analysis, 15-minute bond quotes, FX analysis, yield curves, federal policy analysis, calendars, and more.

- ✔ **CNNfn** (www.cnnfn.com) is affiliated with Cable News Network (CNN) and provides links to financial sites, investment articles, market information, and online research sources. Market information includes graphs showing the averages of the New York Stock Exchange, the American Stock Exchange, and NASDAQ. For mutual fund data, click on Stock Quotes. Enter the ticker symbol for your mutual fund or stock. CNNfn provides charts and company snapshots of selected firms. For mutual funds, CNNfn provides the latest performance data from Lipper Analytical.

- ✔ **Data Broadcasting Online** (www.dbc.com) retrieves up to seven ticker symbols at one time. Stock quotes include last price, change, currency, percent change, opening price, day low, day high, previous day's closing price, and volume. For mutual fund and stock quotes, markets, and portfolio information, you need to go to separate financial market menus. For access to premium data and real-time quotes, the firm charges $29.95 per month.

✔ **PC Quote** (www.pcquote.com) offers five levels of service that range from $75 per month to $300 per month or $750 per year to $3,000 per year for real-time quotes, charts, and more. (See the Web site for details.) Free services include ticker symbol lookup, current mutual fund and stock prices, fundamental data, Market Guide company snapshots, Zacks Investment Research broker recommendations, annual earnings and earning estimates, current company news, charts of the company's stock price history and volume, and market indexes. Overall, you can search for stocks, bonds, futures, options, mutual funds, and indexes. You can also maintain up to five portfolios with 20 ticker symbols in each portfolio.

Understanding the real cost of sales fees

One of the advantages of mutual funds is that you can purchase them directly from the mutual fund company. If you purchase mutual funds through a broker or a financial planner, you're charged a sales fee. If you have to pay a sales charge for purchasing your mutual fund, deduct this amount from your yield for the year. For example, if you pay a 5-percent sales charge for your $1,000 investment in mutual funds, the amount invested in the funds is $950. If the fund increases by 10 percent in one year, you have a $1,045 investment. Your true yield is $95, or 9.5 percent ($95 ÷ $1,000) — not the full 10 percent.

On the other hand, if you purchase a no-load mutual fund, your yield is 10 percent because you don't pay the sales fee. Your original $1,000 investment in mutual funds is now worth $1,100, which is $55 more than the fund with the sales fee.

Here are a few examples of firms that can sell you a mutual fund without a sales charge (or load):

✔ **Invesco** (www.invesco.com) provides plenty of information about its no-load funds. If you're a beginning investor, you'll appreciate the useful advice at this site. The site includes online prospectuses, charts to compare rates of return, and a list of the firm's financial services.

✔ **Janus** (www.janus.com) has a family of no-load funds. The site provides account access, brief overviews of fund performance, application forms, investor chats, and articles. If you want a prospectus, just ask for one at this Web site; Janus mails one to you.

✔ **T. Rowe Price** (www.troweprice.com) uses its Web site to provide information about tax law changes, access to your account, daily prices, brief updates of fund performance, information about its discount brokers, international investing, and information about the firm. You have the option of downloading a prospectus or having one sent to you by mail.

✔ **Vanguard** (www.vanguard.com), one of the largest mutual fund families, has around 90 funds that don't charge sales fees. The Vanguard Web site includes brief fund descriptions, downloadable prospectuses, and an education center. This site offers an online library, online calculators, a portfolio planner, a listing of their upcoming events (such as end-of-the-year returns), and investment articles.

For more details about buying mutual funds and minimizing fees, see *Investing For Dummies* by Eric Tyson, MBA.

Opening a mutual fund account

Before you invest in a mutual fund, read the fund's prospectus so that you understand exactly what you're investing in. Next, fill out the online account application form for the mutual fund company. SEC regulations require your signature to open an account. For specific details about opening an account, contact the fund company or broker. In general, you need to complete the following steps:

1. **Indicate your fund selections.**

2. **Mark what type of account you want: individual, joint, or trust.**

3. **Include your social security number.**

4. **Mark whether you want check-writing privileges.**

5. **Indicate whether you want direct or automatic deposits from a checking account or paycheck.**

6. **Mail your completed account application form and your check, made payable to the mutual fund.**

A better way to buy mutual funds

I suggest that you visit the Schwab site (www.schwab.com) for the details on a revolutionary way to purchase mutual funds. One Source Schwab offers 350 no-load mutual funds from 50 families. (The total universe of mutual funds consists of about 600 fund families, and more than 9,000 mutual funds.) You can purchase several mutual funds in the same fund family and thus save time and effort because you don't have to call several mutual fund companies to open accounts and make your purchases.

If you are unhappy with one of the mutual funds, you can swap it with another mutual fund in the same family at no cost. At the end of the month, you receive only one statement that covers all your funds.

Schwab also provides you with one statement for your taxes. This statement makes calculating the tax you owe on your profits easier than usual.

Figure 6-2 shows the application form for Lipper Funds, Inc., at
`www.lipper.com/howto.htm`. This site indicates all the necessary steps for
opening an account.

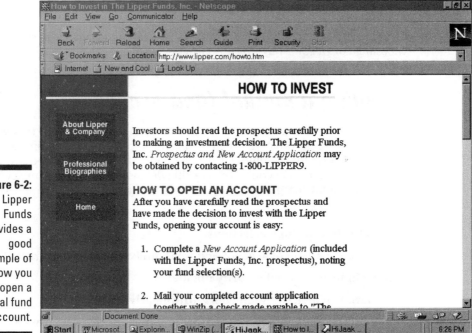

Figure 6-2:
Lipper
Funds
provides a
good
example of
how you
can open a
mutual fund
account.

Selling Your Mutual Funds

The prospectus of a mutual fund details how you can sell your funds.
Liquidating your shares may take a little time, so don't wait until the last
minute to sell. Generally, the selling process works like this:

1. **Call your fund company or your broker.**

2. **Direct the representative to sell your shares.**

   You get that day's closing price, provided that you call before 4:00 EST.

If you are holding the certificate shares of a mutual fund, the selling process
involves additional steps:

1. **Write a letter to the fund's agent requesting redemption of your fund
   shares at their market value at the time your request is received.**

2. **Enclose the certificates you hold.**

   If a custodial bank holds your shares, this step isn't necessary.

3. **Sign the letter and the certificates.**

4. **Have your signature guaranteed by your local bank or broker-dealer who is a member of the New York Stock Exchange (NYSE) or the National Association of Securities Dealers (NASD).**

5. **Insure the mailing for the full market value of the securities on the date they're sent.**

   Federal law requires redemption within seven days of when the fund's agent receives your request.

Starting Your Mutual Fund Account with as Little as $50

You don't need a great deal of money to buy a mutual fund. Before you start reading prospectuses, find out which mutual funds have automatic investment plans (AIPs). A mutual fund with an automatic investment plan often allows you to invest as little as $25 per month.

The Internet provides information about which mutual funds offer AIPs. Here are a few examples of online mutual funds with automatic investment plans:

- **TD's Green Line Family of No-Load Mutual Funds** (www.tdbank.ca) has a pre-authorized purchase plan of more than 30 funds to choose from. Invest quarterly, monthly, weekly, or even on your payday. Minimum initial and subsequent investments can be as low as $25. You can change your investment amount, frequency of purchase, and choice of funds at any time.

- **Strong Automatic Investment Plan** (www.strong-funds.com/strong/ LearningCenter/aipbroch.htm), shown in Figure 6-3, has an automatic investment plan for 36 of its no-load funds. The program allows you to invest at predetermined intervals for as low as $50. No charges are required to establish or maintain this service.

- **Vanguard Fund Express** (www.vanguard.com/catalog/service/ 5_3_1_2.html) is a plan that allows monthly, bimonthly, quarterly, semiannual, and annual automatic payment to be transferred to your Vanguard account. The maximum amount is $100,000, and the minimum amount is $25.

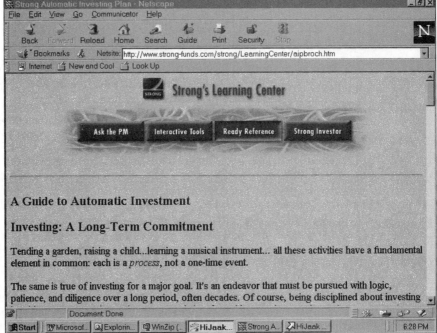

Figure 6-3:
Strong's
AIP allows
you to open
a mutual
fund
account
with as little
as $50.

> ✔ **T. Rowe Price** (www.troweprice.com) has two no-load funds in its automatic investment plan that allow monthly, bimonthly, quarterly, semiannual, and annual automatic payments. Minimum payments can be as little as $25.

After you select several mutual funds with AIPs, ask for the funds' prospectuses and application forms. You can request the forms online, by telephone, or by mail. Fill out the section marked automatic investments and complete the form. You are authorizing the mutual fund company to make regular electronic withdrawals from your checking account. Many funds let you decide how much you want to invest. For example, you may decide to invest $50 per month or $25 every payday. AIPs let you enjoy the benefits of compounding and when you reinvest, your dividends and capital gains can add up quickly.

Don't Want to Select Your Own Mutual Funds? Join an Online Investment Club

If you want to invest in mutual funds but just don't know where to start, consider joining an investment club. Investment clubs usually have three purposes:

✔ Finding out about investing

✔ Having fun

✔ Making money

To find out about the investment clubs in your area, see Investment Clubs at `www.computerland.net/missouri/investment_club.htm` and the National Association of Investment Clubs (NAIC) at `www.better-investing.org/clubs/clubs.html`.

Investment club members use leads from breaking news, which they get at Web sites such as Reuters (`www.reuters.com`) and Bloomberg Personal (`www.bloomberg.com`). They tap into Web sites that provide free information (for example, `www.investorguide.com`), they download business reports (such as the ones you can find at `personal12.fidelity.com80`), and they monitor Usenet newsgroups and Listserv mailing lists. They use e-mail to swap tips, leads, and other information with their fellow investment club members. (For details about newsgroups and Internet mailing lists, see Chapter 3.)

The goal of most investment clubs is to help beginning investors become smart investors — that is, to educate investors in a disciplined approach to successful investing, portfolio management, and wealth building. The people who belong to these investment clubs often believe that finding new sites and investments and meeting new people with the same interests can be very helpful and profitable.

Want to try your hand at an investment club before you actually join one? Figure 6-4 shows The Investment Club (`www.investmentclub.com`), a free investment club simulation. You don't need any investment experience to join. Just register online, and you receive a fictional $100,000 to invest. Follow the rules and regulations and see how well you do, compared to your fellow investors. The investor who makes the most profit at the end of each month receives a prize from Apogee Information Systems.

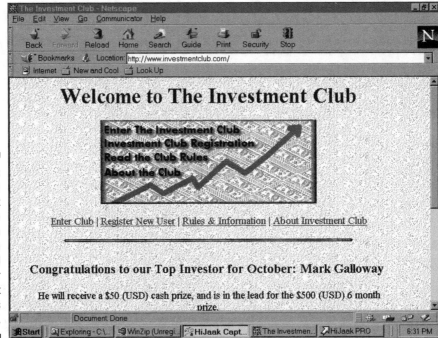

Figure 6-4:
Join The
Investment
Club
simulation
and see
how well
your
investment
strategies
work.

Chapter 7

The Keys to Successful Internet Mutual Fund Investing

. . . .

In This Chapter

▶ Understanding mutual fund types, fees, and risks

▶ Locating and reading online prospectuses and other information

▶ Using online screening tools to find mutual funds that meet your requirements

. . . .

*T*his chapter provides you with all the basic online tools for identifying mutual fund candidates. I present some general information about mutual fund investment, including types of funds, fees, and potential risks. I offer suggestions about where to find mutual fund facts and figures online. I also describe five online screening tools that can help you choose the mutual fund that best meets your needs. These mutual fund screens vary from simple to more advanced. By the way, the best online mutual fund screen is the one that includes the investment criteria you feel are important.

Mutual Fund Basics

With more than 9,000 funds to choose from, selecting a mutual fund has become a complex process — meaning that online screening tools are more important than ever before. When you select your investment criteria, you need to consider several factors:

✔ How long do you plan to own the mutual fund?

✔ How much risk to your principal can you tolerate?

✔ Which mutual fund category meets your personal financial objectives?

The funds you select will be based on the answers to these questions. If you need your money in a year, and can't afford much risk, because, for example, you plan to use the money to purchase a house, you want to consider a safe, short-term bond fund. On the other hand, if this money is your retirement fund that you don't plan to tap for 10 years, and you can stomach some ups and downs, you should consider a growth stock fund.

Before you start screening mutual fund candidates, you need to understand some general information: the types of funds you can choose, the fees that mutual fund companies charge, the types of risk associated with mutual funds, and the way to read a prospectus.

Discovering the differences between open-end and closed-end mutual funds

An o*pen-end mutual fund* has an unlimited number of shares. You can sell these shares either through the mutual fund company or your broker. The Securities and Exchange Commission requires that each mutual fund company calculate the NAV of each fund every day at the close of business.

A *closed-end mutual fund* has a limited number of shares, does not stand ready to purchase its own shares from its owners, and rarely issues new shares beyond its initial offering. You can only buy or sell these shares through a broker on the major stock exchanges. Most closed-end funds repurchase their shares in the open market. The value of these shares isn't calculated by using the NAV methodology. Instead, shares are valued by using a method similar to bonds and are traded at either a discount or a premium. Market prices of publicly traded closed-end mutual fund shares are published daily.

Minimizing fees

Loads are the fees with which mutual fund companies compensate the broker who sold you the fund. About half of all stock and bond funds have loads; money market funds normally don't have loads. Loads and other fees are important because they are deducted from your investment returns.

Loading it on

A *front-end load* is the most common type of fee that mutual fund companies charge. Investors pay this fee when they purchase shares in the mutual fund. No additional fees are charged for redeeming or selling your mutual fund shares. By law, front-end loads can't be greater than 8.5 percent. Loads average 5 percent for stock funds and 4 percent for bond funds.

The less common *back-end load* fee is charged when you sell or redeem the shares. Back-end fees are usually based on time, starting at 5 percent during the first year and declining a percentage point a year — by year 5, no fees are charged. However, back-end load funds often have Rule 12b-1 fees, which are usually the amounts charged to investors for promoting the mutual fund. Regulations state that fees can't exceed 0.75 percent, and other fees for shareholder services can't exceed 0.25 percent.

Generally, funds with back-end fees are more expensive than funds with front-end fees due to the high Rule 12b-1 fees. However, if you are willing to hold your investment for five years or more (which really, you ought to, if you're investing in stocks), you pay no load (back-end loads usually disappear after five years).

Excluding the maximum fee for front-end loads of 8.5 percent, mutual funds can't charge more than 7.25 percent for the life of the investment. Overall, load fees vary from 4.0 percent to 8.5 percent of the NAV for the shares purchased.

What does all this fee information mean? If you purchase 300 shares at $10 per share with an 8-percent front-end fee, you pay $3,240 for a $3,000 investment. In other words, your investment needs to increase by $240 just to break even.

Taking it off

Some funds have no loads, which means that they have no front-end or back-end fees. These no-load funds generally don't have a sales force. Nevertheless, no-load funds do charge service fees, proving that there's no such thing as a free lunch. Mutual fund companies charge annual fees for their management services, deducting these amounts before calculating the NAV. The SEC doesn't regulate or cap the maximum amount that firms can charge, but service fees average around 1.5 percent.

Some mutual fund companies may have low up-front fees but charge high rates for managing fund operations. The prospectus details whether the mutual fund charges these fees.

For more information on operating expenses and other fees, see Chapter 8 of *Investing For Dummies* by Eric Tyson, MBA (published by IDG Books Worldwide, Inc.).

Understanding Mutual Fund Risks

Mutual funds provide statements about their objectives and risk posture (which is briefly explained in qualitative terms in the prospectus). Rather than provide precise information to help you evaluate the riskiness of a mutual fund, however, these statements typically offer vague, general explanations of a fund's approach to risk. For more precise, statistical evaluations of a fund's risks, you can turn to independent mutual fund rating services such as Morningstar (www.morningstar.net).

Morningstar and other independent rating services calculate such statistics as the standard deviation of a fund's return. I don't want to turn this chapter into an introductory statistics course, but I can tell you that standard deviation helps you judge how volatile, or risky, a fund is. This statistic shows you how much a fund has deviated from its average return over a period of time. Figure 7-1 shows Morningstar's standard deviation calculation for a mutual fund, which you can find at www.morningstar.net/nd/ndNSAPI.nd/Research/ViewMFRisks?ticker=GATEX#Volatility.

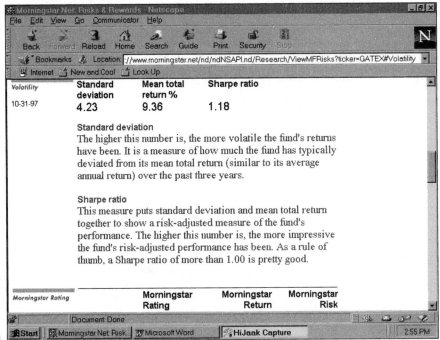

Figure 7-1:
The standard deviation calculations by Morningstar.

Standard deviation offers a clear indicator of a fund's consistency over time. A fund's standard deviation is a simple measure of the fund's highest and lowest returns over a specific time period. Just remember this point: The higher the standard deviation, the higher the fund's risk.

For example, if the 3-year return on a fund is 33 percent, that statistic may mean that the fund earned 11 percent in the first year, 11 percent in the second year, and 11 percent in the third year. On the other hand, the fund may have earned 28 percent in the first year, 5 percent in the second year, and 0 percent in the third year. If your financial plan requires an 11 percent annual return, this fund is not for you!

A Fund for You, a Fund for Me

You can choose from a wide variety of mutual fund categories. As a matter of fact, so many types of funds are available that you're almost guaranteed to find a fund that is an excellent fit for your personal financial objectives. You can summarize the funds into six groups:

- **Aggressive growth funds:** Aggressive growth funds are investments in small, young companies and may involve the use of options and futures to reap greater profits. If the stock market is hot, these funds often provide the biggest return of all mutual funds, mostly due to the capital gains of the stocks in the fund. They typically drop the most, when the market is cold. Their volatility makes them a poor choice for the short-term inverstor.

- **Growth funds:** Growth funds are similar to aggressive growth funds but have less risk. They may invest in larger, well-established firms with a long track record of earnings that may continue to grow faster than average. In addition to stocks, these funds generally include bonds and cash equivalents. Growth funds are best for investors with medium- to long-term objectives.

- **Growth and income funds:** Funds in the growth and income category target a steady return with protection of the principal. They often invest in companies that are growing as well as companies that are paying high or increasing dividends. Growth and income funds are more diverse than growth funds and are, therefore, less risky, but they reap fewer rewards if the stock market soars.

- **Bond funds:** Bond funds usually have less risk than funds with stocks. Bond funds are usually good investment choices for short-, medium-, and long-term investors who desire low risk. For more information on bonds, see Chapter 10.

> ✔ **International funds:** International funds include a mix of stocks and bonds from other nations or governments. These funds are subject to several types of risks that domestic mutual funds don't experience, such as political risk and exchange rate risk (losing money because of changes in the currency exchange rate).
>
> ✔ **Money market funds:** Money market funds provide less return and less risk than other types of mutual funds and are good investments for short-term investors. The principal advantage of these funds is their safety. Also, if you ever need to get to your money fast, money market funds may be the type of fund for you.

Table 7-1 provides a brief overview of the time period and risk tolerance level of each type of mutual fund. For more explanation about the various types of mutual funds, check out *Investing For Dummies* by Eric Tyson, MBA.

Table 7-1	Choosing the Right Type of Mutual Fund	
Investment Time Period	*Risk-Tolerance Level*	*Category of Mutual Fund*
Less than 2 years	Minimum risk to principal	Money market fund (not a money market deposit account, or MMDA)
	Some risk to principal	Bond fund (short to intermediate bond fund)
Between 2 and 4 years	Minimum risk to principal	Money market fund (not an MMDA)
	Some risk to principal	Bond fund (short to intermediate term)
	Moderate risk to principal	Bond fund (intermediate to long-term)
Between 4 and 6 years	Minimum risk to principal	Money market fund (not an MMDA)
	Some risk to principal	Bond fund (short to intermediate)
	Moderate risk to principal	Growth and income funds
	Excessive risk to principal	Growth funds and international funds

Average rates of return for different funds

Setting realistic expectations for your investment choices is important. The Internet provides many information sources about the average rates of return for different types of mutual funds. One good example is from the American Association of Retired Persons (AARP) at www.aarp.org. Among other types of information, this site reports the five-year average rate of return for several types of funds.

Finding Facts and Figures Online

Here is a list of online information services that can assist you in finding the right mutual fund:

- ✔ **Invest-o-rama Directory of Mutual Funds** (www.investorama.com/funds.html), shown in Figure 7-2, is a directory of more than 5,000 mutual funds.

- ✔ **The Mutual Funds Directory** (nestegg.iddis.com/mutfund) provides a comprehensive directory of more than 9,297 funds in more than 540 fund families. All mutual funds are listed alphabetically and have hyperlinks to more information.

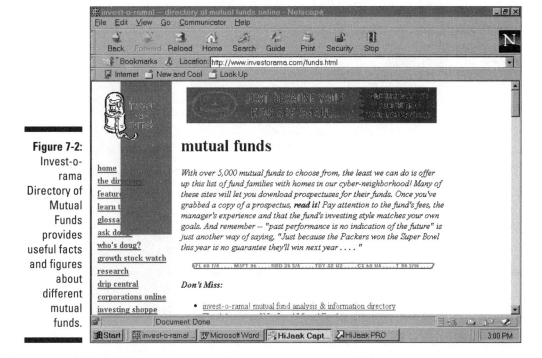

Figure 7-2: Invest-o-rama Directory of Mutual Funds provides useful facts and figures about different mutual funds.

- ✔ **Mutual Funds Interactive** (The Mutual Funds Homepage) (`www.fundsinteractive.com/index.shtml`) offers tutorials for beginning mutual fund investors, interviews and descriptions of fund strategies with top mutual fund managers, analyses of the mutual funds market, and links to mutual fund home pages.

- ✔ **NewsTracker Mutual Funds** (`nt.excite.com`), from Excite, provides free mutual fund and business news articles. Additionally, NewsTracker has links to the Excite business and investing channel, investing news links, mutual funds online, and NETworth mutual fund manager.

- ✔ **The Wall Street Journal** (`interactive.wsj.com`) provides information on mutual funds as part of its Money & Investing section. This free information includes news and features, statistics on the top performers in various fund categories, mutual fund profiles, scorecards, and closed-end fund prices.

- ✔ **The Street.com** (`www.thestreet.com`) provides fund profiles and scorecards at `www.thestreet.com/MutualFundProfiles/funds.asp`, as shown in Figure 7-3. You can search Lipper Analytical's top performers for the week. Additionally, you can search funds by asset size, category, fund symbol, or fund name.

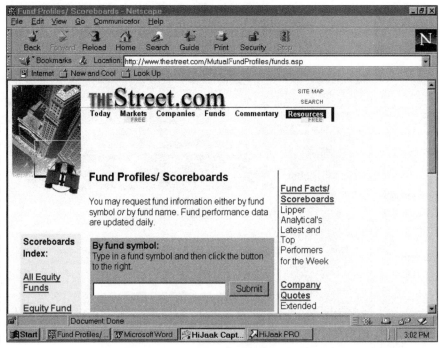

Figure 7-3: The Street.com provides mutual fund profiles, scorecards, and the capability to search for mutual fund reports and statistics.

Locating and Reading the Prospectus

Fast EDGAR Mutual Funds Reporting is located at `edgar.stern.nyu.edu/mutual.html`. This Web site, shown in Figure 7-4, provides prospectuses for more than 7,000 mutual funds. If you know the name of the fund you're interested in, you can investigate the fund's activities at this site. Target your search by determining the range of dates you're interested in, which filing forms (quarterly, annually, and so on) you want to read, and the name of the specific fund you're interested in.

If you don't know the exact name of the fund you want, refer to Morningstar at `www.morningstar.net`. Morningstar provides a mutual fund search engine. Just enter what you know of the mutual fund's name. The search engine's results provide you with several mutual funds that have similar names. It is likely that the mutual fund you are seeking is one of the funds listed.

After you find the prospectus you want, download it to your computer so that you can read it at your leisure. Here's how you download a prospectus that you have accessed via the EDGAR for Mutual Funds Web site:

1. **With the prospectus displayed in your Web browser, choose File⇨Save.**

   Your browser displays the Save As dialog box.

2. **Enter a file name for the prospectus and select the directory in which you want to save the file.**

3. **Click on Save.**

   Your browser saves the prospectus on your computer. If you have a dial-up connection to the Internet, you can disconnect from your ISP.

4. **Minimize your Internet browser.**

5. **Open your word-processing program.**

6. **Open the prospectus file.**

   You can now read the prospectus at your leisure offline.

When you read the prospectus you have downloaded, look for the following information:

- ✔ **Investment objectives:** The first paragraph of the prospectus describes the fund's investment objectives and lists the types of securities the fund invests in. If the fund doesn't meet your investment objectives, you can stop reading and start evaluating another fund.

- ✔ **Fees:** The SEC requires all mutual funds to list all fees, costs, and expenses in a table at the front of the prospectus.

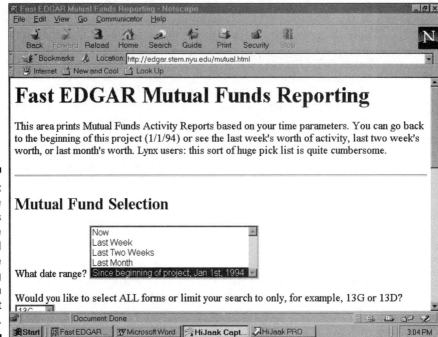

Figure 7-4:
Get the
prospectus
for the
mutual fund
you're
investigating
online from
Fast
EDGAR.

✓ **Additional expenses:** Additional expenses may be for extra services such as printed shareholder materials, toll-free telephone numbers with 24-hour service, accumulation plans that reinvest your distributions (shareholder profits), and related support and guidance.

✓ **Performance:** Year-to-year data for the last ten years (or less if the fund isn't that old) in condensed financial statements indicates the fund's performance. Statistics track the fund's NAV, shareholder distributions, and expenses. For funds that include stocks, dividends and price information also may be included. Many funds provide graphs that show how a $1,000 investment in the fund increased or decreased over a ten-year period.

✓ **Statement of additional information:** This section of the prospectus covers complex items such as the biographies of the fund's directors, the fund's objectives, and contracts for professional services. These reports are free to the fund's shareholders that request them.

The SEC requires the prospectus to indicate what fees the fund charges for a $1,000 investment with a 5-percent return redeemed at the end of one year, three years, five years, and ten years. Keep in mind that both load and no-load funds have management fees and operating expenses that are charged to the fund.

How to Screen Mutual Funds Online

The Internet provides a variety of mutual fund screening tools that sort more than 9,000 mutual funds by criteria that you select. For example, you may want one type of fund for your children's education — something long-term because you don't need the funds for 10 to 20 years — and a different fund for your retirement to help you reduce your current tax liabilities. With these online screening tools, you can evaluate several funds that meet your financial needs.

Most of the stock-screening sites on the Internet are free. These database searches are an inexpensive way to isolate mutual funds that meet your special criteria. Some databases list funds incorrectly or have outdated information. However, they are useful for pruning a large list of candidates to a manageable short list.

Some mutual fund screening programs — for example, Quicken (www.quicken.com) and MSN Investor (investor.msn.com) — are for beginners to use. Others, such as ResearchMag (www.researchmag.com), require some practice. Some mutual fund screens allow you to download the data to your spreadsheet so that you can do additional analysis.

Each screening site uses different criteria to sort mutual funds. You have to decide which criteria you care about and then use the site that offers the criteria you want. Anyway you look at it, the selection of the right mutual fund is still up to you.

Here's an overview of the features of five mutual fund screens that are best for beginning online investors:

- ✔ **Investor Square** (www.investorsquare.com), shown in Figure 7-5, has a mutual fund screen called Mutual Fund Explorer. This screen is one of the best mutual fund screens available for beginning investors. The free service screens, ranks, and profiles more than 9,500 mutual funds using up to 100 different variables. The program is designed to help you find the best 25 performers by category, detailed objective, or specific category (like short-term or long-term bond fund). Just highlight the category and click on Submit.

- ✔ **Microsoft Investor** (investor.msn.com/home.asp?) charges $9.95 per month for a full package of features that include mutual fund and stock screens. A 30-day free trial period is available. The mutual fund screen is easy to use, and you can copy the results to your spreadsheet. Figure 7-6 shows how you select your criteria to build a list of mutual funds.

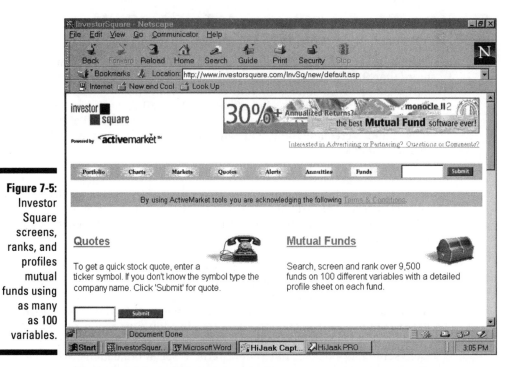

Figure 7-5:
Investor
Square
screens,
ranks, and
profiles
mutual
funds using
as many
as 100
variables.

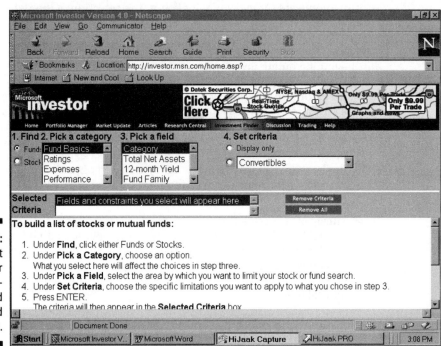

Figure 7-6:
Microsoft
Investor
has well-
designed
mutual fund
screens.

(Used by permission from Microsoft Corporation.)

✔ **Morningstar (**www.morningstar.net**)** offers a free, independent service that evaluates more than 6,800 mutual funds. At Morningstar's home page, click on Mutual Fund Screen to access the Morning Star Mutual Fund Screen. One drawback of the program is that you can't copy screen results to a spreadsheet.

✔ **Quicken.com (**www.quicken.com**)** provides its mutual fund screen free of charge. At the Quicken.com home page, click on Mutual Fund Screen to access the mutual fund screen shown in Figure 7-7. The screen's values are updated on a monthly basis. You can copy screen results to a spreadsheet.

✔ **ResearchMag (**www.researchmag.com**)** is a free service that is definitely for the experienced investor. However, after you get familiar with its 40 research variables, the service is easy to use. ResearchMag requires your free registration. To access the screen from ReseachMag's home page, click on Mutual Fund Screens. To save time and to avoid making the same mistake over and over, be sure to keep a list of what works and what doesn't. The program searches more than 3,500 equity mutual funds. You can copy screen results to a spreadsheet.

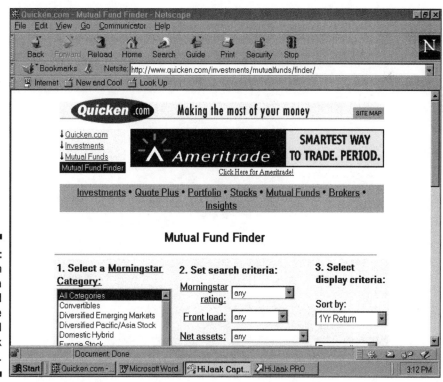

Figure 7-7:
Quicken.com
provides a
useful and
easy-to-use
mutual fund
stock
screen.

✔ **Thomson Investors Network** (www.thomsoninvest.net) charges $9.95 per month for a full package of features, including mutual fund and stock screens. Guests and members need to log in before using the Mutual Fund Screen. Click on Research. Next click on Mutual Fund Screen and select the characteristics of the mutual fund you are seeking. Click on Submit to enter your choices. You can't copy search results to a spreadsheet program.

Chapter 8

The Basics of Stocks
and Rates of Return

. . . .

In This Chapter

▶ Getting your financial house in order to begin wealth-building

▶ Matching your investment objectives to the right investments

▶ Finding and reading online stock quotes

▶ Locating news about potential investments

. . . .

*T*he focus of this chapter is stock selection. The savvy online investor prospects all possible stock candidates, looking for companies that are exceptional in some way and positioned to perform well in the future.

In this chapter, I discuss using the Internet to decide which types of securities are right for you. I also show you how to keep current with online news services, read a stock table, and find the ticker symbols of securities online, so that you can make wise investment decisions.

Taking Stock of You . . .

Most people spend the bulk of their income on no-frills necessities such as housing, food, transportation, and education. People who don't invest often believe that they can't afford to do so. Investing today usually means giving up some immediate pleasure, such as a European vacation, taking the family to see a play, or going to that great new restaurant. However, even a small amount of money invested each month can make a big impact on your long-term financial security.

Investing can help you stay ahead of inflation and assist you in accumulating real personal wealth with the power of compounding. Successful investing has several key factors, some of which must be in place before you invest your first dollar:

✔ **Know yourself.** How much risk to your savings can you tolerate and still sleep at night? How much experience, technical knowledge, and time do you have for making investment decisions?

✔ **Know your goals and the time you have to accomplish those goals.** Understand exactly what's needed to achieve your financial objectives.

✔ **Decide how you want to allocate your assets into the three main classes: stocks, bonds, and cash.** You decide how much you want to invest in each class based on how much risk you can tolerate, your required rate of return, and the investment time period.

✔ **Select specific investment candidates in the three asset classes.** Bear in mind the importance of compounding and the impact of taxes and fees on your returns.

✔ **Determine your investment criteria for selecting the right investments.** For example, how much risk can you take? How long can you invest your cash? What is your required rate of return? (For more help in determining your personal investment criteria, see Chapter 9.)

✔ **Keep current with changes in the economy and other factors that affect your investments.** Strive to make proactive rather than reactive investment decisions. You can keep current by using the online news services listed in this chapter and in this book's Internet Directory. I offer additional how-to information in Chapter 13.

✔ **Decide how you plan to define success for your investment selections.** Monitor your investments and keep good financial records.

You can find many asset allocation worksheets on the Internet. Check out the worksheet from Community Financial Planning Services, Inc. (`www.comfin.com/assetq.html`). This free, easy-to-use worksheet can immediately assist you in matching your risk tolerance levels to your financial goals. However, this is a commercial site, so be forewarned that ComFin will try to sell you something. For more information about getting your financial house in order, check out Chapter 3 of *Investing For Dummies* by Eric Tyson, MBA (published by IDG Books Worldwide, Inc.).

Understanding Stocks

When you buy shares of a company, you purchase part ownership in that company. As a shareholder, you're entitled to periodic cash dividends (as decided by the board of directors). The amount of cash dividends paid per year can vary, but they're generally predictable.

As a shareholder, you also expect to receive *capital appreciation* on your investment — that is, the difference between your purchase price and the market price of your shares. If the company prospers, your shares of stock increase in value. If company performance declines, the market value of your shares decreases.

The *annual return* is the percentage difference of the stock price at the beginning of the year from the stock price at the end of the year. The price at which you can buy or sell a share of common stock can change radically. As a matter of fact, stock prices are so volatile that accurately predicting annual returns is impossible. (If we had this gift, we would all be rich!)

Common stock returns can vary — for example, from a depressing –43.34 percent in 1931 to a thrilling 53.99 percent in 1933. However, investments in the stock market have consistently outperformed any other type of investment. Total stock returns over the last 50 years have averaged 13 percent, meaning that a stock investment of $500 in 1947 would be worth $1,729,670 today.

Picking the Right Stock for the Right Goal

Selecting your own stocks can be hard work. The exciting thing is that the Internet has much of the information you need, and most of this information is free. With the power of your computer, you can utilize Internet data to gain real insight. As you start to determine which stocks you're interested in, you should be aware of the different types of stocks. Stocks have distinct characteristics, and as general economic conditions change, they behave in special ways.

Write a short list of your financial goals, and then investigate how different types of stock relate to those objectives. Different stocks have different rates of return — some are better for young, aggressive investors; others are better for retirees or for people in high tax brackets. Here are a few examples of the different types of stocks:

- ✔ **Blue-chip stocks:** Usually the most prestigious stocks on Wall Street. They're high-quality stocks that have a long history of earnings and dividend payments. These stocks are often good long-term investments.

- ✔ **Cyclical stocks:** Stocks of companies whose fortunes rise when business conditions are good. When business conditions deteriorate, their earnings and stock prices decline. These companies are likely to be manufacturers of automobiles, steel, cement, and machine tools.

✔ **Seasonal stocks:** Similar to cyclical stocks; their fortunes change with the seasons. Good examples of seasonal companies are retail corporations whose sales and profits increase at Christmastime.

✔ **Defensive stocks:** Tend to be stable and relatively safe in declining markets. Defensive stocks are from companies that provide necessary services, such as electricity and gas, that everyone needs regardless of the economic climate. Companies in this category also provide essentials such as drugs and food, so their sales remain stable when the economy is depressed.

✔ **Growth stocks:** Growth companies are positioned for future growth and capital appreciation. However, their market price can change rapidly. Rather than pay dividends, growth companies typically spend their profits on research and development to fuel future growth. These stocks are good for aggressive, long-term investors who are willing to bet on the future. If you're in a high tax bracket, these stocks may be for you; low dividends mean fewer taxes. However, if expected earnings don't match analyst predictions, expect a big decline in stock price.

✔ **Income stocks:** Purchased for their regular, high dividends. Income stocks usually pay better than industry averages for similar products and services. Income stocks are attractive to retirees who may depend on their dividends for monthly expenses. Income stocks are often utilities companies and similar firms that pay higher dividends than comparable companies. These companies are often slow to expand because they spend most of their cash on dividend payouts. During times of declining interest rates, bonds are better investments.

✔ **International stocks:** Investors in these stocks often believe that U.S. domestic stocks are overpriced. These investors are seeking bargains overseas. However, these stocks include some risks that U.S. stocks don't have, such as higher than normal market volatility; reduced liquidity; social, political, and currency risks; and a lack of public information.

✔ **Speculative stocks and initial public offerings:** Easy to identify because they have price-earnings ratios that are between 50 and 100 when other stocks have multiples of 15 to 20. Another type of speculative stock is an initial public offering (IPO). This type of stock has no track record. A good example of speculative stock is Netscape; its stock price is high and revenues are small.

✔ **Value stocks:** Some Wall Street analysts consider these stocks to be bargains. These stocks have sound financial statements and increases in earnings but are priced less than stocks of similar companies in the same industry.

For more information on achieving success in the stock market, pick up a copy of *Investing For Dummies* by Eric Tyson, MBA.

How to Read a Stock Chart or Table

Most newspapers and many Internet sites, such as The Wall Street Journal Interactive Edition (www.wsj.com) and Barron's (www.barrons.com) have a listing of the day's stock activities. Table 8-1 shows the information you find in a typical listing from The Wall Street Journal Interactive Edition. (The values in the table are hypothetical.) The stock detailed is Compaq (CPQ). Compaq designs, develops, manufactures, and markets a wide range of computing products, including desktop and portable computers.

Table 8-1 Reading the Stock Pages at The Wall Street Journal Interactive Edition

Entry	Value
Date	November 16, 1998
Last	$66 \, ^{7}/_{16}$
Change	$+3 \, ^{7}/_{8}$
Volume	14,122,200
Time	4:21 p.m. EST
Exchange	NYSE
Day Open	$64 \, ^{7}/_{8}$
Day High	$67 \, ^{3}/_{16}$
Day Low	$64 \, ^{1}/_{8}$
Close	$62 \, ^{9}/_{16}$
Change	$+ \, ^{5}/_{16}$ (Previous day)
Volume	9,323,900 (Previous day)
52-Week High	$79 \, ^{9}/_{16}$
52-Week Low	$28 \, ^{13}/_{32}$

Here's how to interpret all this information about Compaq's stock:

  ✔ **Last: 66 $^{7}/_{16}$.** The dollar amount of the last price for the Compaq stock. (All stock prices are customarily shown in fractions instead of dollars.)

  ✔ **Change: +3 $^{7}/_{8}$.** The change in the current price to the closing price.

  ✔ **Volume: 14,122,220.** The volume or number of shares traded that day.

✔ **Time: 4:21 p.m. EST.** The time of the price quote. Some Internet quote services provide real-time quotes; others may be delayed as much as 20 minutes.

✔ **Exchange: NYSE.** The exchange that the stock is traded on. Compaq is traded on the New York Stock Exchange (NYSE).

✔ **Day Open: 64^7/$_8$.** The price of the stock at the beginning of the day.

✔ **Day High: 67^{13}/$_{16}$.** The highest stock price of the day.

✔ **Day Low: 64^1/$_8$.** The lowest stock price of the day.

✔ **Close: 62 ^{9}/$_{16}$.** The closing price from the previous day. The market closes on Saturday and Sunday, so the previous day for Monday, November 16, 1998 is Friday, November 13, 1998.

✔ **Change: + ^{5}/$_{16}$.** The change from the closing price of the previous day.

✔ **Volume 9,323,900.** The number of shares traded as of this time, on the previous day.

✔ **52-Week High: 79^9/$_{16}$.** The highest stock price in the last year.

✔ **52-Week Low: 28^{13}/$_{32}$.** The lowest stock price in the last year.

Finding Ticker Symbols and Stock Prices Online

A ticker symbol is the letter code representing the company's name in the listing for a publicly traded security. For example, if you want to find the current price for a share of Compaq's stock (as I do in the preceding section of this chapter), look for the company's ticker symbol — CPQ. Ticker symbols for companies traded on the NYSE have between one and three letters, stocks traded on NASDAQ have four or five letters.

Many commercial organizations provide ticker symbols and quotes on the Internet. Figure 8-1 shows one such company, called PC Quote. PC Quote (www.pcquote.com) is an excellent quote service that has a link to a symbol lookup page and other features that make it a good place to start researching stock prices. For example, you can type in the partial name of a company, and the PC Quote program automatically finds the ticker symbol.

If the program can't find the company's ticker symbol based on the partial name you enter, it suggests several candidates, including the ticker symbol, company name, and stock exchange. You can scroll through the companies until you find the one you want. Click on the company's name, and the program fetches the latest stock prices. (The free service is delayed 20 minutes. For subscribers, quotes are real-time.)

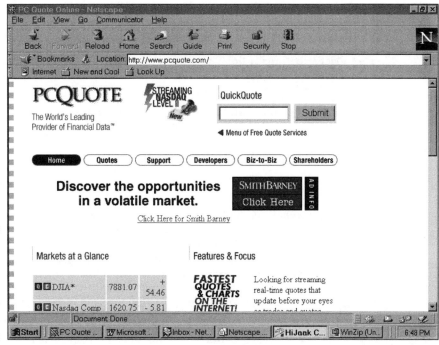

Figure 8-1:
PC Quote can help you find a ticker symbol.

One of the advantages of PC Quote is that it can look up five ticker symbols at a time; just leave a space between each company's name or ticker symbol as you enter them. Many other quote services can accommodate only one ticker symbol or company name at a time.

PC Quote provides links to charts, news, earnings information, fundamental analysis data, and Securities and Exchange Commission (SEC) filings that detail the company's financial position. Stock price data includes the amount of the last sale, time of the last sale, net change, percent change, highest sale of the day, name of the exchange, previous closing price, opening price, and volume. PC Quote also shows the following information:

- **52 week high:** The highest stock price in the last year.
- **52 week low:** The lowest stock price in the last year.
- **Annual dividend:** Cash payments made to stockholders by the corporation.
- **Earnings per share (EPS):** The company's earnings for the last 12 months divided by the number of common shares outstanding.
- **Dividend yield:** The current annualized dividend paid on a share of common stock, expressed as a percentage of the current market price of the company's common stock.

- **Beta:** The relationship between the investment's returns and the market's average returns, expressed as a number with one decimal point.

- **Price/earnings ratio:** The price the market places on the firm's earnings. For example, if a firm has earnings per share of $2 and a stock price of $50, its price/earnings ratio is 25 ($50 ÷ $2).

- **Amount of shares outstanding:** The total number of shares the firm has issued to common stockholders.

Here are a few examples of Internet quote services:

- **PC Quote** (www.pcquote.com) offers five levels of service that range from $75 per month to $300 per month or $750 per year to $3,000 per year for real-time quotes, charts, and more. See the PC Quote Web site for details. Free services include ticker symbol lookup, current stock prices and fundamental data, Market Guide company snapshot, Zack's Investment Research broker recommendations, annual earnings and earning estimates, current company news, charts of the company's stock price history and volume, and market indexes. You can search for stocks, bonds, futures, options, mutual funds, and indexes. You can also maintain as many as five portfolios of 20 ticker symbols each.

- **Data Broadcasting Online** (www.dbc.com) retrieves as many as seven ticker symbols at one time. Quotes include last price, change, currency, percent change, opening price, day low, day high, previous day's closing price, and volume. The ticker symbol lookup requires you to click on the title of where the stock is traded (for example, North America) and then click on the first letter in the company's name. Next you have to scroll through a list of all stocks beginning with that letter. For access to premium data and real-time quotes, the firm charges $29.95 per month.

- **Briefing.com** (www.briefing.com) provides a free introductory service that includes market comments, quotes, charts, portfolio tracking, sector ratings, and an economic calendar. Briefing.com has two levels of premium service. The first level, called Stock Analysis, is $6.95 per month (with a free trial) and includes stocks on the move, technical stock analysis, earnings calendar, splits calendar, stock ratings, upgrade/downgrade reports, and company reports. The highest level of service, called Professional, is $25 per month (with a free trial) and includes many advanced investor services.

Using News Summary Services to Find Stocks

As you prospect the Internet looking for stock candidates, you may wish that someone would automatically bring information to you. Your wish has been granted. Many organizations provide news summaries free of charge, and some services give you news for a fee.

Often news summaries that are sent to your e-mailbox are the best way to keep in touch with changing events and information about potential investments. Here are a few examples of online newsletters that are automatically delivered to you:

- ✔ **Edupage** is a summary of news about information technology. It's provided three times a week as a service of Educom, a Washington, D.C.-based consortium of leading colleges and universities seeking to transform education through the use of information technology. To subscribe, send an e-mail message to listproc@educom.unc.edu. Leave the subject line blank. Type the following text in the body of the message: **subscribe edupage** *John Smith* (type your name in place of *John Smith*).

- ✔ **Individual NewsPage** (www.newspage.com), shown in Figure 8-2, allows you to set a personal profile that makes this online newspaper your personal clipping service. Its home page provides breaking news, company links, news searches, and quotes. To subscribe, go to the Web site and fill out an enrollment form. Daily e-mail basic service is free. If you want more than news summaries, standard service is $6.95 per month, and premium service is $9.95.

- ✔ **InfoBeat** (www.infobeat.com) is a free daily online newspaper sponsored by the *San Jose Mercury News*. You can select user profiles that highlight finance, news, weather, sports, or entertainment. To subscribe, just go to its Web site and enroll.

- ✔ **InvestorGuide Weekly** (www.investorguide.com) is designed to keep you informed of Web-related developments in the areas of investing and personal finance. The site includes links to articles on how to use the Internet for investing, new and improved Web sites, investing in Internet companies, and electronic commerce. For a free subscription, send a blank e-mail message to weekly@investorguide.com.

- ✔ **Kiplinger Online** (www.kiplinger.com) provides news of the day, business forecasts, personal finance, stock quotes, lists of top funds, online calculators, retirement advice, listings of great Internet sites, and financial FAQs. You can subscribe online to all the Kiplinger publications. For example, *Kiplinger's Personal Finance* is $23.95 a year, and the *Kiplinger Letter* is $76 a year.

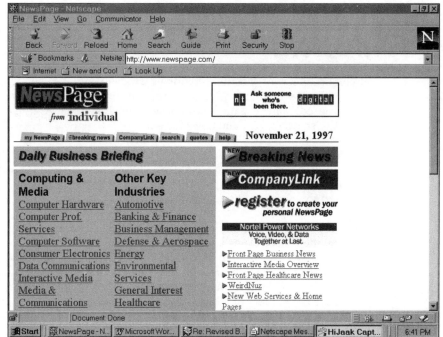

✔ **Online Money** (www.pathfinder.com) is designed for online investors and individuals interested in personal finance. To subscribe, all you have to do is provide your name and e-mail address. One of this site's best features is how it's organized. It starts with the headlines of top stories and personal finance hot links and then provides the news summaries.

✔ **Research on Demand** (www.gsnews.com) is a high-end service from Goldman Sachs that offers *Research Headlines,* a daily update of rating and estimate changes. Research on Demand also offers *U.S. Research Viewpoint,* a weekly review of the impact of earnings and rating changes. Subscriptions start at $1,500 per quarter; a la carte pricing is also available.

✔ **The Economist** (www.economist.com), shown in Figure 8-3, sends free weekly summaries of the magazine's "Business this Week" and "Politics this Week" columns to your e-mailbox. To subscribe, send an e-mail message with the message join economist-business or join economist-politics to newscaster@postbox.co.uk or subscribe when you visit www.postbox.co.uk/economist.htm.

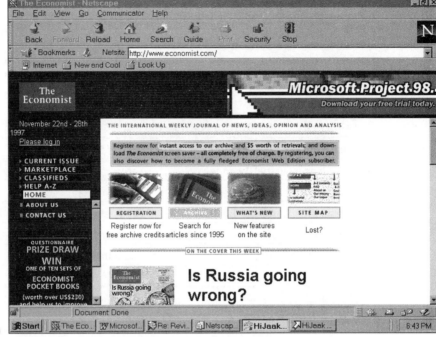

Figure 8-3: The Economist sends free weekly news summaries directly to your e-mailbox.

What Does the S&P 500 Have to Do with Anything?

You can measure how good or bad an investment is by comparing it to a market index. For example, the Standard & Poor's (S&P) 500 tracks a broad group of large capitalized stocks that are traded on the New York Stock Exchange, the American Stock Exchange, and NASDAQ. You can see the S&P Web site at www.stockinfo.standardpoor.com.

Each stock in the S&P 500 index is weighted by the relative market value of its outstanding shares. Overall, the index represents the performance obtained in the stock market for large capitalized stocks. (I define the term *large capitalized stocks,* or *large cap stocks,* later in this section.) This index provides performance information so that you can compare the stocks in your portfolio to "the market." If your returns are better than the market, you're doing well. If your returns are lower than the market, you need to re-evaluate your stock selections.

When you compare the performance of your stock to a market index, you can determine whether the stock outperformed the market, maintained the market rate, or underperformed. As Table 8-2 shows, however, not all market indexes are alike. For example, the Dow Jones Industrial Average is the most well-known index, but it includes only 30 large, mature, consumer-oriented companies. The Wilshire 5000 is the most comprehensive index of common stock prices regularly published in the U.S. and may be the best indicator of overall market performance. As you can see in Table 8-2, the S&P 500 tracks the performance of large capitalized stocks. In other words, the S&P 500 isn't the appropriate index for evaluating the performance of your small capitalized stock.

Table 8-2	Comparing Apples to Apples with the Right Index
Index	*Type of Security*
Dow Jones Industrial Average	Large capitalized stocks
Financial Times World	World stocks
Lehman Bros. Corporate Bonds	Corporate bonds
Lehman Bros. Government Bonds	U.S. Treasury bonds
Morgan Stanley EAFE	International stocks
Russell 2000	Small capitalized stocks
S&P 500	Large capitalized stocks
Wilshire 5000	Entire market

Source: Jim Jubak, *The Worth Guide to Electronic Investing* (1996, Harper Business, New York, NY).

Table 8-3 helps to explain why the S&P 500 may not be the appropriate index to compare to your small capitalized stock. *Capitalization* (or *cap*) is the total number of shares outstanding multiplied by the current stock price of those shares. For example, a firm with 1 million common shares outstanding at $55 per share has capitalization of $55 million, which makes the company a small cap firm. Table 8-3 shows a quick estimate of how the capitalization of different companies sorts out.

Table 8-3	Defining the Capitalization of Companies
Category	*Capitalization*
Micro Cap	Less than $50 million
Small Cap	$50 million to $500 million
Mid Cap	$500 million to $5 billion
Large Cap	More than $5 billion

According to Standard & Poor's, small capitalized stocks have outperformed large capitalized stocks over time. Over certain short-term periods, however, this may not hold true. From 1983 to 1990, small capitalized stocks, as a group, underperformed larger capitalized firms. From 1991 to 1993, both small and mid capitalized firms have outperformed large capitalized companies.

Valuing Stocks

Many ways exist to value common stock. Overall, the value of a stock is the present value of all its future dividends. However, common stockholders aren't promised a certain dividend each year. The dividend is based on the profitability of the company and the board of director's decision to pay dividends to stockholders.

The second source of return for a stock is the increased market price of the stock. If the company decides not to pay dividends and reinvests profits in the firm, the company's stock price should increase.

Fundamental analysis seeks to determine the intrinsic value of securities based on underlying economic factors. It is the most widely accepted method for determining a stock's true value, which you can then compare to current prices to estimate current levels of mispricing. Fundamental analysts usually forecast future sales growth, expenses, and earnings.

Warren Buffet is the famous investor and chairman of Berkshire Hathaway. He shared his investment analysis methodology with Robert Hagstrom who wrote a book about it. If you're interested in his successful stock analysis techniques, you can download an Excel spreadsheet (available for both PC computers and Macintosh) from www.investorweb.com/MembersIndex.asp and analyze your investment candidates using "The Warren Buffet Way."

Technical analysis is another way to value stocks primarily using historical and volume trends. Technical analysts focus on charts of stock prices, patterns, and trading volumes. They don't consider the underlying economics of these changes. Technical analysts believe that the future can be predicted when a beginning pattern is identified. They don't investigate causes for trends of price and volume changes.

Technical analysts may talk about "accumulations" to describe stock price increases on large trading volumes. They may believe that demand is stronger than supply if stocks are moving from what they consider "weak hands" to "strong hands." The technical analyst may consider such movements a sign of sustainable change in the stock price. If the trading volume was light, the technical analyst might consider the change transitory.

These meaningful statements have no direct connection to the underlying economics of the company's stock. Generally, large volume changes are associated with some new information about the company, not its past trends. However, technical analysis can't be ignored because some large institutional investors use their vast computing power to conduct technical analyses. These organizations often suggest using fundamental analysis for a round of investigation, followed by technical analysis to double-check those results.

If you're interested in technical analysis, visit the following sites for more information:

- ✔ **Invest-O-Rama** provides an extensive tutorial on technical analysis at www.investorama.com/features/ssg_00a.html.

- ✔ **Trendvest** (www.trendvest.com) offers a Trading Simulator and Multiple Ratings System. Trendvest provides free samples of its services.

- ✔ **Wall Street City** (www.wallstreetcity.com) provides a good technical analysis tutorial.

For more explanation on valuing stocks, check out *Investing For Dummies* by Eric Tyson, MBA.

Chapter 9

Internet Stock Screening

● ●

In This Chapter

▶ Getting familiar with online stock screens

▶ Building your first stock screen

▶ Locating online and PC-based stock screens

▶ Using prebuilt stock screens

▶ Getting online stock recommendations from the experts

● ●

Stock screening boils down to finding the answer to one fundamental question: Which stock (among all stocks) should I buy right now? Of course, finding the answer to this question requires asking many more specific questions about stocks — questions that are difficult to answer without the help of computerized databases.

This chapter shows how you can use the Internet and PC-based stock screening tools to whittle down the universe of stocks to a manageable few candidates. You can then analyze your short list of stocks for gems that may bring you above-average returns. This chapter also tells you where to find daily or weekly results of prebuilt stock screens.

Finding the Best Stock Electronically

Screening is a process that permits investors to discover and distill information within a larger set of information. The Internet provides many screening tools that help you prospect stock issues. The goal of stock screens is to point out which stocks are worth your research and analysis time.

Some people believe that using a stock screen is like panning for gold. You use your computer to screen ("pan") for investment "nuggets" from a long list of possibilities. The online investor sets the objectives of any single screen. Different people get different results because no two people have exactly the same selection criteria or investment philosophy.

Overall, the benefit of stock screens is that they let you generate your own ideas — ideas that generate profits based on your investor savvy. Stock screening programs allow you to go beyond finding good stock investments and assist you in finding the very best stocks.

To identify investment candidates, the stock screen uses your preset criteria, such as *growth* (stocks that are expanding faster than the market or their peers); *value* (stocks that have strong financial statements but are selling at prices below their peers); or *income* (stocks that provide higher than average dividends).

Depending upon the criteria you select, you may have to run several iterations of the stock screen. For example, your first screen may result in several hundred possibilities. Because you can't investigate and analyze so many candidates, you have to run a second screen of these results. This fine-tuning should lead to a manageable list of investment candidates that you can research and analyze — perhaps between 10 and 20 candidates. It is likely that you can quickly whittle this number down by using common sense and your investor savvy.

Choosing the criteria for your first stock screen

Typically, you build a stock screen by accessing an online stock screening tool and filling out an online form. I offer examples of the variables used in these forms later in this chapter, in the section "Important ratios for screening stocks." The first stock screen that you develop may include quantifiable variables that you believe are the most important — for example:

- ✔ **Earnings growth:** The percentage of change between current earnings and earnings for the last quarter or last year.
- ✔ **Recent earnings surprises:** The difference between predicted and actual earnings.
- ✔ **Price-earnings ratio:** The current price of the stock divided by the earnings per share — that is, net income divided by the total number of common shares outstanding. For example, value stocks have P/E ratios below 10 or 12, and growth stocks have P/Es above 20.
- ✔ **Dividends:** The annual cash dividend paid by the company.
- ✔ **Market capitalization:** The number of outstanding shares multiplied by the current stock price of those shares. Market capitalization is sometimes abbreviated to *cap.* This value is a measurement of the company's size. Firms with high market capitalization are called "large cap" and companies with a low market capitalization are called "small cap."

Fine-tuning your stock screen

After you select your initial screening criteria, you click on Submit, Sort, or a similar command. A list of stock candidates appears. Often this list includes several hundred stocks. This number is still too large to research, so you should narrow this list by selecting more variables.

You may have some special knowledge about the industry you work in. You may have used certain products over the years and can use your knowledge to your advantage. However, keep in mind that a good product doesn't necessarily mean a good company. You may want to filter out companies that you just don't understand. You may also want to filter out companies about which you lack information. Without at least some basic information, you can't perform a complete analysis.

Using your stock screen results

After you complete your second stock screen and sort the data, you should have a list of about 10 to 20 companies. Start a file for each firm and begin to gather data for your analysis. At this point, you may discover that some companies aren't worth additional research — a finding that further reduces your short list. For example, the company may have filed for bankruptcy, or it may be targeted for federal investigation. Maybe the company recently paid a large fine for shady dealings, or the executive management was recently indicted for fraud, misconduct, or some other crime.

Check out the stock screen at StockTools (www.stocktools.com). After you reach the StockTools homepage, click on *stock screen*. You can query the StockTool's database for fundamental and historical stock information by using your own investment criteria.

Important ratios for screening stocks

Every industry tends to have its own language, and the financial industry is no exception. In the following sections, I define the key terms that the finance industry uses for stock screening variables.

Figure 9-1 shows Hoover's StockScreener (www.stockscreener.com), which uses up to 20 variables. It sorts the results alphabetically. Hoover's StockScreener screens more than 7,800 publicly traded companies, including major foreign companies and most NASDAQ small cap stocks. (For more information about small cap stocks, see Chapter 8.) Each stock screen's results are hyperlinked to a Hoover's *company capsule* (a snapshot of the company), as well as the company's home page, stock quotes and charts, SEC filings, and investment news.

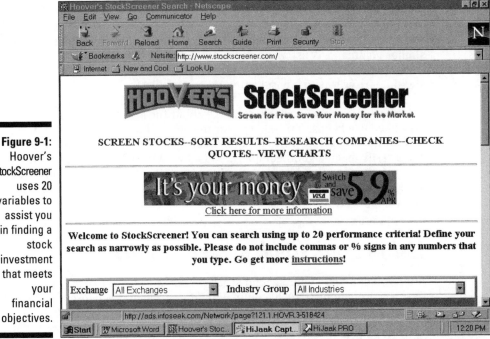

Figure 9-1:
Hoover's
StockScreener
uses 20
variables to
assist you
in finding a
stock
investment
that meets
your
financial
objectives.

(Reprinted with permission. Copyright © 1997 Hoovers, Inc.)

Beta

Beta is the measurement of market risk. It is the relationship between investment returns and market returns. Risk-free Treasury securities have a beta of 0.0. If the beta is negative, the company is inversely correlated to the market — that is, if the market goes up, the company goes down.

Book value

Book value is the original cost less depreciation of the company's assets less the outstanding liabilities. (*Depreciation* is the means by which an asset's value is expensed over its useful life for federal income tax purposes.)

Cash flow to share price

The ratio of *cash flow to share price* is the company's net income plus depreciation (expenses not paid in cash) divided by the number of shares outstanding. For companies that are building their infrastructure (such as cable companies or new cellular companies) and, therefore, don't yet have earnings, this ratio may be a better measure of their value than earnings per share (EPS).

Current ratio

Current ratio is current assets divided by current liabilities. A current ratio of 1.00 or greater means that the company can pay all current obligations without using future earnings.

Debt to equity ratio

To determine the *debt to equity ratio,* divide the company's total amount of long-term debt by the total amount of equity. (*Equity* is defined as the residual claim, by stockholders of company assets after creditors and preferred stockholders have been paid.) This ratio measures the percentage of debt the company is carrying. Many firms average a debt level of 50 percent. Debt to equity ratios greater than 50 percent may indicate trouble. That is, if sales decline, the firm may not be able to pay the interest payments due on its debt.

Dividends

Dividends are paid quarterly out of retained earnings. However, some high growth companies reinvest earnings and don't pay dividends.

Dividend yield

Dividend yield is the amount of the dividend divided by the most current stock price. You can use dividends as a valuation indicator by comparing them to the company's own historical dividend yield. If a stock is selling at a historically low yield, it may be overvalued. Companies that don't pay a dividend have a dividend yield of zero.

Earnings per share (EPS)

Earnings are one of the stock's most important features. After all, the price you pay for a stock is based on the future earnings of the company. The consistency and growth of a company's past earnings indicate the likelihood of stock price appreciation and future dividends. *Earnings per share* is often referred to as EPS.

Market capitalization

Market capitalization is calculated by multiplying the number of outstanding shares times the current stock price of those shares. Market capitalization is sometimes called *market value.*

P/E ratio

You calculate the *price-earnings ratio* by dividing the price of the stock by the current earnings per share. A low P/E ratio indicates that the company may be undervalued. A high P/E ratio indicates that the company may be overvalued.

Price-to-book value

Price-to-book value is tangible assets less liabilities, and the price/book value is the current price of the stock divided by the book value. If the current stock price is below the price-to-book value, the stock may be a real bargain. On the other hand, impending unprofitability may be the reason.

Return on equity (ROE)

Return on equity (ROE) is usually equity earnings as a proportion of net book value. You divide the most recent year's net income by shareholders equity (*shareholders equity* is assets minus liabilities) to calculate ROE.

Shares outstanding

The term *shares outstanding* refers to the total number of shares for a company's stock. This is a number that beginning investors often get wrong because it changes on an almost daily basis. To determine the firm's out-standing shares, you need the most recent data.

Investment Risks

No one invests in securities to lose money. However, each security has its own fine print. The Securities and Exchange Commission (www.sec.gov) has put together a list of some things to watch for:

- ✔ The higher the return, the greater the risk. You may lose some or all of your investment.
- ✔ Some investments can't be easily sold or converted to cash. For example, you may have a hard time selling a municipal bond before it matures.
- ✔ If you want to sell an investment quickly, you may have to pay some penalties or transaction charges.
- ✔ Investments in new companies or companies that don't have a long history may involve greater risk.
- ✔ Securities, like mutual funds, are not Federal Deposit Insurance Corporation (FDIC) insured.
- ✔ The securities you own may change due to corporate reorganizations, mergers, or third-party actions. You may be asked to sell your current shares, or you may be offered new shares due to this activity. Make certain that you understand the complexities of this investment decision before you act.
- ✔ Past performance of a security is no guarantee of future performance.

Using Online Stock Screens

The Internet provides a variety of stock screens. Some are easy to use, and others are more complex. The more advanced stock screens require some learning time.

Web-based stock screens can require between 2 and 30 variables. Their computerized stock databases can include anywhere from 1,100 stocks to more than 9,000 stocks. Additionally, some computerized stock databases are updated daily, weekly, or monthly. The best stock screen is the one that includes your personal investment criteria. Here are a few examples:

- ✔ **Market Guide's NetScreen** (netscreen.marketguide.com) allows you to screen for stocks by using any of 20 variables. This screen features comparisons of variables, user-defined variables, comparison of variables to a constant, use of a variable more than once, and use of operators (greater than, less than, equals, and so on). The database is updated weekly. The stock screen was started in September 1997. Your screening results are limited to no more than 200 companies at a time. The program doesn't allow you to view screen results of more than 200 companies.

- ✔ **IQ Net Basic Stock Scan** (www.iqc.com/scan) uses less than ten variables to screen stocks. Stock data is updated daily, about $2^{1}/_{2}$ hours after the close of the U.S. markets. The use of this Web site is free. The company also has a more advanced product called IQ Suite. The monthly subscription fee for IQ Suite is $18.95, with a free one-month trial.

- ✔ **MSN Investor** (investor.msn.com) has a stock screen called Investment Finder that searches 8,000 companies to find securities that meet your specific criteria. The program uses dozens of variable combinations. The monthly subscription fee is $9.95, with a free one-month trial.

- ✔ **Wall Street Research Network (WSRN)** (www1.wsrn.com) has a Quick Search Report that uses a maximum of 20 variables. You can quickly access the stock screen by heading to www1.wsrn.com/dataset/search.html.

- ✔ **Stock Tools Database Query** (www.stocktools.com) uses less than ten variables and is easy to use. Screen results can be highlighted and pasted into Excel spreadsheets (Office 97 and newer versions).

- ✔ **ResearchMag** (www.researchmag.com) requires your free registration before you begin. The stock screen has 12 basic variables that screen more than 9,000 stocks. The service is free of charge, but you need to be a subscriber to use the advanced stock screen. Subscriptions are based on the number of reports you use per year. Rates start at $55 for 25 of any combination of three reports. See the Web site for details.

Using Stock Screening Software

PC-based stock screens use their own stock screening software and databases. The advantage of these programs over Web-based stock screens is that they use hundreds of variables to screen stocks. I describe a few examples in this section.

Investor's Prospector (www.better-investing.org/computer/stbpro.html) is a product of the National Association of Investors Corporation (NAIC). The NAIC (www.naic.com) has negotiated an agreement with Standard & Poor's to provide stock selection data for more than 3,500 stocks traded on the New York Stock Exchange, the American Stock Exchange, and NASDAQ. The NAIC software imports data directly from S&P database. Each company has its own datafile. This special datafile has 5 to 10 years of fundamental data, S&P Analyst estimates for 5-year EPS growth, and current year EPS. Datafiles are updated quarterly. Annual subscriptions start at $179 for NAIC computer group members, $209 for NAIC members, and $244 for nonmembers. See the Web site for more information.

Equis International — MetaStock (www.equis.com) is a technical analysis software product that includes a stock search engine, real-time charting, and an analysis tool. The program is compatible with Microsoft Office 97, which means that you can download data to an Excel spreadsheet or embed charts in Word programs. You set the rules to identify trends and highlight important ratios. Click on a stock price, and the program links your Internet browser to a free Web site that provides the current stock prices. When you purchase the software, you receive a CD-ROM with a historical database of more than 2,100 different U.S. securities, Canadian stocks, mutual funds, futures, and indexes. The price of MetaStock 6.5 for Windows is $349.

Figure 9-2 shows the home page of MetaStock software. The makers of Metastock use their software program to make stock recommendations. For example, they show the top five stocks that had the biggest gains (more than $5 a share) over the last week. Gains are measured on a percentage basis. For example, a $20 stock that increases in price to $25 has a $5 gain or a 25 percent gain.

American Association of Individual Investors (www.aaii.org) has a downloadable library of stock software and screens for members. Its Stock Investor program and database provides fundamental data for 7,000 stocks and includes a screening engine with more than 350 variables for each company, covering eight quarters of quarterly data. Data includes earnings estimates for 4,000 companies and information about business sectors and industries. Annual subscriptions are $99 for members and $150 for nonmembers.

Figure 9-2: MetaStock can assist you by screening stocks and providing real-time price analyses.

(Courtesy of Equis International, a Reuters Company.)

Telescan's Pro Search Module (www.telescan.com) allows you to target your best investment opportunities with its stock screening program. Select from 207 variables to isolate stocks that have the highest performance based on your investment goals. The program includes the Analyzer Module, which performs in-depth technical and fundamental analysis using data from Telescan's 20-year historical database. The program, which sells for $395, also includes Quotelink, a data downloader, and Optimizer programs.

Telescan provides many screen results of the Telescan Prospector online. This Web page shows the results of various Telescan stock searches. The company computes more than 25 million search combinations every week to find the searches that have worked the best or worst over the last 12 months. The latest searches are available every Monday. The firm displays the best 25 stocks for categories that include micro cap stocks, NASDAQ stocks, NYSE stocks, AMEX stocks, small cap stocks, medium cap stocks, large cap stocks, all stocks, and industry groups.

Using Those Terrific Prebuilt Stock Screens

The Internet provides many prebuilt stock screens that use preselected criteria. Some of these screens may make your work easier because they already include the investment criteria that you feel is most important. In the following paragraphs, I describe a few examples.

Quicken.com — Popular Stock Searches (www.quicken.excite.com/investments/stocks/search/) uses a large database that is owned by an independent financial information company called Disclosure. Figure 9-3 shows the Quicken.com prebuilt stock screen. This prebuilt stock screen uses four search categories:

✔ **Growth:** Growth stocks are defined as stocks that have higher than average growth over the last five years. This area has two stock screens. The first screen looks for stocks with high historical growth in revenue, earnings, and net income. The second stock screen searches out large cap stocks with high historical growth in revenue, earnings, and net income.

✔ **Earnings strength:** This category includes stocks that have a history of earnings strength and have exhibited that strength in their most recent annual report. This category sorts stock into groups of high historical growth in EPS and high EPS.

✔ **Yield:** This stock screen locates stocks that produce the highest dividend yield for their owners (stocks with high yields).

✔ **Valuation:** Using the P/E ratio as an indicator, these searches identify stocks that may be undervalued or overvalued by the market. Two prebuilt stock screens exist for this category. The first is lowest P/E ratios; the second is highest P/E ratios.

Wall Street Voice (www.wsvoice.com), shown in Figure 9-4, provides easy to use, prebuilt stock screens with only two variables. When you get to the home page, click on Stock Screening. The screens at this site use the following variables:

✔ **Beta:** This variable is a measure of the sensitivity of an investment's return compared to the market. A beta of zero (0.0) is usually associated with risk-free investments like Treasury securities. A beta of between 0.0 and 1.0 is usual for defensive stocks (stocks with products and services — such as utilities, prescription drugs, food, and so on — that are necessary regardless of the economy). Small cap stocks have betas that are usually greater than 1.0 and more volatile. If a stock has a

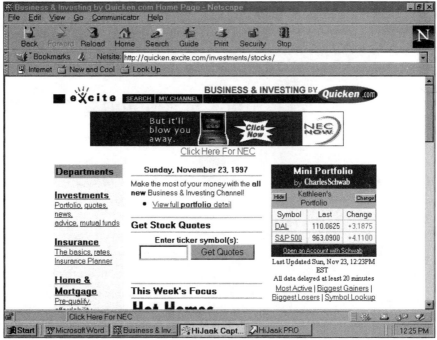

Figure 9-3:
Quicken.
excite.com
provides
prebuilt
stock
screens to
assist you
in your
stock
selection.

beta of 2.0, then the stock should provide twice the rate of the market return (as indicated by the S&P 500 or some other index) in a *bull* (up) market. In a *bear* (down) market, a stock with a beta of 2.0 falls twice as fast as a stock with a beta of 1.0.

✔ **S&P Five Star Recommendations:** Standard & Poor's staff continuously reviews each stock ranking by using one of five performance categories. Analysts rate stocks from one star (sell) to five stars (buy). From 1987 to the present, Standard & Poor's analysts' recommendations have returned twice the S&P 500.

The database of 1,100 stocks in 103 industry groups is updated weekly.

Market Player (www.marketplayer.com) provides a more advanced stock screening engine. Instructions for using the engine are easy to understand, but you should allow some time for getting used to the program. Market Player has many prebuilt screens that you may find useful. (If you're an experienced online investor, the prebuilt screens may provide some ideas about how you can improve your own screens.) Here are a few examples of the Market Player's prebuilt screens:

✔ **Short sales:** Market Player provides a near term short selling screen (for experienced investors). I explain short selling in Chapter 16.

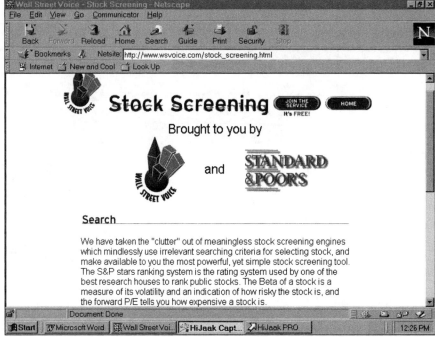

(Copyright © 1997 CharSher Corp.)

Figure 9-4:
Wall Street
Voice
provides a
way to sort
Standard &
Poor's
recommended
stocks.

✔ **Valuation screens:** Market Player has four valuation screens: Low P/E; Low Relative P/E; Low Price Book, Dividend Yield, Price/Sales; and Low Price and Normalized Earnings.

✔ **Earnings surprises screens:** Market Player has two earnings surprises screens: Recent Earnings Surprises and Biggest Stable EPS surprise.

The Motley Fool (www.fool.com) offers a weekly discussion of its stock screens. Motley Fool provides screen results that pick out companies that missed or beat analysts' consensus estimates by 9 percent or more. Stocks are listed alphabetically as well as by descending percentages.

The other two screens that Market Player provides are for rising or falling margins. *Margins* are defined as *profit margins* (what's left after all expenses have been paid), *operating margins* (what's left after sales expenses, administration expenses, and general nonproduction overhead expenses are paid), and *gross margins* (what's left after labor and materials have been paid). When earnings are increasing faster than sales, the company is performing better than ever. In general, companies that are increasing their margins tend to produce the best earnings over time. In contrast, companies with falling margins may be on the decline.

Determining Your Own Investment Criteria for Stock Screens

Many ways exist for setting up stock screens that can be beneficial for your information mining. In the following sections, I offer a few examples of ways that you can build stock screens to discover specific categories of stocks. I've chosen the categories of growth stocks, income stocks, and value stocks for these examples.

Screening for growth stocks

Growth stocks are expanding at rates faster than their counterparts. They have different degrees of risk and are a way of betting on the future.

Your stock screen for growth stocks may consider the following criteria:

- ✔ **Basic growth:** Any stock that has growth of 15 percent or more in one year.

- ✔ **Long-term growth:** Any stocks that grew 15 percent or more in one year over the past five years. (Companies must have historical EPS records of over five years.)

- ✔ **Earnings for growth:** Stocks that have a price-to-earnings ratio that is equal to or less than the growth rate of the stock plus its dividend yield.

- ✔ **Aggressive growth companies with low P/E ratios:** Stocks with annual earnings growth of more than 24 percent and P/E ratios of less than 15. (P/E ratios of less than 15 are preferable, but rare in the current market.)

Screening for income stocks

Income stocks tend to be stodgy, boring, slow-growth companies that are steady income producers. You may want to include dividend yield in your stock screen for income stocks. For example, you may screen for any stocks with a dividend yield that's at least equal to the S&P 500 and never falls below 4 percent. (This criterion rules out growth stocks that don't pay dividends.)

Screening for value stocks

Value stocks are companies that have strong financial statements and good earnings but are traded at stock prices that are less than their industry peers.

Here are some criteria that you may want to include in your stock screen for value stocks:

- **Book value:** Stocks for which the book value of the company is less than 80 percent of the average S&P 500 stock.

- **Debt-equity ratio:** Stocks for companies with a debt/equity ratio of 50 percent or less.

- **Price-earnings ratio:** Stocks for which the average of the company's five-year earnings is not less than 70 percent of the average P/E ratio of the S&P 500. Don't include stocks with a P/E ratio greater than 12. (A low P/E ratio may indicate that the stock is selling at a bargain price.)

- **Underpriced stocks:** Three criteria exist for this stock screen:

  - Small cap stocks with *quick ratios* (current assets less inventory divided by current liabilities) greater than 1.0 and return on assets (ROA) greater than 0.0

  - A price to earnings ratio (P/E ratio) that is half of that industry's average

  - A price-to-book value ratio of 80 percent or less, and a price-to-sales ratio of 33 percent or less

Your Judgment and Hot Stock Picks

The Internet provides many stock recommendations. These hot stock picks are usually free. Some investors would say that that's about what this information is worth — nothing. However, stock recommendations may be helpful indicators of general market trends.

Accepting someone's advice is always subject to your judgment. Keep in mind that seeing something written on the Internet doesn't necessary mean that it's true. Whenever you get investment advice, you should consider what the advice-giver has to gain.

Investigations by NASDAQ regulators indicate that the prices of stocks that are "talked up" in Internet chat rooms often increase due to a flurry of buying and selling. After the discussions stop, the stock trades at a less feverish level, and prices tend to level off. What this finding means is that you're unlikely to find an *underpriced* stock in an Internet chat room. However, general observations and discussion about changes in the market by savvy investors can be very valuable.

Here are a few examples of Internet sites that provide stock recommendations:

- ✔ **First Advisors** (`firstadvisors.com`) offers free stock recommendations, quotes, and portfolio tracking. The service lets you watch the investments that professional money managers select by following four different professional managers and five investment types: Arbitrage by Gabelli Asset Management, Large Cap Value by the Edgar Lomax Company, Large Cap Growth by Cornell Capital Management, Tactical Fixed Income by Central Plains Advisors, and Mid Cap Growth and Equity by Cornell Capital Management. Reports sent by U.S. mail are $19.95 per month; e-mail reports are $24 per year; and faxed reports are $36 per year.

- ✔ **Investors Guru** (`home.istar.ca/~invguru`) focuses on small capitalized stocks. The site includes many features, stock watch lists, research forums, newsletters, e-mail alerts, and links to related investor sites. The site uses a program called Mega Search to access free quotes, charts, and news, from the Internet's most popular corporate financial information providers.

- ✔ **Streetnet** (`www.streetnet.com`), shown in Figure 9-5, indicates the hottest sectors and industries. Additionally, it provides you with the fundamental data for the 12 hottest stocks ($2 to $10 and $10 and up). For contrarians, Streetnet provides the same information for the biggest losers. When you reach this site, be sure to click on the What's Up button and the What's Down button.

 Most Internet investor advice is intended to stimulate your thinking and to help you avoid some of the common mistakes that others have made. Peter Lynch, author and former money manager at Magellan Fund, suggests that you spend as much time on your $1,000 investment as you would on the purchase of a $1,000 refrigerator.

Figure 9-5:
Streetnet
provides
stock
recommen-
dations.

Chapter 10

Going with Bonds: Which Type Is Best for You?

In This Chapter

▶ Understanding the basics of bonds

▶ Finding online information about the four general types of bonds

*B*onds are similar to stocks because you make money in two ways. The first way is *capital appreciation;* the bond increases in value if interest rates decline, which means that you can sell the bond at a *premium.* That is, you can sell the bond for more money than you paid for it. (By the way, the profit you make is called *capital gains.*) The second way to make money is the periodic interest payment that you receive during the bond term.

Bonds are often called *fixed income investments.* They represent debts or IOUs from the issuer. The amount of the loan is the *principal;* the compensation given to the investor is called *interest payments.* In this chapter, I show you how the Internet provides information about Treasury, federal agency, municipal, and corporate bond auctions and offerings, historical and current yield rates, education, tax information, and more.

Bonds can be virtually risk-free and guaranteed by the U.S. government, or they can be speculative, high-flyers that can crash and go into default. You may decide that these investments aren't for you, but if you own a mutual fund, you may already be invested in the bond market.

Bond Basics

DSBonds are usually purchased through a broker. Treasury securities (bills, notes, and bonds) can be purchased without a broker directly from the government.

The most popular bonds are often long-term debt that matures in ten or more years. A bond is a commitment by a public or private entity to pay the bondholder certain interest payments at specific times and the *principal* (the original investment) at the end of a specified time period.

Bonds have clearly stated terms and maturity dates. These terms can be as short as 13 weeks or as long as 30 years. Sometimes you can't recover your investment until the bond matures. If you have to sell the bond before it matures, you may have a difficult time finding a buyer. The broker's commission takes some of your return, and you lose the sizable return you were going to receive on your investment.

Bonds have their own terminology that you need to understand:

- **Par value:** Refers to the face value of the bond and the amount returned to the bondholder at maturity. The par value of bonds is generally set at $1,000.

- **Coupon interest rate:** Indicates what percentage of the par value of the bond is paid out annually in the form of interest.

- **Maturity:** Indicates the length of time until the bond issuer returns the face value to the bondholder and terminates the bond.

- **Current yield:** Refers to the ratio of the annual interest payment to the bond's current selling price. For example, assume that the bond has an 11 percent coupon rate, a par value of $1,000, and a market value of $700. It has a current yield of 15.71 percent ($[0.11 \times \$1,000] \div \$700$).

- **Yield to maturity:** Indicates how much you would pay today for the future benefits of the bond. It is the investor's required rate of return used as the discount rate to determine the present value of future interest payments and the repayment of the principal at maturity. (See Chapter 9 for an example of determining the present value.)

For more information about investing in bonds, check out *Investing For Dummies* by Eric Tyson, MBA (published by IDG Books Worldwide, Inc.).

Finding bond indexes and historical data online

Bond indexes are designed to represent either the average yield to maturity or the average price on a portfolio of bonds that have certain similar characteristics. Historical data can also provide bond performance insights.

The Internet offers several sources for these averages and historical data. Here are a few examples:

- **Moody's Investor Services** (`www.moodys.com`) provides long-term corporate bond yield averages based on bonds with maturities of 20 years and above. Corporate bond averages are sorted into average corporate, average industrial, and average public utility groups and by bond ratings.

- **Bondsonline** (`www.bondsonline.com/bcgraphs.htm`) provides charts and historical data that compare various bond market sectors — for example, comparison of the 30-year Treasury bonds, 10-year Treasury notes, and the Dow Jones Industrial Average. This site also offers a comparison of tax-free municipal yields as a percentage of U.S. Treasury yields.

- **Federal Reserve Bank of St. Louis** (`www.stls.frb.org`) lists the monthly interest rate for each type of Treasury security. Files for specific Treasuries (for example, the one-year Treasury bill rate — auction average) and a downloadable zipped file that contains all the Interest Rate Series (historical archives of interest rate data) are available.

Rating bond risk

Moody's, Standard & Poor's, Fitch, and DCR are the best-known and most prominent credit-rating agencies. These companies assess the risk of bonds by studying all the bond's information and then assign the bond a rank that reflects the issuer's ability to meet the promised principal and interest payments. This rating may change during the life of the bond, and a change in the rating can dramatically change the value of the bond. All the bond rating companies rate bonds in descending alphabetical order from A to C, but each company uses a somewhat different letter scheme.

The rating agencies warn investors that a bond's rating isn't a "buy" recommendation. However, due to the risk-reward ratio, bonds with higher ratings offer lower yields; bonds with lower ratings, which represent a riskier investment, offer higher yields.

The Four Basic Types of Bonds

Many organizations issue bonds, but the following types of organizations issue most bonds:

  ✔ The federal government (Treasury securities)

  ✔ Federal government agencies

  ✔ State and local government agencies (municipal bonds)

  ✔ Corporations

In the following sections, I briefly discuss each type of bond.

Uncle Sam's bonds: Treasury securities

Treasury securities are U.S. government securities called Treasury bills, notes, and bonds. These securities are a major source of government funds and a key investment for many consumers. The U.S. government is highly unlikely to default on its Treasury securities, but if it does, your dollar is also probably worthless, so your investment is, essentially, risk-free.

The disadvantage of the risk-free rate of Treasury securities is that it's generally considered the bottom of the yield pile — the lowest yield you can get. As the level of risk gets greater, the reward also increases. You can expect a better yield (but more risk) from corporate bonds with similar maturities.

You can purchase Treasury securities without a broker, directly from the government, in a program called Treasury Direct. For information about Treasury Direct and instructions on how to open an account, see www.publicdebt.treas.gov/sec/sectrdir.htm.

The Treasury Direct program allows investors to participate in regularly scheduled auctions. The minimum investments are $10,000 for bills, $5,000 for notes maturing in less than five years, and $1,000 for securities that mature in five or more years. Your interest payments are paid into your Treasury Direct account, as is a security's par value at maturity.

For information about Treasury auction dates, see the Bureau of Public Debt's Web page at www.publicdebt.treas.gov/of/ofannce.htm.

Treasury bills are sold for less than their face value. The discount represents the interest the investor earns. Interest income on Treasuries is usually exempt from state and local taxes but is subject to federal taxes.

Internet information on Treasury securities

For more information on U.S. Treasury securities, see the following Web sites:

✔ **Kirlin: About Investments** (www.kirlin.com/aboutinv/ust.html) provides a good overview of Treasury securities. This tutorial includes information on safety and availability.

✔ **Media Logic** (www.mlinet.com/mle/ec_1000.htm) provides links to Treasury security auction results, Treasury quotes, government bond indexes, historical treasury yield information, and more.

✔ **Winstar** (www.winstarsecurities.com/index.html) is a brokerage that specializes in buying and selling Treasury securities and government agency bonds.

Figure 10-1 shows a forecast of the yields on U.S. Treasury securities for the next six months (www.neatideas.com/economic/tbond.htm). Forecasts are based on data from the last ten years and a forecasting methodology. You may find this information useful for spotting market trends.

Savings bonds: The easiest way to save

Series EE savings bonds are easy to buy. You can purchase them at any bank. In addition, some employers have savings bonds automatic investment programs. The employee has a certain amount of money deducted from his or her paycheck, and that money is used to purchase savings bonds. For some people, this kind of investment program is the easiest and only way they can save money.

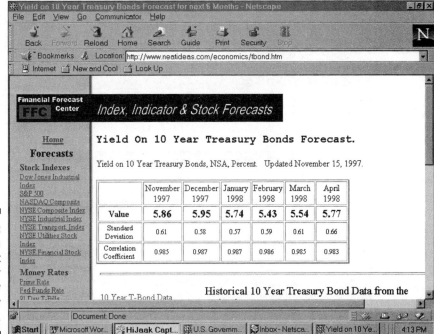

Figure 10-1: Looking in all the right places for Treasury security trends.

The full faith and credit of the United States back U.S. savings bonds. The Series EE savings bonds that you buy today earn market-based rates for 30 years. However, you can cash in the bonds at any time after six months from the purchase date.

Income from U.S. savings bonds is exempt from state and local income tax. You can also defer paying federal income tax on the interest until you cash in the bond or until it stops earning interest in 30 years. If you use savings bonds for educational purposes, they may provide you with additional tax savings.

Figure 10-2 shows the Web site for the Bureau of Public Debt at `www.publicdebt.treas.gov/sav/sav.htm`. This site provides information about the different types of savings bonds and notes that are available.

Federal government agency bonds

Agency bonds are similar to Treasury bonds but have marginally higher risk and higher returns. They can be sold at $1,000 to $25,000 and sometimes more. Federal agencies issue bonds to support housing (either with direct loans or the purchase of existing mortgages); export and import activities with loans, credit guarantees, and insurance; the postal service; and the activities of the Tennessee Valley Authority.

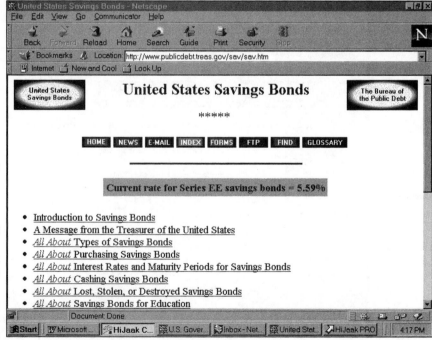

Figure 10-2:
The Bureau of Public Debt provides a vast amount of information on savings bonds.

For additional information on government agency bonds, see MoneyLine's The Bond School at `www.moneyline.com/mlc_fagc.html`.

Not all government agency bonds are equal. The full faith and credit of the U.S. government guarantees many issues. Although government agency bonds aren't a direct obligation of the U.S. government, they offer little, if any, credit risk. However, some bonds (for example, those of the Tennessee Valley Authority) do not have this guarantee.

The beauty of tax-free municipal bonds

Towns, cities, and regional and local agencies issue municipal bonds. Municipal bonds usually have lower interest rates than comparably rated corporate bonds and Treasury securities. Income from a municipal bond investment is generally exempt from federal, state, and local taxes, so the securities are very attractive to investors in high tax brackets. You treat capital gains on such bonds as normal income.

The minimum amount required for investment in municipal bonds is $5,000, and municipal bonds are sometimes issued at a discount. This discount is to compensate investors for the additional risk that some of these bonds have, due to the financial difficulties of some local governments.

Three primary types of municipal bonds exist. Each bond type has special features:

- ✔ **General obligation bonds** are backed by the full faith and credit of the issuing agency. For municipal bonds, full faith and credit also means the taxing power of the issuing agency.

- ✔ **Revenue bonds** are backed by the funds from a designated tax or the revenues from a specific project, authority, or agency. These bonds are not backed by the full faith and credit (or the taxing power) of the issuing agency. In other words, revenue bonds are only as good (and as creditworthy) as the ventures they support.

- ✔ **Industrial development bonds, called IDBs,** are used to finance the purchase or construction of industrial facilities that are to be leased to businesses. Leasing fees of the facilities are used to meet construction expenses and the repayment requirements of the bonds. Often these bonds provide inexpensive financing to firms choosing to locate in the geographical area of the issuer. Examples of IDBs are bonds for the construction of piers and wharves.

Municipalities can also issue short-term securities called tax-exempt commercial paper and variable-rate demand obligations.

You can see the Nuveen Research Web site at `www.nuveenresearch.com`. This Web site is an excellent source for information on new municipal bond issues, municipal prospectuses, research reports, and more.

Floating with corporate bonds

Corporate bonds are a major source of corporate borrowing. When corporations make corporate bonds, they "float a bond issue." Such bond issues take the form of either debentures, which are backed by the general credit of the corporation, or asset-backed bonds, which are backed by specific corporate assets like property or equipment. Income from these bonds is taxable. However, top-rated corporate bonds are often almost risk-free and have a higher return than Treasury securities.

Corporate bonds are generally considered safer than stocks due to two factors:

✔ The bonds state exactly how much the corporation will pay the bondholder. Shareholders are entitled to cash dividends, but payment and the amount of the dividend is at the discretion of the corporation.

✔ Bondholders are creditors. They receive payment before the corporation can distribute any cash dividends to shareholders, which means that bondholders have greater protection in getting at least some return on their investment. (In bankruptcy, bondholders are paid from corporate assets before common stockholders.)

Some risk of default always exists. In the 1980s, many companies used junk bonds to finance highly leveraged takeovers of rival companies. Their bonds were rated noninvestment grade and speculative by the bond-rating agencies. Due to the additional risk, these bonds paid above-average interest rates. For some bondholders, these bonds were a windfall. For bondholders who invested in the corporate bonds of companies that failed, their bonds went into default and became worthless junk. Professional money managers are required by law to buy investment-grade securities, so they can't purchase junk bonds.

Figure 10-3 shows Bondtrac (`www.bondtrac.com`), a bond-tracking software company. Bondtrac provides a partial list of its services to demonstrate the use of its data and the functionality of its software. The free services don't show offer, concession, price, yield, or dealer information; these types of information are considered restricted information for licensed security brokers. With your free registration, you can look up corporate bonds, as well as municipal bonds and U.S. government agency bonds by using a variety of search criteria. Your screen results include information about bond amount, minimum purchase amount, rating, symbol, description, coupon, and maturity date.

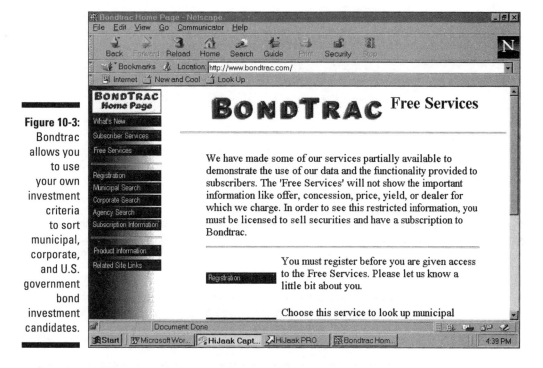

Figure 10-3:
Bondtrac allows you to use your own investment criteria to sort municipal, corporate, and U.S. government bond investment candidates.

Two new types of bonds

These relatively new types of bonds may be of interest to online investors:

- **Zero coupon bonds:** Zero coupon bonds offer no interest payments but are put on the market at prices substantially below their face values. The return to the investor is the difference between the investor's cost and the face value received at the end of the life of the bond. If you don't rely on interest payment income, zero coupon bonds may be the way to go (for example, if you're saving for your child's college education and need the cash for tuition in ten years).

- **Eurobonds:** Investments in foreign securities typically involve many government restrictions. Eurobonds are bonds offered outside the country of the borrower and usually outside the country in whose currency the securities are denominated. For example, a Eurobond may be issued by an American corporation, denominated in German deutsche marks, and sold in Japan and Switzerland. The Eurobond market is unique because it is relatively unregulated and untaxed.

For additional information about Eurobonds, see the following sites:

- Bradynet CyberExchange (`www.bradynet.com`) provides bond prices, analysis, research, ratings, news, information about new issues, forums, and more. Enter **Eurobonds** in the Search engine on the homepage and select Search Bradynet. You get a page that includes a demonstration program that searches for specific Eurobond issues.

- Petercam Eurobonds (`www.petercam.be/eurobonds/eurobond1.html`) provides valuation techniques for Eurobonds, benchmarks, and information about Eurobond primary and secondary markets.

As shown in Figure 10-4, J.P. Morgan & Company, Inc. (`www.jpmorgan.com`) provides a government bond index that is a widely used benchmark for assessing and quantifying risk across international fixed-income bond markets. If you're looking for benchmarks, go to the J.P. Morgan homepage and click on Index.

The indexes measure the total, principal, and interest returns in each market and can be reported in 19 currencies. You can compare Eurobonds to the index to provide a realistic measure of market performance.

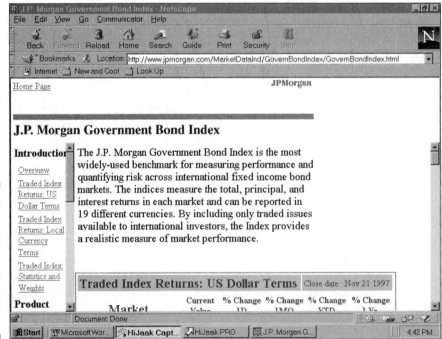

Figure 10-4: J. P. Morgan & Company provides a benchmark for international bonds.

(Reprinted with permission from J.P. Morgan & Co., Inc.)

Part III
Paying the Right Price

"I suppose coins and stamps might have been a more prudent collectible to invest in."

In this part . . .

The Internet offers plenty of resources that can help you turn your hunches into investment strategies. The chapters in this part of the book show you how to use the Internet to locate hard-to-find financial information so that you can analyze investment candidates. This part of the book shows you how to buy and sell mutual funds online, as well as how the World Wide Web can assist you in finding annual reports and other data about companies that you fancy. In this part, you find out how to evaluate stock prices like a pro, you explore one of the easiest ways available to value bonds, and you discover how to reduce the purchase costs of buying your favorite stocks by using direct purchase and dividend reinvestment plans.

Chapter 11

Online Analysis, Buying, and Selling of Mutual Funds

*W*hen selecting a mutual fund, investors often look for relative performance over the last ten years, five years, and three years to see how the fund reacts to different economic conditions and stock market environments. Other factors in selecting a mutual fund include evaluating the fund manager's experience and record, the fund's level of consistency, and the fund's major investment holdings.

In this chapter, I show how you can match your financial objectives and risk-tolerance level to the right mutual funds. As a result, you can decide how much you should invest in a particular type of fund. I also describe how you can use online mutual fund ratings to assist you in selecting the very best mutual funds for your personal portfolio. Finally, this chapter shows you how to buy and sell mutual funds online.

Going Online with Mutual Funds

Mutual funds are great for investors who lack capital, technical knowledge, and the time to establish and maintain a diversified stock or bond portfolio. The advantages of mutual funds are easy access to your assets, the ability to sell the funds if you need to, and professional management.

A wide difference exists in the kinds of mutual funds available. Many large mutual fund companies manage *families* of funds. A mutual fund family is a group of mutual funds all under the same management. Today, you can select from more than 9,600 different mutual funds from over 700 fund families. Most likely, one of these funds meets your personal objectives and risk-tolerance level. If you aren't satisfied with the fund you select, you can always switch from one fund to another in the same fund family without any additional exchange costs.

You can find information about a fund's goals, strategies for reaching those objectives, performance, management, and fee structures in the fund's prospectus. Prospectuses are often located at the fund's Web site (for example, T. Rowe Price's site at www.troweprice.com), and they're also filed at the Securities and Exchange Commission's Web site at www.sec.gov.

Mutual funds fall into two main categories: *open-end funds* (which can continuously acquire new funds for investment through the sale of additional shares) and *closed-end funds* (which initially raise capital by selling a fixed number of shares, and then those shares are bought and sold on a stock exchange).

For more information about the two types of mutual funds, see Chapter 7. For more explanation about investing in mutual funds, take a look at *Investing For Dummies* by Eric Tyson, MBA (published by IDG Books Worldwide, Inc.).

Different funds have different fees. Some funds have *up-front loads* (a sales commission when you buy the fund) or *back-end loads* (a sales commission when you sell the fund), and some funds have *no loads* (no sales commissions).

For a list of a few no-load mutual funds, see www.noload.com.

All funds have fees and expenses, but the amounts vary. By law, sales commissions can't be greater than 8 percent of the amount invested. All funds have a management fee — usually around 2 percent of the fund's total assets — that is paid to the professional money managers. Some funds have Rule 12b-1 fees, which allow the fund's managers to charge investors for marketing the fund and distributing fund information. By law, Rule 12b-1 fees can range between 0.25 percent and 1.25 percent of the fund's annual return.

Figure 11-1 shows the Web site for the 100% No-Load Mutual Fund Council (www.100noloadfunds.com). You may be interested in what it has to say about its membership. The site provides links to profiles of no-load mutual funds, and you can request a prospectus from the mutual funds company.

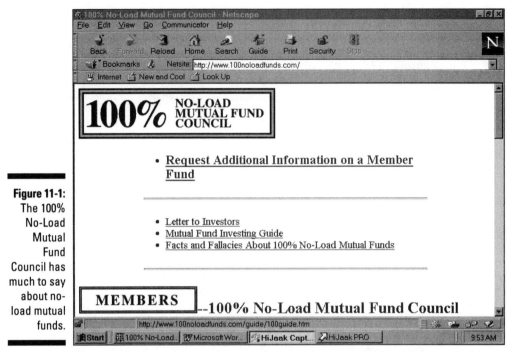

Figure 11-1:
The 100%
No-Load
Mutual
Fund
Council has
much to say
about no-
load mutual
funds.

(Copyright granted by the 100% No Load Mutual Fund Council.)

Finding the Right Mix of Investments

Asset allocation is the specific amount of money that you spend for each type of investment. In Wall Street-speak, it's how you diversify your financial assets (stocks, bonds, and cash) by amounts that you determine. It also means trying to squeeze every bit of return out of each asset type, given the level of risk.

Overall, the right asset allocation approach is the one that works best for you. It should take into consideration your age, the amount of time you can invest your money, your financial goals, your risk-tolerance level and the impact of taxes on your investment decisions.

Table 11-1 shows all the ingredients for finding the combination of assets that may be just right for you. The source of this guideline is Value Line (www.valueline.com). The table shows Value Line's definitions of nine investor types. The types are categorized as conservative, moderate, and aggressive. The investment time frame fills out the picture. The investment period can be short-term, medium-term, or long-term.

Table 11-1	Mutual Fund Asset Allocations Based on Investor Risk-Tolerance Levels		
Risk	Time Frame		
	Short-term (0 to 2 years)	Medium-term (3 to 5 years)	Long-term (6 years and greater)
Conservative	#1	#2	#3
Stocks	0%	30%	50%
Bonds	0%	25%	50%
Cash	100%	45%	0%
Moderate	#4	#5	#6
Stocks	10%	55%	65%
Bonds	30%	35%	35%
Cash	60%	10%	0%
Aggressive	#7	#8	#9
Stocks	30%	70%	100%
Bonds	30%	30%	0%
Cash	40%	0%	0%

Source: Value Line Mutual Fund Survey, *How to Invest in Mutual Funds* (1995), Value Line Publishing, Inc., New York, NY.

Many mutual funds match the asset allocation table shown in Table 11-1. You can start with one mutual fund, or you can purchase a mutual fund for each allocation. If you purchase several mutual funds, you can diversify your risk even more. For example, to complete your portfolio, you may want to buy a money market fund, a stock mutual fund, and a fixed-asset (bond) mutual fund. It's your money and your choice.

Matching Mutual Funds to Your Financial Objectives

Table 11-2 shows how you can match mutual fund categories to your financial objectives and risk-tolerance level. After you read Table 11-1, decide which of the nine investor types most closely matches your personal financial plan and risk-tolerance profile. For more detail about the investor types, visit the Value Line site at www.valueline.com. Table 11-2 shows what categories of mutual funds are right for your investor type. The percentages listed in Table 11-2 match the recommended allocations shown in Table 11-1. (For details about fund types, see Chapter 7.)

Table 11-2 Suggested Mutual Funds for Nine Types of Investors

Investor Type	Cash	Stocks	Bonds
1	(100%) Money market fund		
2	(45%) Money market fund	(30%) General equity	(25%) Intermediate fixed income partial equity funds (asset allocation), Tax-free fixed income funds (municipal bonds)
3	(0%)	(50%) General equity funds (income, growth	(50%) Taxable fixed-income funds (government agency, and income) Fixed-mortgage), income partial equity funds (asset allocation)
4	(10%) Money market fund	(30%) General equity funds income	(60%) Short-term fixed-income funds (diversified), Fixed-income partial equity funds (asset allocation and balanced)
5	(10%) Money market fund	(55%) General equity funds (growth income)	(35%) Intermediate fixed-income funds (diversified), Intermediate fixed-income partial equity funds (balanced), Tax-free fixed-income funds (municipal bonds)
6	(0%)	(65%) General equity funds (growth, growth and equity)	(35%) Fixed-income bonds (diversified, corporate), Fixed-income partial equity funds (balanced), Tax-free fixed-income funds (municipal bonds)

(continued)

Table 11-2 *(continued)*

Investor Type	Cash	Stocks	Bonds
7	(40%) Money market fund	(30%) General equity funds (aggressive growth, small cap)	(30%) Short-term fixed-income funds (corporate high-yield), Short-term fixed-income partial equity funds (convertible)
8	(0%)	(70%) General equity funds (aggressive growth, small cap), Specialty equity (technology, other)	(30%) Intermediate fixed-income (corporate high yield), Intermediate fixed-income partial equity funds (flexible), Tax-free fixed-income funds (municipal bonds)
9	(0%)	(100%) General equity funds (aggressive growth, growth, growth and income, and small cap equity funds), Small cap equity funds, Specialty equity (technology, other), International equity (European, foreign, global, or Pacific stock)	(0%)

Interested in finding specific mutual funds in the categories that match your personal finance profile? Stock Smart (www.stocksmart.com) can assist you in finding the mutual fund that's right for you. When you reach the Stock Smart home page, click on the Fund icon at the top of the screen. Next, click on the Smart Stock Fund Wizard icon. On the questionnaire that appears, answer the questions about what you're looking for in a mutual fund. The Wizard uses your preferences to find funds that best match your specific needs.

Using the Internet to Help You Choose the Best Funds in Each Class

Past performance doesn't guarantee future performance. However, annualized returns are often used to compare funds. The Internet offers tables of fund comparisons for each month and for periods ranging from one month to ten years or more. For example, Business Week (www.businessweek.com) has a Mutual Funds Corner that provides listings of the returns for the best funds, bond fund leaders, the worst funds, and so on.

Comparing a fund to similar funds is a good way to examine a fund's performance. Organizations such as Morningstar (www.morningstar.net) have mutual fund tables that make comparisons easy by grouping top-rated fund classes and including the averages for each category. A fund's capability to consistently outperform similar funds is one sign of good quality. In contrast, you should avoid funds that have consistently underperformed for three years or more.

Make certain that the funds you're comparing are similar. A big difference exists between an aggressive growth fund and a growth fund. To verify your analyses, check the prospectus of each fund. The fund's investment objectives are listed in the first paragraph. You may discover that the fund that looked so attractive at first is too risky for you.

Following a mutual fund checklist

As you select your first mutual fund, consider several factors, which I describe in the following checklist:

- ✔ **The fund manager:** Often a fund is only as good as its management. If the fund manager has shown great performance in the past, future performance is likely to be above average. If the fund manager has been replaced, past performance becomes less meaningful and may even be worthless. A poor-performing fund that gets a new fund manager may turn around and become a top performer.

- ✔ **The stability of the fund's philosophy:** If the fund seems unclear about its financial goals and is switching investment methods, it may be in trouble.

- ✔ **The size of the fund:** Good fund candidates have at least $50 million under management and should be large enough to keep up with institutional investors. At the opposite end of the spectrum, funds with more than $20 billion tend to have problems with being too large.

✔ **The objectives of the fund:** Some funds focus on specialty or sector funds (gold funds, biotech funds, and so on) and often offer great returns. However, they aren't good funds for the online investor who wants to own just one mutual fund. If you own just one specialty fund, you lose the advantage of diversification.

✔ **Fees:** A debate has raged during the last ten years about which is better: no-load or load mutual funds. All the studies indicate that paying a sales commission doesn't ensure a greater return. However, investing in a fund with high fees and high returns is better than investing in a fund with low fees and poor performance.

✔ **Purchase constraints:** Although some funds require a minimum initial investment of $5,000, many good funds don't have this requirement. Additionally, if you enroll in a fund's automatic investment program, the minimum initial investment amount is usually waived.

For additional information about selecting mutual funds, see Morningstar (www.morningstar.net). Morningstar has a learning section (just click on Learn) and helpful articles. One such article is titled "Select Your First Fund."

Assessing mutual fund performance

By comparing statistics for two mutual funds that are in the same category, you can assess the performance of each fund. Table 11-3 shows statistics for the Fidelity Magellan fund. Table 11-4 shows statistics for the Janus Growth and Income fund. These November 1997 statistics are from Morningstar (www.morningstar.net).

Table 11-3	Fidelity Magellan (FMAGX) Mutual Fund Statistics						
	1992	*1993*	*1994*	*1995*	*1996*	*YTD*	*3-Year Average*
Total Return %	7.02	24.66	−1.81	36.82	11.69	24.68	
S&P 500	7.62	10.06	1.32	37.53	22.95	30.40	
+/− S&P 500	−0.60	14.60	−3.13	−0.71	−11.26	−5.72	
Standard Deviation							15.50
Mean Total Return %							20.52
Beta							0.91
Morningstar Rating							2 Stars
Morningstar Risk							1.09

Table 11-4		Janus Growth and Income (JAGIX) Mutual Fund Statistics					
	1992	1993	1994	1995	1996	YTD	3-Year Average
Total Return %	5.35	6.70	−4.87	36.35	26.03	32.27	
S&P 500		7.62	10.06	1.32	37.53	22.95	30.40
+/− S&P 500		−2.27	−3.36	−6.19	−1.18	3.08	1.87
Standard Deviation							20.52
Mean Total Return %							26.76
Beta							1.10
Morningstar Rating							4 Stars
Morningstar Risk							1.13

Tables 11-3 and 11-4 provide the following information about the two funds:

✓ **Total Return %:** The percentage annual return (less all management fees and fund expenses) for the mutual fund.

✓ **S&P 500:** The percentage annual return for Standard & Poor's 500 index, which you can use as a benchmark to see how well the fund is performing compared to the market.

✓ **+/− S&P 500:** The difference (plus or minus) between the fund's returns and the S&P 500.

✓ **Standard Deviation:** A measure of how much the fund has deviated from its mean total return (similar to its average annual total return) over the past three years. The higher the number, the more volatile the mutual fund's returns.

✓ **Mean Total Return %:** The mean (a statistic that's similar to average) of the fund's annual return for the last three years.

✓ **Beta:** A measure of volatility. A beta of one or greater for a mutual fund indicates that the fund is more volatile than the index to which it's being compared. A beta of less than one indicates that the fund is more stable than the index.

✔ **Morningstar Rating:** The star rating attempts to put together a measure of risk and return. The rating assesses how well the fund has compensated investors for its level of volatility. The ratings listed are an average of the fund's rating over the last three years.

✔ **Morningstar Risk:** A rating of the fund's volatility on the downside (how it has performed compared to U.S. Treasury bills) relative to that of other funds in its asset class. A score of 1.0 is average. Scores greater than 1.0 indicate more than average risk over the last three years.

Here's what Tables 11-3 and 11-4 tell you about the two funds:

✔ A comparison of the annual returns to the S&P 500 over the last five years shows that both funds did not regularly outperform the market.

✔ Looking at each fund's annual returns, you can see that both funds lack consistency.

✔ Comparing the annual return of the two funds, the mean total return of the Janus Growth and Income (JAGIX) mutual fund is 26.76 percent and the return of the Fidelity Magellan fund is 20.52 percent. An investor in the Janus fund was rewarded with a significantly better return, and with less risk — hence the Janus fund's four star rating and the Fidelity fund's two star rating.

✔ Comparing the risk of the two funds, the risk of the Janus fund (as measured by the standard deviation) is greater. The standard deviation for the Fidelity Magellan fund is 15.50, and the standard deviation of the Janus Growth and Income fund is 20.52. These numbers indicate that the risk of achieving a higher return is greater with the Janus fund.

The Ratings War

Mutual fund companies don't show you the standard deviation and the betas of their mutual funds. However, you don't have to make your investment decision without these bits of vital information. Many Web sites offer information on the ranking of mutual funds. Rankings are useful because they help you digest important performance and risk statistics into one measure.

Here are a few examples of Web sites that offer information on the ranking of mutual funds:

✔ **Barron's** (www.barrons.com)

✔ **Business Week** (www.businessweek.com)

✔ **Forbes** (www.forbes.com)

✔ **S&P Mutual Fund Profiles and Stock Guides** (www.stockinfo.standardpoor.com)

Two of the most popular rating services are Morningstar and Value Line. Morningstar (www.morningstar.net) is a free service. Value Line (www.valueline.com) is a fee-based service.

The Morningstar rating system

Morningstar is an independent, Chicago-based firm that has been evaluating mutual funds and annuities since 1984. The organization currently evaluates more than 7,500 mutual funds.

Morningstar uses historical data to develop its ratings. The unique feature of the rating system is that it penalizes mutual funds for risk. Morningstar rates funds for consistently giving the highest returns and adjusts for risk as compared to funds in the same category.

Morningstar's five-star system is as follows:

- **Five Stars:** In the top 10 percent of performance; produces substantially above-average returns

- **Four Stars:** In the next 22.5 percent of performance; produces above-average returns

- **Three Stars:** In the middle 35 percent of performance; produces average returns

- **Two Stars:** In the lower 22.5 percent of performance; produces below-average returns

- **One Star:** In the bottom 10 percent of performance; produces substantially below-average returns

The Value Line dual rating system

Value Line uses a dual rating system that includes overall rank and measures various performance criteria, including risk. Funds are ranked from one to five, with one having the highest rank (the best risk-adjusted performance) and the best risk ranking (the least risky). For more details about Value Line, see Chapter 6 of *Investing For Dummies* by Eric Tyson, MBA.

Value Line uses historical data to develop its ratings. The five-number system is as follows:

1. In the top 10 percent; highest overall performance and lowest risk

2. In the next 20 percent; above-average performance and lower risk

3. In the middle 40 percent; average performance and average risk

4. In the lower 20 percent; below-average performance and higher risk

5. In the lowest 10 percent; lowest average performance and highest risk

Value Line has a software package that includes no- and low-load versions of Value Line's fund-analysis software. Launched as a less extensive alternative to the full Mutual Fund Survey for Windows, the program features the same sophisticated sorting, screening, filtering, portfolio analysis, and graphics capabilities. Its database presents essential information on more than 3,000 no- and low-load funds. The program is available on CD-ROM or 3$\frac{1}{2}$-inch disk. One-year subscription prices are $149 for monthly service and $95 for quarterly updates. A two-month trial subscription is available for $29. You can download updates from Value Line's Web site at www.valueline.com. A free, downloadable demo version of the software and database is available.

When using mutual funds ratings, you must keep two things in mind. First, past performance does not predict future performance. Second, comparing the ranks of two different mutual fund categories is meaningless. For example, you can't compare the ranks of a municipal-bond fund against an aggressive-growth fund.

Forecasting Your Mutual Fund's Future

After you look into rating systems such as the ones I describe in the preceding section, you may be interested in an online site that forecasts future returns. Just for the fun of it, check out the A. Bull & Co. Power Ratings for 600+ No-Load Funds at www.angelfire.com/biz/mutualfunds/POWER.html.

The company provides free analyses of the 600 most popular no-load mutual funds in the U.S. Each analysis includes a listing of a fund's total returns for the last three months and the last month as well as forecasts of the mutual fund's annual return. The forecast is based on price changes and weighted returns (including distributions) for the next year.

A. Bull & Co. also provides a free current update of its forecasts for 600 well-known no-load mutual funds in a generic spreadsheet format that allows you to sort and screen funds by using your own criteria. In addition to the data shown at the company's Web site, you can order a full report that includes ticker symbols, risk measurements based on three-year standard deviations, and more. To receive the full free update by e-mail, just send your request to mutualfunds@mailexcite.com.

Buying Mutual Funds Online — No Broker Needed

You can purchase a mutual fund without a broker. All you have to do is contact the company directly. Table 11-5 lists a few online mutual fund companies. The table shows the name of the mutual fund company, its Internet address, the minimum investment required, the number of funds the mutual fund company has, and whether the company has an automatic investment program. Usually, if you enroll for the automatic investment plan, you don't have to deposit the required initial minimum investment amount.

Table 11-5	Examples of Online Mutual Fund Sources			
Company	**Internet Address**	**Minimum Investment (Non-IRA Accts)**	**No. of Funds**	**Automatic Investment Plan?**
AIM Funds	www.aimfunds.com	$500	45	Yes
Alliance Funds	www.alliancecapital.com	$250	118	Yes
American Century Funds	www.americancentury.com	$2,500	60+	Yes
Columbia Funds	www.columbiafunds.com	$1,000	12	Yes
Dreyfus Funds	www.dreyfus.com	$2,000	150+	Yes
Evergreen Funds	www.evergreen.com	$1,000	70+	Yes
Fidelity Funds	www.personal.fidelity.com	$2,500	253	Yes
INVESCO Funds	www.invesco.com	$1,000	48	Yes
Janus Funds	www.janus.com	$2,500	19	Yes
John Hancock Funds	www.jhancock.com	$1,000	71	Yes
Kemper Funds	www.kemper.com	$1,000	43	Yes
Merrill Lynch Funds	www.plan.ml.com/products_services	Varies	100+	Yes
Nations Funds	www.nationsbank.com	$1,000	44	Yes
Oppenheimer Funds	www.oppenheimerfunds.com	$1,000	49	Yes
Paine Webber Funds	www.painewebber.com	$25,000	86	No

(continued)

Table 11-5 *(continued)*

Company	Internet Address	Minimum Investment (Non-IRA Accts)	No. of Funds	Automatic Investment Plan?
Prudential Funds	www.prudential.com	Varies	168	Yes
Putnam Funds	www.putnaminv.com	$500	209	Yes
Schwab Funds	www.schwab.com	$1,000	29	Yes
Scudder Funds	funds.scudder.com	$2,500	47	Yes
Smith Barney Funds	www3.smithbarney.com	$1,000	60+	Yes
Stein Roe Funds	www.steinroe.com	$2,500	21	Yes
Strong Funds	www.strong.com	Varies	30	Yes
Van Kampen	www.vkac.com	$500	30+	Yes
Vanguard Group	www.vanguard.com	Varies	90	Yes

Buying Mutual Funds Online: Using an Electronic Broker

You can purchase mutual funds through registered representatives of banks, trust companies, stockbrokers, discount brokers, and financial planners. To purchase mutual funds via the Internet, go to an online broker's Web site. (I list a few examples later in this section.)

Register by completing the online application form. You have to provide information about your income, net worth, social security number, and the type of account you desire. Sometimes you can open an account based on the quality (creditworthiness) of your information.

However, to have a fully functioning account, brokerages are required to have your signature on file. After they have your signature on file, you can buy or sell as much as you want.

After you open your account, you can log on to the Internet, go to your brokerage Web site, and enter orders by completing the online form. You can access your account at any time, check all your investments, and monitor your investments by using online news or quote services.

You have the following options for selecting an electronic broker:

- ✔ **A deep-discount broker:** The least expensive type of broker; offers no recommendations; contacting a human if an error occurs is often difficult

- ✔ **A discount broker:** Less expensive than full-service brokerages; no recommendations; minimum human contact

- ✔ **A full-service broker:** Full commissions, recommendations, advice, and personal service

Here are a few examples of online deep-discount brokers:

- ✔ **American Express Financial Direct** (www.americanexpress.com) requires an initial investment of $2,000 to open an account. This firm trades stock and mutual funds for a flat rate of $24.95.

- ✔ **Ameritrade** (www.ameritrade.com) is a New York-based firm that charges a flat rate of $8.00 per trade. This firm trades stocks, funds, and options. An initial investment of $2,000 is required to open an account. If you're wondering where this firm came from, the organization is a consolidation of Ceres, Aufhauser, and eBroker.

- ✔ **Discover Brokerage Direct** (www.lombard.com) is a San Francisco-based firm that requires an initial investment of $2,000 to open an account and charges $14.95 per trade. The firm trades stocks, funds, and options.

- ✔ **Donaldson, Lufkin, & Jenrette (DLJ Direct), formerly PC Financial Network,** (www.dljdirect.com) is based in New York. Figure 11-2 shows the Web site for this firm, which requires a $5,000 minimum initial investment to open an account. Trades are $20 for up to 1,000 shares. Trades of over 1,000 shares add $.02 per share. The company trades stocks, funds, bonds, and options.

- ✔ **E*Trade** (www.etrade.com) is a Palo Alto, California-based firm that charges a flat rate of $19.95 for the first 5,000 shares traded and then $0.01 for shares above that amount. It's also available on America Online and CompuServe.

- ✔ **Investexpress** (www.investexpress.com) doesn't require an initial investment to open an account. The firm trades stocks, funds, and options, and charges $13.95 per trade.

- ✔ **National Discount Brokers** (www.NDB.com) is a Chicago-based firm that requires an initial investment of $2,000 to open an account, and charges $14.75 per trade. The firm trades stocks, funds, and options.

- ✔ **Net Investor** (www.netinvestor.com) is a Chicago-based firm that requires an initial investment of $5,000 to open an account. Trades are $19.95 plus $.01 per share and a $4.45 transaction fee. The company trades stocks, funds, bonds, options, and CDs.

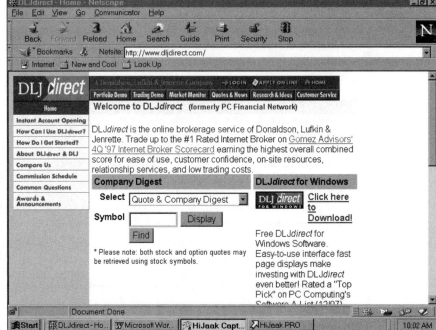

Figure 11-2:
Donaldson,
Lufkin, &
Jenrette
can assist
you in
purchasing
mutual
funds.

The Right Time to Sell Your Mutual Funds

If your fund becomes one of the worst performers, consider selling. However, you need to look at more than just the fund's rating. Here are a few guidelines for determining when to sell a fund:

- ✔ Compare the fund's returns to the appropriate index. For example, check the S&P 500 at www.stockinfo.standardpoor.com for mutual funds with large cap stocks.

- ✔ Compare your fund to other funds in the same category. If your fund consistently trails its peers, it may be a loser.

- ✔ Keep track of changes in your fund's management. If the fund hires a new money manager, that person may have a different investment strategy.

✔ If the fund increases by three or four times its original size in a short time period and its performance starts to decline, you may want to sell. As the fund keeps growing and growing, the professional money manager can't invest in the securities he or she knows and loves best, so the fund may start to acquire poor or average performing assets.

✔ Consider your needs. If you purchased the fund for a specific purpose and your life circumstances change, you should sell the fund and purchase one that meets your needs — even if the fund is doing well.

Figure 11-3 shows FundAlarm (www.fundalarm.com), a free, noncommercial Web site. FundAlarm provides objective information to help individual investors decide whether to sell a mutual fund. For details about how you can be automatically notified about when it's time to sell your mutual funds, see the Web site.

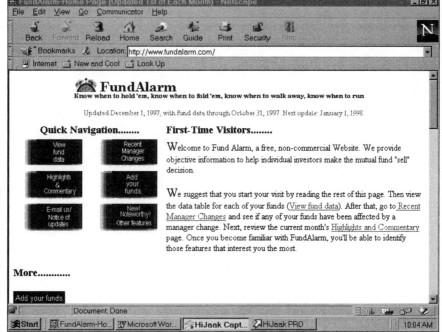

Figure 11-3: FundAlarm automatically notifies you about changes in your mutual fund.

When not to sell your mutual funds

In 1997, investors poured $11.5 billion dollars per month into mutual funds. Most investors are happy with their choices in mutual funds. According to Morningstar (www.morningstar.net), the average return on mutual funds is 21.7 percent. However, you'll probably want to change the funds or sell your mutual fund at some point. How do you know when it's time to sell?

Mutual funds offer diversification of market risks. However, some funds are likely to decline more than others during bear (down) markets. If your mutual fund is experiencing a temporary setback, it isn't time to sell; the market always has increases and decreases. You can't sell your fund every time it declines because you'll never accumulate long-term capital appreciation and experience the power of compounding.

Funds that underperform in the short term can still be sound investments. For example, Fidelity Magellan and Janus Income and Growth funds didn't outperform the market in the last three years; however, their average total returns over the last three years were 21.7 percent and 27 percent, respectively.

Chapter 12

Researching Individual Stocks

● ●

In This Chapter

▶ Finding annual reports online

▶ Downloading, printing, and saving annual reports

▶ Analyzing company annual reports

▶ Using prepared company data to make your investment decision

● ●

*I*n the past, only large financial institutions had access to high-quality financial data. Clients didn't have anywhere else to go for stock advice, which meant that bankers and stockbrokers charged customers hefty commissions for their research and recommendations. Much of this data is now available on the Internet. Some of the databases are free, and some are fee-based. Databases that charge fees require subscription fees — payment by the month, by database, or by document.

Even with free or low-cost information, however, researching stocks is still hard work. Doing so requires good judgment, the ability to fit all the bits and pieces of information together, and excellent decision-making skills. If you're thinking about investing in stocks, you need to research the following information:

✔ **Companies:** Profiles, management, financial health, insider trading, potential mergers, and acquisitions

✔ **Industries:** Industrial markets, industrial standards, and trends

✔ **Economic indicators:** The national, regional, and local economics

✔ **Other factors:** New legislation, technological breakthroughs, and new stock offerings

Often the best starting point for researching the stock of a certain company is the annual report. The best place to find annual reports is on the Internet. This chapter shows you how to locate annual reports by using a search engine, special company locator sites, investor supersites, and EDGAR — the Securities and Exchange Commission's online database.

Publicly traded companies are required to file quarterly reports with the Securities and Exchange Commission (www.sec.gov). These reports provide updates of the company's activities since it filed its annual report. If the company is going through a momentous change (such as a merger or acquisition), it's required to file more often.

You can find important information about a company in the annual report, but annual reports require careful reading. This chapter shows you how to download an annual report and analyze any publicly traded company. After all, reading a company's annual report is a little like kicking the tires of a used car. You want to make certain that you get what you think you're buying.

Finding Financial Statements Online

If you're a stockholder, you automatically receive the company's annual report. Annual reports are also free for the asking to anyone else. All you have to do is call the firm's investor relations department and request that they mail you a copy.

For online investors, getting annual reports is even easier. The Internet provides three sources for annual reports:

- ✔ **Company Web sites:** Many companies have Web sites that include their annual reports. You can use special corporate linking sites and commercial search engines to find these Web sites.
- ✔ **Investor compilation sites:** These investor supersites often include annual reports, company news, earnings forecasts, and other useful information.
- ✔ **Securities and Exchange Commission (SEC) filings:** The SEC does a good job of making electronically filed company reports available to the public.

In the following sections, I show you how to find annual reports using these sources.

Using a search engine to find an annual report

Many publicly traded companies have Web sites on the Internet. These sites often include the company's annual report as part of the firm's public relations and investor services.

To find these annual reports, you can start with a commercial search engine such as AltaVista (www.altavista.digital.com), Infoseek (www.infoseek.com), or Excite (www.excite.com). After you access one of these *search engines* (Web-based tools that enable you to hunt for Web sites on topics that you specify), you simply enter words or phrases that describe the information you want to find, and then you click on the Search button. To find a company report, you enter the company name, a plus sign (+), and the words *annual report* in quotation marks, as in the following example:

```
Microsoft + "annual report"
```

Using Boolean operators (which I discuss in Chapter 3) forces the search engine to stack all the annual reports on top of the retrieved Web pages.

Using Web sites that link to company home pages

Many Web sites provide links to the home pages of large businesses. Here are two examples of these sites:

- ✔ **Global Securities Information, Incorporated** (www.gsionline.com): This site provides links to the home pages of large corporations.

- ✔ **Web100** (www.w100.com): Figure 12-1 shows Web100, a site that provides links to the 100 largest U.S. and international businesses on the Internet. You can sort the database by industry and Fortune 500 rankings.

Finding online annual reports: Investor supersites

If using a commercial search engine or a special business Web site locator doesn't lead you to the annual report you desire, try an investor supersite. You can find many such investor directories on the Internet. Here are a few examples:

- ✔ **Hoover's Online Company Profiles** (www.hoovers.com): This site includes company profiles and annual report information on more than 25,000 publicly traded, private, and international firms. You can get capsule information for free; you pay a fee for access to the entire database.

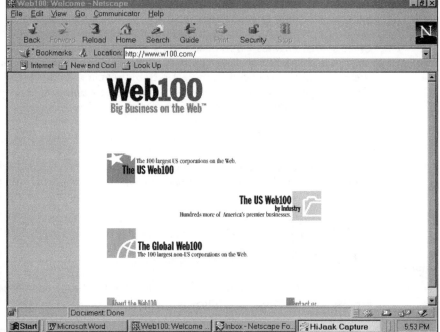

Figure 12-1:
Web100
provides
links to the
home pages
of the 100
largest
businesses
on the
Internet.

✔ **Invest-o-Rama's Publicly Traded Corporations Online**
(www.investorama.com/corp.shtml): This site provides links to more
than 1,000 publicly traded companies. Many of these pages include
links to the firms' annual reports.

✔ **The Annual Reports Library** (www.zpub.com/sf/arl/index.html):
Founded in 1983, the Annual Reports Library includes more than 1.5
million original annual reports from corporations, foundations, banks,
mutual funds, and public institutions located throughout the world.

✔ **Wall Street Research Net** (WSRN.com): This site provides the annual
reports for more than 16,000 publicly traded firms.

✔ **Zacks Investment Research** (www.zacks.com): Figure 12-2 shows the
Web site for Zacks Investment Research. This firm's database includes
more than 5,000 U.S. and Canadian companies. It also tracks 200
industry groups.

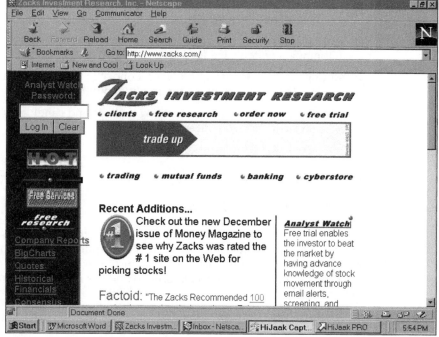

Researching a company's SEC filing

The SEC's EDGAR service (www.sec.gov) provides downloadable performance data. Annual reports can be more than 50 pages long and have lengthy accounting notes. For example, the 10-K annual reports include descriptions of the business, business properties, legal proceedings, stockholder voting matters, selected financial data, management's discussion of the firm's financial condition and results of operations, financial statements and supplementary data, changes in accounting procedures and financial disclosures, insider transactions, executive compensation, and leasing agreements.

When you search the EDGAR database, you're asked for the report number of the document you want. The reports are numbered in the following manner:

- ✔ **10-K Reports:** Annual reports that include shareholder information covering the firm's fiscal year

- ✔ **10-Q Reports:** Quarterly reports that include shareholder information for the firm's last quarter

- ✔ **8-K Reports:** Interim reports covering an odd period due to a merger, acquisition, or other event

- ✔ **S-1 Registration:** Forms required for businesses that want to offer stock to the public; often used for initial public offerings

- ✔ **S-3 Registration:** Registration of a secondary offering; necessary form to offer stock to the public after an initial public offering

- ✔ **14-A Form:** Information about voting matters and candidates seeking election to the board of directors

Downloading SEC filings in just three clicks

When you find the annual report you want, save it to a floppy disk or your computer's hard disk. After you download the report and save it on your computer, you can read the file at your leisure. You can also use your word processor's snappy text search features to find the important information you need.

After you find the report you want, you can save the data in just three clicks:

1. **Click on the File menu at the top-left corner of your Internet browser screen.**

2. **Click on Save.**

   Your browser displays a dialog box asking you which drive you want to save the data on and which name you want to file it under.

3. **Enter a name for the file and specify where you want to save the file.**

   Use the company's name or initials for the filename and a file extension of .txt or .doc.

4. **Click on Save.**

   You're finished downloading a 50-page document from the Internet.

To read the file, just start your word processing program and open the file.

If the columns are out of alignment, you may need to adjust the font size for the entire document.

Trivia from the Annual Reports Library

Can you name . . .

1. The oldest library in the world still operating?

2. The first people who used handwriting?

3. Who founded the first "members only" library? and when?

4. Where and when was the first tax-supported library?

5. Who said, "Never judge an annual report by its movie"?

6. The oldest printed annual report?

7. The world's longest printed annual report?

8. The first annual report with CD-ROM and diskette copies?

9. The annual report with sunflower seeds?

10. The annual report that included a saliva drug screening kit?

11. The smallest/shortest annual report?

12. The annual report that had a penny glued to the cover?

13. The annual report that smelled of spices?

14. The annual report that came wrapped in a reusable canvas sack?

15. The annual report that included water?

16. The first annual report that included coupons for all the company's products?

17. Who said, "The real purpose of a library is to trap the mind into doing its own thinking"?

18. The annual report cut into the shape of a deck of playing cards?

19. The annual report that's covered with a laced-up sleeve that you have to unlace before you can read the report?

20. The annual report that reads like and follows along like a game of monopoly?

21. The annual report that put a warning on its front cover stating, "WARNING: This Report is NOT interactive NOR entertaining"?

22. The annual report that came inside a bank coin bag which, when unzipped, revealed a simulated checkbook and $100 bills all wrapped together and, when opened, revealed the annual report?

Give up?

For the answers, see The Annual Reports Library at www.zpub.com/sf/arl.

Analyzing a Financial Statement

Companies often use their annual reports to attract new investors; you can guess that these reports contain some marketing fluff and exaggerations. Most of this embellishment is self-evident. Analyzing a company with a calculator, paper, and pencil will take you about an hour.

The results of this examination can help online investors make investment decisions. Buying stock in a company without reading the annual report is like buying a used car without seeing it. Here's a checklist of the information you need to consider while you review a company's annual report:

- ✔ **Profitability:** How much money did the company make last year?

- ✔ **Survivability:** How is the company coping with competition?

- ✔ **Growth:** Is the company expanding? How fast is this expansion?

- ✔ **Stability:** Is the company subject to radical changes from year to year?

- ✔ **Dividends (if any):** Is dividend growth constant? How does it compare to the industry averages?

- ✔ **Problems:** Does the company have any pending lawsuits? Any other problems?

- ✔ **Risks:** Is the company subject to any environmental, political, or exchange rate risks?

- ✔ **Other factors:** Is the management team experienced? Does the company need more executive talent?

Prepared Online Ratio Analysis

Many organizations provide online annual reports that include ratio analysis, performance statistics, accounting notes, and other relevant information. You can download, print, and save all these reports. Much of the downloaded data is ready for your spreadsheet program and your analytic skills; however, you may need to reformat some data, and some data you can't change into a spreadsheet.

Here are two online sources of prepared online ratio analysis and company information:

- ✔ **Thomson Investor Net, formerly MarketEdge Reports,** (www.marketedge.com or www.thomsoninvest.net) provides more than 7,000 in-depth company reports updated twice a month. For stock research, the company provides stock quotes, company information, stock screening, a list of the month's top performers, and more. Company reports include comparison of the firm's ratios to industry averages, but you can't download the reports to your spreadsheet. Monthly subscriptions are $9.95 and include 25 in-depth company reports and 25 mutual fund reports. Additional company reports are $2.50 ($1.50 for mutual fund companies).

- ✔ **Yahoo Market Guide Report** (yahoo.marketguide.com), shown in Figure 12-3, provides free information on "What's Hot" and "What's Not," a sector listing, an industry listing, the company of the day, and educational information. This service charges for quick company facts, company profiles, detailed company reports, and specialized reports that include ratio comparisons and a peer group report. Earnings estimates, detailed financial statements, and stock screening are also available. Prices are by report ($1.00 to $7.95) or monthly by report types ($4.95 to $19.95). You can retrieve reports even if they aren't included in your subscription plan, and you can download company reports to your spreadsheet.

Financial statement analysis involves examining the company's annual report and ratio analysis. However, looking beyond the firm's numbers and evaluating changes in accounting procedures that may hide serious problems is also important. For example, how the firm accounts for depreciation and the valuing of inventory can radically vary between similar firms in the same industry. These accounting procedures can result in earnings per share (EPS) that aren't truly representative of the firm's performance, especially when they're compared to the company's previous EPS and the industry standard. An inaccurate EPS number can lead to big surprises toward the end of the year when the company doesn't perform as expected.

Figure 12-3:
Yahoo!
Market
Guide
Reports
calculate
company
ratios and
provide
comparisons
to the
industry.

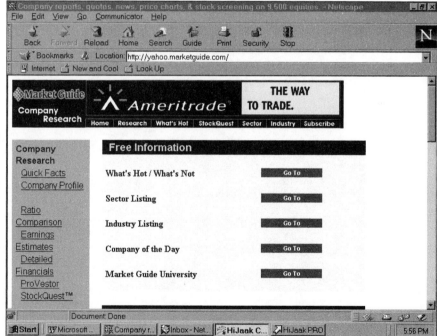

Chapter 13

Digging Deeper

. . . .

In This Chapter

▶ Turning your hunches into investment strategies

▶ Comparing stock returns to other investments

▶ Getting hard data on the economy

▶ Researching stocks online with hard facts

. . . .

*Y*ou may use an online stock screen (see Chapter 9) to whittle down the number of common stock investment candidates you're considering. Or you may select a few companies because you know something about the products they sell. Maybe you work in the industry or have used the company's products or services over a long period of time.

After you find a few investment candidates, you use online sources to download the annual reports of the companies that you find interesting (see Chapter 12). You read the financial statements, and you calculate the ratios that are important to investors. You may think that you're done, but you need to do a little more research before you contact your online broker.

The next step involves digging deeper to understand the economic environment in which your investment candidate operates. In this chapter, I help you locate the online sources that you can use to determine where the company stands in its industry and what type of marketing techniques it's using to maintain and increase revenues. I show you where to find out what the experts are saying about your stock pick and where to go online to find analyst earning estimates. I also point out where you can get historical stock price information. After you have all of these hard facts, you can make your investment decision.

Many investors do not have the confidence to select their own stocks. This chapter shows how you can conduct your own online research to find winning investments. Many of the sources I list in this chapter are the same sources that full-service brokers use in their stock analyses.

Turning Your Hunches into Investment Strategies

Every online investor has his or her own research system for investigating investment candidates. What makes any system work is that it is repeatable and that it ensures that you don't make investment decisions based on emotional factors. The following guidelines can assist you in turning your hunches into investment strategies. You begin by gathering all the facts:

1. **Find the candidates that you want to research.**

   Match your hunches about stocks that are positioned to be top per-formers to your investor profile and use a stock screen or some other method to identify investment candidates. (For more information about researching individual stocks, see Chapter 12. For in-depth coverage of Internet stock screens, refer to Chapter 9.)

2. **Trim your list of candidates.**

   Locate the online annual reports for your short list of stock candidates using the techniques I outline in Chapter 12. Conduct your analysis and reduce the list to several companies

3. **Find out more about each company.**

   Use this background information to put each company into a broader context using the sources I detail in this chapter. For example, is the company a market leader?

   The good news is that the Internet has tons of this type of information, and most of it is free. Here are some examples of sources for this information (I list Internet resources for these categories of information later in the chapter):

   - **News:** Read the company's press releases and keep current with breaking news. Try to connect isolated news articles to spot trends.

   - **Industry:** Read news articles and industry trade journals to spot patterns that may indicate technological breakthroughs or new products. Does the industry have problems with oversupply, and if so, how does this situation affect the profits of the company you're researching?

   - **Economics:** Note how changes in the national, regional, and local economies affect your investment candidates. Will a rising dollar lower corporate returns? What are the Wall Street economists saying?

- **Market:** What's happening in the stock market? Are prices and trading volume increasing?

- **Analysts' evaluations:** Most publicly traded companies have Wall Street analysts who often provide opinions about the firm. Study what the analysts are saying about the company. What they say may provide you with leads for additional research.

- **Earnings estimates:** Keep current with the earnings estimates of professionals. Are the estimates going up or down?

- **Historical prices:** Sometimes you can tell where a company is going by seeing where it has been. Evaluating a company's past stock prices may provide you with new insights.

4. **Decide whether the company is a low-priced, high-quality stock or a loser.**

   When you put all the facts together, you gain a good understanding of what causes the company's stock price to rise or fall. Additionally, you know what's normal for the company.

5. **Ask yourself "What if?"**

   For example, what if sales drop by 10 percent, like they did five years ago? What if the material the company uses to manufacture its product becomes scarce — would this scarcity cause the cost of goods to increase? Would such a change reduce profits so much that the company couldn't pay its interest expense? Would the company be forced into bankruptcy?

6. **To complete your investment strategy, determine how risky the stock is.**

   Could you lose your entire investment? If so, you need to add a *risk premium* to your required rate of return. This risk premium compensates you for the additional risk of your investment. Should the return be ten times your investment or maybe even 50 times your initial investment? Making this decision can be difficult, because everyone defines risk differently and everyone tolerates a different level of risk. So what's normal anyway?

Conquering Uncertainty with Online Research

You can use the Internet to get background company information by accessing one of the many free and fee-based databases, where you can dig up all kinds of facts and opinions about a company. Some of this information can provide you with new insights, ideas, and leads about additional research.

Overall, this information can provide you with an understanding of how a company works within the economy, how it copes with the competition, and how it ranks within its industry. This information is often critical to your investment decision.

With millions of Web pages on the Internet, finding exactly what you're looking for can be a challenge. However, uncovering one small fact can make the difference between purchasing a mediocre stock and buying a stock that can bring you exceptional returns. As you surf the Internet, you may encounter sites that discuss stocks, markets, online trading, and more. In the following sections, I help you locate the right online sources that can assist you in finding the background information you need to complete your company research.

Gaining new investor insights with breaking news

Daily news and press releases can assist you in keeping current with your investments or investment candidates. These sources often provide the first glimpse of why a stock price is rapidly increasing or falling like a stone. One of the advantages of these online sources is that they have *archives,* where you can check past company events that made news.

Here are a few Internet resources for finding press releases and breaking news:

- ✔ **Bloomberg Online** (`www.bloomberg.com/welcome.html`)**:** Shown in Figure 13-1, this site includes newswire articles, edited columns, audio clips about current market performance, and other information about stocks, bonds, markets, and industry. The site is well organized and provides access to current market statistics, business and financial news, major newspaper stories, Bloomberg columns, and financial analysis tools. (Bloomberg's charges a fee for subscribing to its magazine, but you can search its Web site for free.)

  Bloomberg's magazine subscribers ($23.95 for ten issues) can access a special area of the Web site that includes free quotes, company profiles, fundamentals of more than 18,000 stocks and mutual funds, and the capability to analyze and store a portfolio with as many as 50 securities.

- ✔ **Commerce Business Daily via the Internet** (`www.issinet.com/cbd`)**:** This paper covers government procurements, contract awards, foreign government standards, surplus property sales, and other information. Online information is available the day before the printed edition is released. Searchable archives for the last six months are available. *Commerce Business Daily* offers a free 30-day trial. Annual subscriptions and access to past issues are available to individuals for $200 per year.

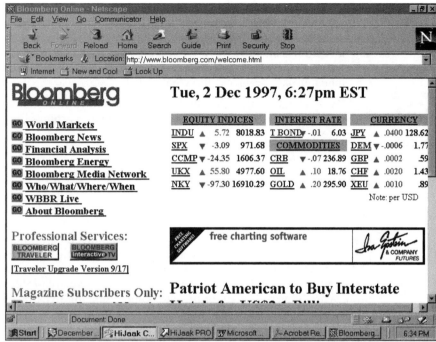

Figure 13-1:
Bloomberg
Online can
provide you
with the
company
news you're
looking for.

✔ **Ecola's 24-hour Newsstand (**www.ecola.com**):** This site contains links to more than 1,500 Web sites for published material from local and specialty papers, magazines, and major news services. You can search titles for keywords.

✔ **Newspaper Indexes:** You can find comprehensive indexes to the online versions of major newspapers at the Newspaper Association of America (www.infi.net/naa) and Newslink (www.newslink.org).

✔ **The Wall Street Journal Interactive Edition (**www.wsj.com**):** This interactive site contains recent news, business, and market columns from *The Wall Street Journal.* Articles have links to charts, graphs, and tables. Daily news is continually updated. The site includes closing stock prices and a summary of each day's activities.

Don't forget The Wall Street Journal Interactive Briefing Books. These handy summaries include a company's background, financial overview, stock performance, company news, press releases, and corporate snapshot.

The firm offers a two-week free trial. Subscribers to the print version of *The Wall Street Journal* pay $29 per year for the Internet version of *The Journal.* Other subscribers pay $49 per year. For an additional fee, you can gain access to a much larger database of business research.

✔ **WSRN** (www.wsrn.com): This site provides a good starting place for your search for company information. WSRN has more than 500,000 links to Internet financial sources to help professional and individual investors. The site is divided into eight sections: company information, economic research, market news, news, research publications, mutual funds, broker services, and what's new.

You can start at the "Research a Company" page and use the links to get SEC filings, quotes, graphs or charts, news, earnings estimates, research reports, and summaries.

Locating company profiles and related data

In much the same way as the literary world includes biographies of famous people, the world of finance has *company profiles*. Company profiles include all the events that make a company what it is today. You can keep all of a company's pertinent facts handy by obtaining a company profile. Company profiles are often designed for investors and highlight investor-related information.

Here are a few online sources for obtaining company profiles:

✔ **Companylink** (www.companylink.com): The database sources for this Web site are Cor Tech Database of Technology Companies — Technology Manufacturers and Developers, Demand Research's Executive Desk Register, and Hoover's Online. The site provides company profiles for publicly traded firms plus the largest private companies in the United States. You can use any profiles marked with the *free* symbol without subscribing. Items marked *SUB* are available for unlimited use by subscribers.

Subscribers can also customize the news they receive. Items marked with a dollar sign ($) are premium content, valued individually; subscribers can purchase these items. Companylink offers a free two-week subscription. Subscriptions are $10 per month. Subscribers get $20 worth of premium services for free (if you didn't use the free trial), access to all full-text articles and summary profiles, and the capability to purchase any of the firm's premium content.

✔ **Hoover's Online** (www.hoovers.com): This site, shown in Figure 13-2, includes free information about 8,500 companies. You can find ticker symbols, company locations, and sales figures at this Web site. Company profiles include the firm's address, phone numbers, executive names, recent sales figures, and company status. This site has links to stock quotes and SEC financial data. Basic service is free. For $9.95 per month or $99.95 per year, you can obtain in-depth information on more than 2,700 companies.

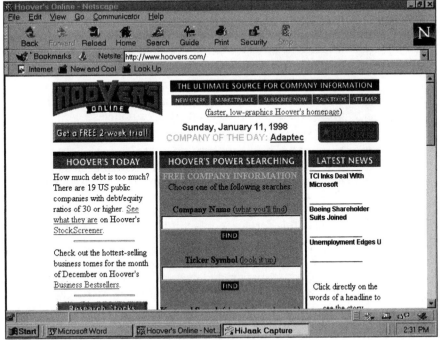

Figure 13-2:
Hoover's
Online
provides
company
information
for more
than 8,500
firms.

(Reprinted with permission. Copyright © 1997 Hoovers, Inc.)

✔ **The Global Network of the Chambers of Commerce and Industry**
(www1.usal.com~ibnet.champshp.html): This site provides general
business information and links to more than 640 U.S. Chambers of
Commerce. The quality of these home pages is diverse. The site also
provides a weekly news service called the *International Business
Monitor.*

Finding industry and statistical information

Annual reports often provide good insights into the forces that drive certain
industries. However, this information may not be enough to answer your
questions.

Independent research about how a company is doing in its industry is often
available from trade associations and periodicals. Market research sites are
helpful for determining how the company of your choice stacks up. Here are
some online sources for industry and statistical information:

✔ **American Society of Association Executives** (`www.asaenet.org`): This organization provides links to Web sites for various industries. The Web sites are generally high-quality industry overviews that often include briefings of industry trends, geographic profiles, and statistics for financial performance analysis.

✔ **Fedstats** (`www.fedstats.gov`): This site allows you to search 14 federal agencies for a specific statistic at the same time. You can also search press releases, regional statistics, or policies.

✔ **Lexis-Nexis** (`www.lexis-nexis.com`): Shown in Figure 13-3, this site has a wide variety of business and legal databases. It recently added a new database of 10- to 20-page market summaries of industry sectors or demographic markets. Additionally, its database includes the *Market Share Reporter* (from 1991 to the present) and *Computer Industry Forecasts*. Pricing for different types of usage varies — if you're interested in this service, contact it for a firm price quote.

✔ **STAT-USA** (`www.stat-usa.gov`): Sponsored by the U.S. Department of Commerce, this site provides financial information about economic indicators, statistics, and news. The site also includes data about state and local government bond rates, foreign exchange rates, and daily economic news about trade and business issues. Statistics include interest rates, employment, income, price, productivity, new construction, and home sales. This site provides the *National Trade Data Bank*, which you can access for an annual fee of $150. New users can take advantage of a free trial of the database.

✔ **Technometrica Market Research** (`www.technometrica.com`): Among other things, Technometrica provides business research that includes industry and market features and trends, market share analysis, market potential analysis, and strategic planning.

✔ **Training Forum Associations Database:** To reach the Associations Database Web page, start at the Training Forum's home page (`www.trainingforum.com`) and click on the *associations* link. This site includes a search engine and a database of professional and trade organizations. Trade associations often collect market data about their industries and want to share it with the public.

Gathering economic and related data

Many individuals try to predict economic trends, but few (if any) are successful. However, having a good understanding of current economic conditions and where they're headed is vital to your comprehension of the company in its broader context. After all, many companies are sensitive to changes in the economy.

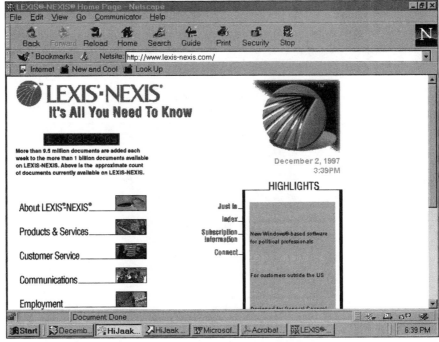

Figure 13-3:
Lexis-Nexis
has an
extensive
database
and
reasonable
rates.

The Internet has many sources for economic information. Here are a few examples:

✔ **Census Bureau (**www.census.gov**):** Shown in Figure 13-4, this site provides information about industry, statistics, and general business. *Current Industrial Reports* provides production, shipment, and inventory statistics. *Census of Manufacturers Industry Series* includes industry statistics (some of this information may be outdated). *The Census of Wholesale Trade* contains data about organizations that sell merchandise to retailers, institutions, and other types of wholesalers. The *Survey* provides updates about current and past statistics of monthly sales, inventories, and stock/sales ratios. *Today's Economic Indicator Report* provides information about government and related entities releasing economic reports on industrial production, consumer sentiment, and so on.

✔ **GSA Government Information Locator Service (**www.gsa.gov**):** Government agencies are now required to provide and maintain a database of the information they provide to the public. Most agencies are using the Internet to meet this requirement. This site includes many U.S. government agency reports in either full text or abstract forms. Most information resources are cataloged and searchable. Searches can include more than one agency.

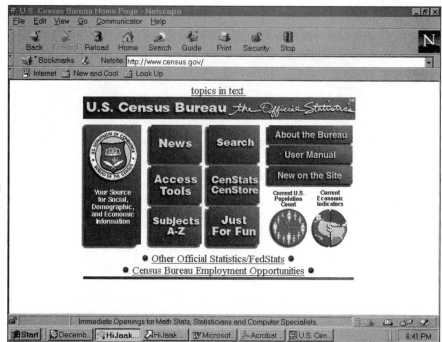

Figure 13-4:
The Census
Bureau has
current
industrial
reports and
other
industry
information.

✔ **Internet Federal Reserve sites** (`www.bog.frb.fed.us/`
`otherfrb.htm`): This site, shown in Figure 13-5, provides links to all the
Fed home pages and gopher sites. Publications by this organization
include high-quality statistics, analyses, and forecasts of regional,
national, and international economic and financial conditions. Publications include *Economic Trends* (from Cleveland), a monthly report on
the GDP (Gross Domestic Product), consumer income, housing starts,
producer price index, and consumer price index. *U.S. Financial Data,*
published weekly in St. Louis, includes statistics on money supply,
interest rates, and securities yields. Regional economic indicators are
published in the *Fed Flash.*

Collecting market information

Understanding the current market environment can help you select a stock
that can provide you with your required return. You need to know how a
company markets its products or services (catalog sales, face-to-face
meetings, and so on) and what share of the total market the company
commands. This information can give you a better understanding of what
drives the company's stock price.

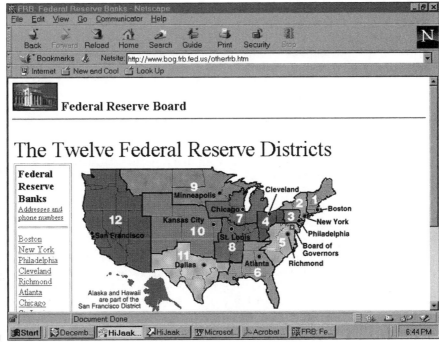

Figure 13-5:
Internet
Federal
Reserve
sites often
have the
best
economic
statistics
around.

Here are some online sources for market information:

- **E-Line** (www.financials.com): This site provides stock ratings and market data, as well as links to DBC (Data Broadcasting Corp.) U.S. Industry Market Summaries, U.S. company stock prices by industry, Griffin Financial Services "Weekly Market Outlook," and Market Vision's "World Markets at a Glance" data about foreign exchange, futures equity, indexes, and U.S. Treasuries.

- **Holt Stock Report** (metro.turnpike.net/holt): This online resource provides indexes; averages; information about foreign markets; issues trades; new highs and lows; currency; gold; interest rates; most active issues on the NYSE, NASDAQ, and AMEX; stocks whose trading volume was up by more than 50 percent that day; and stocks that reached new highs and lows.

- **MSU-CIBER** (ciber.bus.msu.edu/busres.htm): This site is a good starting point for international research. It has links to more than 75 national and international news sources, such as the *Australian Financial Review* and *Asia Week Online*. Regional and country-specific information includes statistical data and listings of international trade shows.

✔ **Quote.com** (`www.quote.com`): Shown in Figure 13-6, this site provides free unlimited delayed security quotes from U.S. and Canadian exchanges; limited balance-sheet data; some company profile information; an unlimited number of updates for a portfolio of up to seven securities; daily, weekly, and/or monthly stock price charts; daily market index charts; daily information for major industry groups; and foreign exchange rates.

Basic service is $9.95 a month. Subscribers get all the free services, updates of two portfolios of up to 50 securities each, *Newsbytes News Network* news, any ten historical data files, any ten customized charts that you may want, and annual reports ordering service (for printed copies sent by U.S. mail). Extra service is $24.95 per month, which includes all the basic services plus more historical data, charts, and reports. Premium service and other types of services escalate from there.

✔ **Thomas Register** (`www1.thomasregister.com`): This site includes buying information for the products and services of more than 155,000 companies, divided into 55,000 categories. The register includes 3,100 online supplier catalogs and is 42,000 pages. After you register and select a password, use of the catalog is free. This site is an excellent source for discovering the chief competitor of a company.

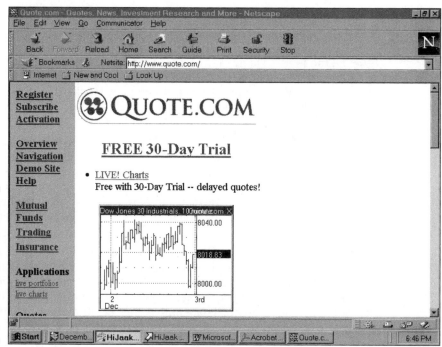

Figure 13-6:
Quote.com
has many
free
services
and offers
more than
stock
quotes.

Checking out analyst evaluations

Often stock prices move because analysts recommend or criticize a company. Although these opinions are "informed," they're still opinions and shouldn't overshadow your good judgment. For example, assume that an analyst suggests buying a stock and forecasts the price to increase to a record high. Over the year, the stock reaches the mark, and then the analyst places a hold on the stock. (A "hold" is a suggestion to investors that they neither sell nor buy the stock.) This hold may look like an unfavorable mark against the stock, but the stock performed just as expected and is currently a good investment.

The Internet now has many analyst reports by individual Wall Street analysts or groups of Wall Street analysts who study a particular stock. However, many of these firms participated in the financing of the companies they're analyzing. Consequently, you rarely see a "sell" recommendation.

Additionally, you may see that analysts' opinions vary. Feel free to disagree with their conclusions, but know what the professionals are saying about a company that interests you.

Wall Street Research Network (www.wsrn.com) has links to three analyst evaluation reports:

- ✔ ACE — Analyst Consensus Estimate Reports
- ✔ Standard & Poor's Enhanced Stock Reports
- ✔ Research Investment Reports

For $4.95, Standard & Poor's (www.stockinfo.standardpoor.com) has basic stock reports, industry reports, news stories, and Wall Street Consensus Reports. The Wall Street Consensus Reports include analyst earnings estimates.

Tracking down earnings estimates

The price you pay for a stock is based on its future income stream. If earnings estimates indicate that the earnings per share is dropping, the stock price you pay today may be too high for the true value of the stock.

Here are several Internet sources for earnings estimates:

- ✔ **First Call** (www1.firstcall.com): The First Call database follows more than 7,500 companies. It also tracks more than 100 industry groups, several commodities and economic indicators, plus the Dow Jones Industrial Averages and the S&P 500. Products and subscription prices vary. Estimates on Demand cost $1.50 to $3 per document retrieved. Historical information is $25 per report, and the Consensus Guide is $25 per month. Other products are available. See the Web site for details.

✔ **NRM Capital** (www.nrmcapital.com): This site provides free earnings announcements, including the company, expected date of the earnings announcement, ticker symbol, estimated amount of the earnings per share (EPS), and last year's EPS.

✔ **Reuters Moneynet** (www.moneynet.com): Reuters Moneynet provides an S&P evaluation of the company you are researching. The evaluation includes a dividends rank, average quality opinion, and date of the next expected earnings report. The consensus earnings per share forecast for the next year and statistics about past earnings are included. Figure 13-7 shows one such report. Reuters Moneynet and WSRN (www.wsrn.com) recently merged, so this site has links to WSRN company reports.

✔ **Stock Smart** (www.stocksmart.com): This site provides earnings estimates for a price. Stock Smart includes a professional portfolio manager, earnings calendar, unlimited stock quotes and graphing, shareholder data, comprehensive research, stock screening, week in review, industry roll-ups, mutual funds, and market information. Subscriptions are $12.95 per month and include a free ten-day test drive.

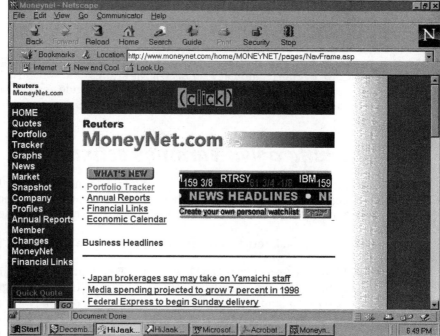

Figure 13-7: Reuters Moneynet provides company earning estimates and much more.

✔ **Zacks Investment Research** (www.zacks.com): This site provides estimated earnings reports based on analyst opinions. The site includes a listing of current earnings surprises, recommendations, and the company's annual balance sheet and income statement. This site is linked to WSRN's (www.wsrn.com) company information report.

Researching historical prices

Seeing where a company has been is always important, in order to get a feeling about where it's going. Here are a few Internet sources for historical prices:

✔ **Standard & Poor's Stock Screens** (www.stockinfo.standardpoor.com/screens/screen10.htm): The Historical & Projected Industry P/E Ratios Report is one of the most useful pages on the Internet. It includes P/E ratios for all the major industries for 1995, 1996, and 1997.

✔ **Quote.com** (www.quote.com): This site provides historical data files as an additional service ($1.95) for current subscribers. Four types of historical data are available:

- U.S. stocks — daily history from October 1988 to the present

- U.S. commodity futures — daily history from April 1994 to the present

- Indexes and indicators — daily history from October 1988 to the present

- Foreign stocks and commodities — daily history from April 1994 to the present

✔ **Stock Tools Data Giveaway** (www.stocktools.com): This site provides a free service but asks individuals not to download information more than 200 times a day. You simply enter the ticker symbol of the company you're researching, and the program automatically retrieves daily data as well as close, high, low, open, and volume data for the last year. You can save the information on a disk and use it in your personal spreadsheet.

Chapter 14

Valuing, Buying, and Selling Bonds Online

. . . .

In This Chapter

▶ Purchasing U.S. Treasury securities without a broker

▶ Understanding why bond values change

▶ Determining the value of any type of bond

▶ Discovering the easiest way to determine your bond returns

▶ Using a hot strategy for reducing bond risk

. . . .

*I*n this chapter, I show you how to analyze, buy, and sell a variety of fixed-income investments. I explore the benefits of savings bonds, I detail new regulations, and I explain the limitations of this type of investment. I also show you where to find the Savings Bond Wizard, which you can use to determine the exact value of your savings bonds.

This chapter also explains how to purchase Treasury securities without a broker. You can't buy Treasuries over the Internet yet, but you can find helpful information — for example, dates of government auctions, Treasury yields, auction results, and instructions about how to open your investor's account at Treasury Direct (the master record of the securities you own that is maintained by the Federal government).

For online investors interested in paying the right price for a bond, this chapter shows how to value all types of bonds and determine bond yields (returns). Doing so may sound complicated, but with a little practice, you'll be calculating your returns in no time. This chapter also explains where to buy bonds online and it offers a hot strategy that can protect you from interest rate risk.

Nice and Simple: Savings Bonds

For many people, the only way they can save money is by purchasing savings bonds. The United States Treasury Department offers two main types of savings bonds:

- ✔ **Series EE:** You pay half the face value of a Series EE bond at the time of purchase, and you receive the face value when the bond matures. The interest rate isn't fixed, so the maturity term is variable. However, most bonds mature in 18 years and don't accrue any more income after 30 years. The minimum denomination is $50, and the maximum denomination is $10,000.

- ✔ **Series HH:** A Series HH bond pays interest directly to your account at a financial institution every six months. These bonds have fixed interest rates for ten years and earn interest up to 20 years. Series HH bonds are available in denominations of $500, $1,000, $5,000, and $10,000.

About 55 million people own savings bonds, and around $15 billion worth of savings bonds are sold per year. Three sources exist for purchasing savings bonds:

- ✔ **Banks, credit unions, and other financial institutions:** Many financial institutions are qualified as savings bond agents. These agents accept the payments and the purchase orders for the EE bonds and forward the orders to a Federal Reserve bank, where the bonds are inscribed and mailed. Allow 15 days for delivery.

- ✔ **Employer sponsored payroll savings plans:** More than 45,000 employers participate in employer-sponsored payroll savings plans, and some banks offer EE bonds through bond-a-month plans.

- ✔ **Federal Reserve banks:** If you write to your local Federal Reserve Bank and ask for an application, you can purchase savings bonds by mail. Figure 14-1 shows the Savings Bond page at the Web site for the Federal Reserve Bank of New York (www.ny.frb.org/pihome/svg_bnds). This site provides the addresses of the 12 regional Federal Reserve banks.

You can get additional information about savings bonds from the following Internet sources:

- ✔ **Market Analysis of Savings Bonds (**www.bondinformer.com**):** An expert provides a market analysis of savings bonds' short- and long-term interest rates at this Web site.

- ✔ **The Bureau of Public Debt (**www.publicdebt.Treas.gov/sav/savbene.htm**):** This site provides information on the benefits of savings bonds and covers interest rates and maturity periods.

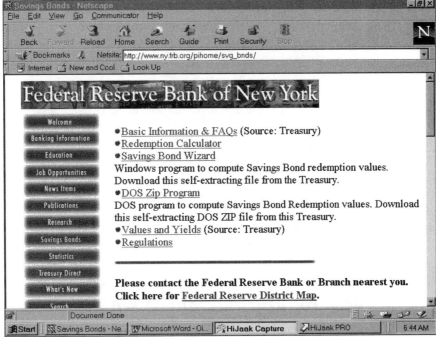

Figure 14-1:
The Federal
Reserve
Bank of
New York
can help
you
purchase
U.S. savings
bonds by
mail.

Check for old bonds in your safe-deposit box or among the papers of elderly relatives. More than $2.3 billion in savings bonds have never been redeemed.

The good and the bad about savings bonds

The returns on savings bonds are so low that they'll never make you rich. In fact, returns are so low that large pension funds and other big investors don't purchase savings bonds. However, for many individuals, savings bonds are the best approach for saving money. Savings bonds offer the following advantages:

✔ **You can save automatically:** Employers who sponsor savings bond programs can automatically deduct an amount that you designate from your paychecks. For many people, this program is a painless way to save money.

✔ **You can diversify your risk:** If you already have investments in stocks and bonds, you may want to invest in savings bonds and thus add a no-risk element to your portfolio.

✔ **Your investment is safe:** In exchange for a low return, savings bonds offer absolute safety of principal — they're no-risk investments.

✔ **You don't pay any sales commissions:** Savings bonds don't require the services of a broker to help you purchase them, and thus you pay no sales commissions.

✔ **Your minimum investment is low:** The minimum investment in savings bonds is $25, and employer-sponsored plans can make the minimum even lower per week.

✔ **You pay no or low taxes:** The difference between the purchase price and the redemption value of EE bonds and the payments made on HH bonds comes in the form of interest. This interest income is subject to federal income tax, but not state or local income taxes. You can defer paying federal income tax on the interest until you cash in the bonds.

✔ **You gain education tax benefits:** For EE bonds purchased after 1989 and cashed to pay tuition and post-secondary education fees, the interest earned is not subject to federal income taxes.

New regulations make savings bonds more attractive

In May 1997, EE savings bonds were radically changed. (EE bonds purchased before May 1997 are not affected by these changes.) The Bureau of Public Debt suggests that purchasers of EE savings bonds understand the following changes:

✔ **Interest rates are calculated in a new way:** The earnings of Series EE bonds issued in May 1997 or after are based on five-year Treasury security yields. The new rate for EE bonds is 90 percent of the average yields on five-year Treasury securities for the preceding six months.

✔ **Interest is compounded more frequently:** Interest is now compounded monthly for these EE bonds. (In the past, interest was compounded every six months.)

✔ **You pay a penalty for cashing bonds before five years:** You can cash in an EE bond after six months, but if you cash a bond before holding it for at least five years, you give up the last three months' interest as a penalty fee.

EE bonds don't pay accrued interest in periodic cash payments like HH bonds do. An alternative investment exists for people who are about to retire and want an investment that pays interest in cash: Sell the savings bonds, pay the tax, and use the proceeds to purchase 20-year Treasury securities. The Treasury securities pay interest in cash so that retirees can use it for living expenses. *Note:* If selling your E and EE bonds puts you in a higher tax bracket, sell them over a two-year period.

Downloading the Savings Bond Wizard

Savings bonds have always been easy to purchase and are popular gifts for new parents and grandchildren. But as easy as these financial instruments are to buy, they are equally difficult to value. This difficulty can be especially troublesome if you need to cash in a bond before it matures. Additionally, bondholders may have problems keeping an accurate inventory of the savings bonds they have on hand.

Recognizing this problem, the Federal government developed a nifty program that does all the work for you. This figure shows a page from the Web site of the Bureau of Public Debt at `www.publicdebt.Treas.gov/sav/savwizar.htm`. This site contains the Savings Bond Wizard, a free savings bond software program. To download the program, just click on the appropriate link.

One of the Savings Bond Wizard's features allows you to print a copy of your bond inventory. (After a flood or fire, this inventory is an invaluable record of the bondholder's investment.)

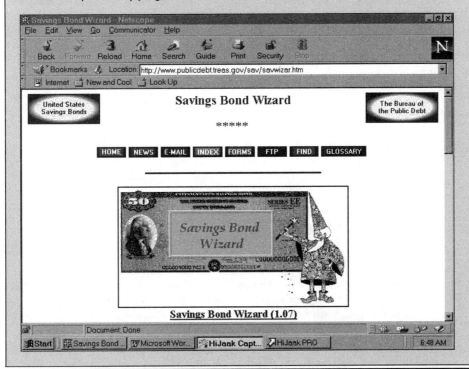

Just Uncle Sam, Treasury Securities, and You

Treasury securities may not look very lucrative if you're used to double-digit returns, but they're excellent investments for investors who can't tolerate risk. In other words, if you're a conservative investor, U.S. Treasury securities may be your type of investment.

At this time, you can't purchase Treasury securities online. However, you can obtain order forms, instructions, auction dates, auction results, and other related information at the Bureau of the Public Debt Web site (www.publicdebt.treas.gov). This site also provides details about how to purchase Treasury securities without a broker (a great money saving feature for investors).

Treasury bills, notes, and bonds are sold at more than 150 auctions held throughout the year. The Bureau of Public Debt provides a three-month calendar of tentative auction dates so you can plan ahead. Official auction dates are announced about seven days before the securities are offered. The Bureau of Public Debt (www.publicdebt.treas.gov) provides auction information.

Treasury bills, notes, and bonds are sold through competitive and noncompetitive bidding:

- **Noncompetitive bid:** You agree to accept a rate determined by the auction, and in return you're guaranteed that your bid will successfully result in purchasing the security you desire. Most individual investors submit noncompetitive bids.

- **Competitive bid:** For a bill auction, the investor submits an offer — or *tender* — specifying a discount rate to two decimal places (for example 5.12 percent). For a note or bond auction, the investor submits a tender specifying a yield to three decimal places (for example, 5.123 percent). Common fractions may not be used. If the bid falls within the range accepted at the auction, the investor is awarded the security. If the bid is at the high rate or yield, the investor may not be awarded the full amount bid. Most financial institutions (banks, insurance companies, brokerages, and so on) submit competitive bids.

The minimum purchase amount for Treasury bills (which mature in one year or less) is $10,000. Treasury bills are sold at a discount from face value and do not pay interest before maturity. Bids for more than $10,000 must be in multiples of $1,000. Noncompetitive bids from individual investors may not exceed $1,000,000 (that's right, a million dollars) for the same offering of Treasury bills.

Treasury notes with maturities of less than five years are purchased in minimum amounts of $5,000 (and in multiples of $1,000). Owners of Treasury notes and bonds receive semiannual interest payments. Treasury notes have terms of more than one year and less than ten years. Treasury bonds have terms that are greater than ten years.

Treasury notes with maturities of between five and ten years are sold in minimum amounts of $1,000 and in multiples of $1,000. Noncompetitive bids from individual investors can't exceed $5 million for the same offering of Treasury notes or bonds.

You can find addresses for all 12 Federal Reserve Banks listed at www.ny.frb.org.

Where to buy 'em

If you purchase Treasury securities directly from the Federal government, they are issued in a book-entry form that is held in the Department of the Public Debt's *Treasury Direct* system. The securities are issued to your individual account. In contrast, if you purchase Treasury securities using a broker, they are issued in a commercial book-entry form. This means that the securities are held in the name of your broker or dealer. The broker then maintains records of each individual investor's Treasury securities.

Treasury Direct is a book-entry system that is managed by the Federal government. After you open a Treasury Direct account, you can purchase bonds from the government without a broker. Treasury Direct provides a statement of account whenever you make a change to your account (for example, when you buy more Treasury securities, sell your securities, reinvest earnings). Maintenance charges are $25 per year for each $100,000 in your account. Treasury Direct provides information about how to open and maintain a Treasury Direct Investor Account at www.publicdebt.treas.gov/sec/secacct.htm.

Tendering your offer

Select the issue you want to bid on and complete the correct *Treasury Direct Tender Information* form at www.publicdebt.treas.gov/sec/secform.htm. Finish the form by making either a competitive or noncompetitive bid, which is called a *tender*. State how many securities you want to buy, the maturity term, and include full payment payable to your local Federal Reserve Bank. You can make payments by direct deposit, certified check, matured Treasury obligation, personal check for notes and bonds, and U.S. currency if presented in person.

When completing the Treasury Direct Tender Information form, you must decide whether you want to send in a competitive or a noncompetitive bid. (Institutional investors always submit competitive bids.) A noncompetitive tender specifies the discount rate with two decimal places that you're willing to pay (for example, 6.12 percent). If your bid is too high and the issue is purchased at a lower rate, you may not get the securities you want.

Detailed directions about how to complete the Treasury Direct Tender Information form and acceptable ways to pay for the Treasuries are available at www.pueblo.gsa and at the Bureau of the Public Debt at www.publicdebt.treas.gov/sec/sectndr.htm.

Selling your Treasury securities

If you need to sell your Treasury security, the Federal government will help you. You can sell directly through Treasury Direct — you don't need a broker. The government will get quotes from different dealers and you get the best price offered. The fee is $34 for each security sold. You can even have the proceeds from the sale of the Treasury security deposited directly to your checking account, less the transaction fee. For additional information, see www.publicdebt.treas.gov/sec/secbsr.htm.

At this time, you can't buy or sell Treasury securities online. However, the Federal government provides lots of individual investor information at the Bureau of Public Debt Web page shown in Figure 14-2 (www.publicdebt.treas.gov/of/ofannce.htm).

You can request that an account be set up before you purchase your first Treasury security by submitting a New Account Request form. Just print the form located at www.publicdebt.treas.gov/sec.sectrdir.htm. Fill in all the required information and mail the form to your local Federal Reserve Bank. Don't send any cash; it's free.

Online sources for more information

Information provided by the government is written in a way that makes purchasing Treasuries seem more difficult and complex than it really is, but don't get discouraged. For more information about understanding and purchasing Treasury securities, refer to the following online resources:

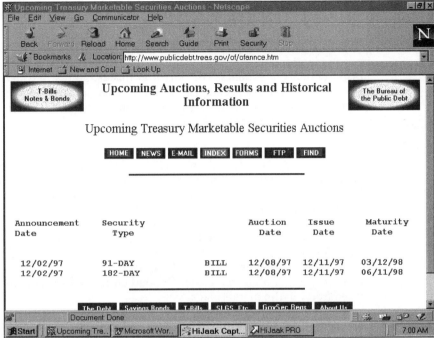

Figure 14-2:
The Bureau
of Public
Debt
provides a
calendar of
upcoming
auction
dates.

- **Economeister:** The Economeister Web site, located at
  `www.economeister.com`, provides auction dates and news about
  Treasury securities.

- **GovPX:** This site, located at `www.govpx.com`, provides quotations of
  U.S. government securities. The site also provides active lists of
  Treasury bonds, notes, and bills with each financial instrument's
  account (CUSIP — Computerized Uniform Securities Identification
  Program) number, coupon rate, and maturity date. Lists include buyers'
  bid prices, sellers' asking prices, changes from the prior trading day,
  and yields.

- **Quote.com Street Pricing:** This site, located at `www.quote.com`,
  provides quotes for Treasury securities and government agency
  securities. Specific information includes interest rates and spreads,
  quotes on active Treasuries, and quotes on government agency securities. Cost is $9.95 per month for the basic service.

- **Zero Coupon Bonds and Strips:** You can get an explanation of these
  more sophisticated Treasury securities from the Federal Reserve Bank
  of New York at `www.ny.frb.org/pihome/fedpoint/fed41.html`.

Calculating Bond Values

A bond issued by a corporation is called a *debt instrument*. The bond states how the debtholder (investor) will be repaid. Generally, these terms are normal debt arrangements. The borrower makes interest payments and then pays the principal at a predetermined date. What makes bonds complicated are provisions to convert the bonds to common stocks at a predetermined stock value and similar issues.

Government agency and municipal bonds are valued in the same way as corporate bonds. However, municipal bonds are generally free from state and local taxes, and government securities are exempt from federal taxes. The return calculated for corporate bonds is somewhat overstated because it doesn't take the impact of taxes into consideration.

The value of the bond is based on the investor's assessment of the bond's value. The receipt of future interest payments, the repayment of principal, and the credit rating or riskiness of the bond usually temper these assessments. You aren't obligated to hold a bond until maturity, and bonds are traded freely in the marketplace.

Calculating the value of a bond involves determining the present value of the interest payments and the eventual recovery of the principal. *Present value* means discounting the future cash flow to calculate how much you're willing to pay today for these future receipts.

The *discount rate* is the investor's required rate of return. This rate includes a risk premium to compensate the investor for the riskiness of the bond. For example, an investor values a bond with a 6 percent annual interest payment lower than its face value.

The Easiest Way to Value Your Bond Returns

Bonds are often quoted at prices that differ from their stated (or *par*) values, a situation that can be troublesome for investors who want to determine the yield of the bond. Many ways exist to calculate the yield value of a bond. In my opinion, the *approximate yield to maturity method* provides the easiest way to determine a bond's current yield.

To calculate the approximate yield to maturity (YTM), you need the following information:

- ✔ Annual interest payment (I)
- ✔ Principal payment (P)
- ✔ Price of the bond (B)
- ✔ Number of years to maturity (M)

Using these values, you calculate the approximate yield to maturity by using the following formula:

$$YTM = (I + ((P - B) \div M)) \div ((0.6 \times B) + (0.4 \times P))$$

For example, what is the yield to maturity on a 12-year, 7 percent annual coupon, $1,000 par value bond that sells at a discount for $942.21? Here are the calculations:

$$YTM = (70 + ((\$1,000 - \$942.21) \div 12)) \div ((0.6 \times \$942.21) + (0.4 \times \$1,000))$$

$$YTM = (70 + (57.79 \div 12)) \div (565.33 + 400)$$

$$YTM = (70 + 4.82) \div 965.33$$

$$YTM = 74.82 \div 965.33$$

$$YTM = 0.0775$$

$$YTM = 7.75\%$$

If your required rate of return is 8 percent, you should *not* purchase the bond because the approximate yield to maturity (7.75 percent) doesn't meet your financial requirements (an 8 percent return). Conversely, if the bond has a return that is equal to or *greater* than 8 percent, the bond meets your objectives and is a "buy" candidate.

Note: If the value of the bond is discounted (that is, sells below its par value — in this case, below $1,000), the yield to maturity (YTM) is greater than the 7 percent coupon rate.

Where to Purchase Bonds Online

The Internet provides many sources for online bond trading. Any of the large brokerages can handle your bond transaction. However, several online brokerages specialize in municipal bonds. Here are a few examples:

- ✔ **Alamo Capital Investment** (www.alamocap.com) is a municipal bond retailer and underwriter that specializes in California municipals, discount trading, and retirement programs.

- ✔ **C. W. Henderson & Associates, Inc.** (cwhenderson.com) is a firm of investment counselors specializing in tax-exempt municipal securities.

- ✔ **Carty & Company** (www.carty.com) deals primarily in municipal bonds.

- ✔ **Corby North Bridge Securities** (www.northbridge.com) is a firm of municipal bond brokers with discount commission rates.

- ✔ **Cutter & Company Brokerage** (www.stocktrader.com) specializes in Treasury securities and publishes a daily update of Treasury bond yields.

- ✔ **Glen Rauch Securities, Inc.** (www.fabkom.inter.net/grshom.html), is a full-service firm specializing in municipal bond brokering.

- ✔ **Lebenthal & Company** (www.lebenthal.com) is a leading municipal bond broker that offers potential customers free advice in its Bond Kit. Request the Bond Kit online, and the firm mails it to you.

- ✔ **Tripp & Co., Inc.** (www.visitus.com/tripp), is a full-service brokerage that specializes in tax-free bonds.

More Online Bond News, Rates, and Advice

For more information about bond markets, commentary, rates, and news, see the following online resources:

- ✔ **Capital Markets Commentary** (www.indata.com/whatsnew.htm) is a weekly fixed-income (bond) market review provided by Interactive Data Corporation, a Financial Times company. The Capital Markets Commentary includes market information about U.S. government agency bonds, U.S. corporate bonds, international bonds, U.S. municipals, and commercial mortgage-backed bonds.

A hot, no-fuss bond strategy

More Americans have invested in bonds than in any other security. Some of the advantages of bonds are that they offer regular interest payments that are higher than money market accounts, they can be tax-exempt, and they offer a way to stay ahead of inflation.

Some of the limitations of investing in bonds are interest rate risk (if interest rates go up, the value of your bond goes down) and credit rating risk (if your bond gets downgraded, its value goes down). Additionally, unless you own a Treasury security, your principal investment isn't guaranteed by the government the way bank deposits are protected by the Federal Deposit Insurance Corporation (FDIC).

Tucker Anthony, an investment counselor, suggests one way to reduce your exposure to interest rate risk. He suggests creating a *bond ladder.* Each rung of the bond ladder consists of a different bond maturity. For example, the first rung of the bond ladder may consist of bonds that mature in one year; the second rung may consist of bonds that mature in two years; and so on for ten years.

The yield of the ten-year bond ladder is less than 20-year bonds, but the ladder provides diversification. As each rung matures, you can reinvest the funds in the same or better ways to conserve your principal. The benefits of this approach are some protection from declining interest rates and low maintenance.

If this bond ladder scheme seems too complex, you can always invest in a bond mutual fund. One of the advantages of a bond mutual fund is that you often get to own a share of bonds that are $50,000, $100,000, or $250,000 each — something that you may not be able to achieve as an individual investor.

✔ **Dow Jones Telerate Bond Commentary** (`www.djmarkets.com`) provides news and commentary on Treasury securities, corporate, and mortgage-backed bonds.

✔ **Tucker Anthony: Yield Alert** (`www.tucker-anthony.com/yield.htm`) is a financial advisor that assists investors by providing various market rates for Treasury securities, government agency securities, corporate bonds, municipal bonds, and zero-coupon bonds. These comparisons are helpful for benchmarking the performance of your bond portfolio.

Investing Online
For Dummies
Internet Directory

The 5th Wave   **By Rich Tennant**

"Well, she's fast on the Keyboard and knows how to load the printer, but she just sort of 'plays' with the mouse."

In this directory . . .

Throughout the pages of *Investing Online For Dummies,* I describe dozens of Internet resources that can assist you in your wealth-building efforts. In this part of the book, I provide you with a listing of the sites you are most likely to use for analyzing investment candidates, selecting the right financial assets for your objectives, monitoring your portfolio, and buying and selling your investments online.

Investing Online For Dummies Internet Directory

The Internet has a wide variety of resources for online investors, and this directory provides a sampling of some of the latest and greatest online investing sites available at this time. I don't claim that this guide is comprehensive. With the constant growth and change that characterizes the Internet, it is almost impossible for anyone to create a directory that lives up to such a claim.

The Internet is a constantly changing resource. Some sites listed in this directory (and elsewhere in this book) may have changed or gone away due to mergers with larger sites. Some Web sites just vanish for no reason. If a site has moved, you may find a link to the new location. If not, try a search engine (like AltaVista or Infoseek) to locate the resource you need.

About Those Micons (Mini Icons)

To give you as much information as possible, this directory uses these *micons,* small graphics that detail some of the special features of a Web site:

$ This site charges an access fee. I use this micon if most of the site's content — or the most important content — is available only to paying subscribers.

You need a special piece of software — a *plug-in,* such as Shockwave or Real Audio — to get the most out of this site.

This site has security features to protect any personal information (such as a credit card number) that you may submit.

This site features shopping opportunities.

The site has software that you can download.

An increasing number of sites on the Internet require your free registration.

The site has interactive message boards that you can use for communicating with other online investors.

This micon identifies sites that offer chat rooms where you interact with other visitors or an investment expert. Participating in chat rooms (and sometimes message boards) often requires registering at the site.

Analyst Evaluations

Finding out what the experts are saying about your investment selection is often useful. Here are a few of my favorite sources for analysts' evaluations.

Research Magazine

www.researchmag.com

$

You can choose from three analyst evaluation reports: ACE — Analyst Consensus Estimate Reports, Standard & Poors Enhanced Stock Reports, and Research Investment Reports. Sample reports are available for downloading.

Standard & Poors Enhanced Stock Reports

www.stockinfo.standardpoor.com

$

To obtain a report from this site, click on the Investor's Center icon, select Order, and then enter the ticker symbol of the company report you desire. The price of the report ($4.95) is displayed, along with information about what the report contains (basic stock report, industry reports, news stories, and Wall Street Consensus Report).

Basics of Investing

If you're looking for good investor starting places, try the Web sites I list in this section of the directory.

Invest-O-Rama

www.investorama.com

Invest-O-Rama is a collection of links to online sources, such as electronic brokers, mutual funds, financial reports, and related investor sources.

InvestorGuide

www.investorguide.com

InvestorGuide features newsletters, articles, stock analyses, and links to thousands of investment sites.

Other Stuff to Check Out

www.investorweb.com
www.pawws.com
www.quicken.com/investments
www.wsdinc.com

Bonds

Bonds (sometimes called fixed income investments) can be short-term or long-term, high-risk (like junk bonds) or low-risk (like Treasury bonds). If you own mutual fund shares, you may already be a bond investor. Check out the following sites for bond-related information.

Bondsonline

www.bondsonline.com/bcgraphs.htm

$

Bondsonline provides charts and historical data that compare various bond market sectors. For example, this site offers a comparison of 30-year Treasury bonds, 10-year Treasury notes, and the Dow Jones Industrial Average.

Bondtrac

www.bondtrac.com

$

Bondtrac is a bond tracking software company. Bondtrac's Web site provides a partial list of the company's services to demonstrate the use of its data and the functionality of its software. With your free registration, you can look up municipal bonds, corporate bonds, and U.S. Government agency bonds using a variety of search criteria.

Other Stuff to Check Out

www.stls.frb.org/fred/data/irates.html
www.moodys.com

Broker Fraud and Complaints

If you suspect that your broker is not as honest as you first thought, you can voice your complaint to the right people using the Internet. Many of these organizations will follow up on your complaint and keep you informed of its status.

Better Business Bureau

www.bbb.org

The Better Business Bureau has an online complaint form. The bureau promises to follow up within two weeks of your complaint.

Securities and Exchange Commission

www.sec.gov

The Securities and Exchange Commission (SEC) has an excellent online complaint process.

National Fraud Information Center

www.fraud.org

The National Fraud Information Center will forward your complaint to the appropriate organizations and include it in the Center's Internet fraud statistics (which may not help you get your money back but may be helpful to other online investors).

Company Profiles

If you're thinking about investing in a company, you can do much of your research online. For example, you can read the company's profile or develop your own company profile based on your online research and analysis.

Companylink

www.companylink.com

Companylink uses the Cor Tech Database of Technology Companies — Technology Manufacturers and Developers, Demand Research's Executive Desk Register, and Hoover's Online databases. All company profiles are for publicly traded firms plus the largest private companies in the U.S.

Hoover's Online

www.hoovers.com

$

Hoover's Online has free and fee-based information on 8,500 companies. Company ticker symbols, locations, and sales can be searched at this Web site. Company profiles include the firm's address, phone numbers, executive names, recent sales figures, and company status.

Direct Public Offerings

In a direct public offering (DPO), a company bypasses an underwriter and offers its shares directly to the public. The Internet provides information and materials about many DPOs.

Direct IPO

www.directipo.com

Direct IPO provides investor resources, information about traditional IPOs and DPOs, an industry spotlight, an IPO contest, a newsroom, and more.

Internet Capital Exchange

www.inetcapital.com

The Internet Capital Exchange is designed to bring companies and investors together to generate funding capital and investment opportunities. Companies that are already public can allow their stock to be traded by investors using an interactive trading system.

Netstock Direct

www.netstockdirect.com

Netstock Direct is an online source of information on direct investing and company materials about direct stock purchase plans.

The Direct Stock Market

www.dsm.com/DSMExt/Home.nsf/
  14beed7583e723a6882564db006bfa0e

The Direct Stock Market provides companies that are issuing direct public offering a central online location for the distribution of their prospectuses and documents. The site is subject to regulatory approval.

Other Stuff to Check Out

www.direct-stock-market.com
www.dpo-council.org
www.virtualwallstreet.com

Dividend Reinvestment Programs

Dividend Reinvestment Programs (DRIPs) allow shareholders to purchase additional shares directly from the company (bypassing brokerage fees) and sometimes at reduced prices (5 percent).

Drip Investor

www.dripinvestor.com

Drip Investor is a guide to buying stocks without a broker. It provides information about companies that are starting DRIP programs, changes to existing DRIPs, tax strategies, how to sell stocks from a DRIP, investment strategies, and more.

Kiplinger Magazine

www.kiplinger.com/magazine/nov96/
  lifetab.html

This page at the Kiplinger Magazine site features an article titled "32 Stocks for Buy and Hold Investors." This article lists 32 companies that have dividend reinvestment plans. You can also purchase shares directly from the companies described in this article.

Other Stuff to Check Out

aries.phys.yorku.ca/~rothery/
  stocks.drips.html
www.aaii.com
www.better-investing.org/store/store.html

Earnings Estimates

When determining the value of a stock, you often need to estimate the company's earnings. Compare your earnings estimates with the experts at the following Web sites.

First Call

www1.firstcall.com

$

The First Call database follows more than 7,500 companies. It also tracks more than 100 industry groups, several commodities and economic indicators, plus the Dow Jones Industrial Averages and the S&P 500.

Reuters Moneynet

www.moneynet.com

 $

Reuters Moneynet provides an S&P evaluation of the company and dividends rank, average quality opinion, fiscal year ending month, and date of the next expected earnings report. The consensus earnings per share forecast for the next year and statistics about past earnings are included.

Zacks Investment Research

www.zacks.com

 $

Zacks provides estimated earnings reports that are based on broker opinions. The site includes a listing of current earnings surprises, recommendations, and the company's annual balance sheet and income statement.

Other Stuff to Check Out

www.moneynet.com
www.nrmcapital.com
www.stocksmart.com

Economic Information

Before you invest, it is always wise to check out the big picture. Find out how the economy is doing, both nationally and regionally. For example, if the economy weakens, how will this change affect your investment selections?

Census Bureau

www.census.gov

 $

The Census Bureau provides information about industry, statistics, and general business. *Current Industrial Reports* provide production, shipment, and inventory statistics. *Census of Manufacturers Industry Series* includes industry statistics (some of this information may be outdated). *The Census of Wholesale Trade* contains data about organizations that sell merchandise to retailers, institutions, and other types of wholesalers. The *Survey* provides updates about current and past statistics of monthly sales, inventories, and stock/sales ratios.

GSA Government Information Locator Service

www.gsa.gov

The GSA Government Information Locator Service includes many Federal agency reports in either full-text or abstract forms. Most information resources are cataloged and searchable. Searches can include more than one agency.

Internet Federal Reserve Sites

www.stls.frb.org/other/websites.html

This Web site provides links to all the Federal home pages and gopher sites. Publications by these organizations include high-quality statistics, analyses, and forecasts of regional, national, and international economic and financial conditions.

Industry Information

Compare the performance of your investment candidate to the industry standard. How is the company performing? Is the company an industry leader or fighting for market share? Find out by researching the company's industry at the following Internet sites.

American Society of Association Executives

www.asaenet.org

American Society of Association Executives provides links to Web sites for various industries. The Web sites are generally high-quality industry overviews that often include briefings of industry trends, geographic profiles, and statistics for financial performance analysis.

Lexis-Nexis

www.lexis-nexis.com

$

Lexis-Nexis has a wide variety of business and legal databases and recently added a new database of 10- to 20-page market summaries of an industry sector or demographic market. Additionally, the Lexis-Nexis database includes the *Market Share Reporter* (from 1991 to the present) and *Computer Industry Forecasts*.

STAT-USA

www.stat-usa.gov

STAT-USA is sponsored by the U.S. Department of Commerce and provides financial information about economic indicators, statistics, and news.

Other Stuff to Check Out

www.fedstats.gov
www.technometrica.com
www.trainingforum.com

Initial Public Offerings (IPOs)

Usually in an initial public offering (IPO), a company offers shares to the public for the first time. Purchasing shares in an IPO may be one way to get in on the ground floor of a new investment opportunity.

Everything About IPOs

**www.moneypages.com/syndicate/
    stocks/ipo.html**

This Web page contains an informative article about the advantages and limitations of initial public offerings.

IPO Central

www.ipocentral.com

IPO Central provides the most recent IPO filings, weekly pricing, commentary, and informative articles.

IPO Interactive

www.fedfil.com/ipo/index.html

IPO Interactive is sponsored by a Dow Jones company that presents Federal filings of IPOs. All IPOs listed exceed $10 million in net proceeds. Online materials include actual and pro forma financial results, operational histories, and background information on each company.

Other Stuff to Check Out

biz.yahoo.com/reports/ipo.html
cbs.marketwatch.com/news/current/
    IPO_rep.htx
www.ostman.com/alert-ipo
www.investhelp.com
www.ipodata.com
www.IPOmaven.com
www.ipomonitor.com
www.techweb.com/investor/ipowatch/
    ipostach.html

Interest Rates

The Internet can help you find the best savings rate in the U.S. Some Web sites even include instructions about how to open out-of-state savings accounts.

Bank-CD Rate Scanner

www.bankcd.com

$

Bank-CD Rate Scanner guarantees its service; if you can find a lower rate at an FDIC-insured institution that accepts nationwide deposits, your $9.95 invoice will be voided.

Bank Rate Monitor

www.bankrate.com

Bank Rate Monitor shows the interest rates offered throughout the nation. The Web site even includes a listing of financial institutions that offer special deals to Internet shoppers.

BanxQuote

banx.com/banx/rates.htm

BanxQuote is a good online source for the best rates for money market deposit accounts. BanxQuote allows searches by location or terms. Data includes the financial institution's name and contact information and the money market account's rate of return.

Investor Compilation Sites

Investor compilation sites are excellent sources for beginning investors. These investor starting points are also good sources for finding new investor Web sites.

Invest-O-Rama

www.investorama.com

Invest-O-Rama includes more than 2,000 investor-related links sorted into categories. The site has a directory that covers bonds, brokerages, dividend reinvestment plans, futures, mutual funds, and more.

InvestorGuide

www.investorguide.com

InvestorGuide is a well-organized directory with links to thousands of investor-related sites. InvestorGuide includes site reviews, summaries, and an extensive section on initial pubic offerings (IPOs).

Morningstar

www.morningstar.net

Morningstar is a Chicago-based, independent rating company that specializes in mutual funds. The site includes information about both stocks and mutual funds, easy-to-use screening tools, and research sources.

The Syndicate

www.moneypages.com/syndicate

The Syndicate includes informative articles on investor topics, more than 2,000 links to related investor sites, and information on brokers, bonds, and more.

Wall Street Research Net

www.wsrn.com

Wall Street Research Net focuses on stock market research. The site includes more than 65,000 links to company information, the economy, market news, investor reports, quotes, mutual fund indexes, and more.

Investor Databases

When researching an investment candidate, investors often use specialized databases to find that elusive piece of data. Here are a few free and fee-based online databases.

FinWeb

www.finweb.com

FinWeb is from the University of Texas at Austin. FinWeb has links to the finance and economics departments of many universities, commercial sources, and financial institutions. This financial supersite includes high-quality recommendations, and all links are screened for content.

Govbot, University of Massachusetts, Amherst

ciir.cs.umass.edu/ciirdemo/Govbot/
    index.html

Govbot is sponsored by the Center for Intelligent Information Retrieval (CIIR). The free database allows you to search more than 200,000 government and military Web pages.

Holt Stock Report

metro.turnpike.net/holt

The Holt Stock Report provides indexes, averages, information about foreign markets, new stock highs and lows, currency exchange rates, gold prices, interest rates, lists of the most active issues on the NYSE, NASDAQ, and AMEX, stocks with today's volume up more than 50 percent, and stocks that have reached new highs and lows.

IBM Info Market

www.infomarket.ibm.com

$

IBM Info Market includes a database that has 75 newswires, 300 newspapers, 819 newsletters, 6,882 journals, and 11 million companies. The site charges by the document.

Other Stuff to Check Out

> www.asaenet.org/Gateway/
> GatewayHP.html
> www.elibrary.com
> www.gsa.gov
> www.lexis-nexis.com
> www.stat-usa.gov

Mailing Lists

Mailing lists are special e-mail programs that re-mail all incoming mail to a list of subscribers. Get new insights and advice from savvy investors by joining a topic-specific mailing list.

CataList

www.lsoft.com/lists/listref.html

CataList has only 14,000 mailing lists but is searchable by site, country, and number of list subscribers. (Sometimes it's a good idea to know how many subscribers will receive your investment question.)

Liszt

www.liszt.com

Liszt is an index of mailing lists arranged alphabetically, by description, name, and subject. The site is searchable.

Reference.Com

www.reference.com

Reference.Com searches 150,000 Usenet newsgroups and mailing lists for the information you want. Instructions about basic and advanced searches are available.

Other Stuff to Check Out

> www.quote.com
> www.smithbarney.com
> www.techstocks.com
> www1.thomasregister.com

Municipal and Treasury Information

State or local units of the government often issue municipal bonds (sometimes called "munis"). Treasury securities (sometimes called "Treasuries") are issued by the Federal government. Both types of investments can help you diversify your portfolio.

Capital Markets Commentary

www.intdata.com/capital.htm

Capital Markets Commentary is a weekly fixed income (bond) market review provided by Interactive Data Corporation, a Financial Times company. The Capital Markets Commentary includes market information about U.S. government agency bonds, U.S. corporate bonds, international bonds, U.S. municipals, and commercial mortgage-backed bonds.

Dow Jones What's New

www.djmarkets.com/nhome/whats-new

This Dow Jones Web site provides news and commentary on Treasury securities, corporate, and mortgage-backed bonds.

How to Purchase Treasury Securities Without a Broker

www.sf.frb.org/treasury/index.html

Avoid brokerage fees by purchasing Treasury bills, notes, and bonds directly from the Federal government. Find out all about it from the Federal Reserve Bank of San Francisco.

Tucker Anthony: Yield Alert

www.tucker-anthony.com/yield.htm

Tucker Anthony is a financial advisor that assists investors by providing various market rates for Treasury securities, government agency securities, corporate bonds, municipal bonds, and zero-coupon bonds.

Other Stuff to Check Out

www.economeister.com
www.govpx.com

Mutual Funds: Automatic Investment Plans

Even if you only have $50 to invest, you can purchase shares in a mutual fund. Automatic Investment Plans (AIPs) allow you to avoid hefty initial minimum investment requirements.

TD's Green Line Family of No-Load Mutual Funds

www.tdbank.ca/tdbank/teleaccess/
   info.html

TD's Green Line Family of No-Load Mutual Funds has a pre-authorized purchase plan of more than 30 funds to choose from. Invest quarterly, monthly, weekly, or even on your payday. Minimum initial and subsequent investments can be as low as $25.

Strong Automatic Investment Plan

www.strong-funds.com/strong/
   LearningCenter/aipbroch.htm

Strong has an automatic investment plan for 36 of its no-load funds. The program allows you to invest at predetermined intervals for as low as $50. There are no charges to establish or maintain this service.

Vanguard Fund Express

www.vanguard.com/catalog/service/
   5_3_1_2.html

The Vanguard Fund Express plan allows monthly, bimonthly, quarterly, semi-annual, and annual automatic payment to be transferred to your Vanguard account. The maximum amount of investment is $100,000 and the minimum amount is $25.

T. Rowe Price

www.troweprice.com

T. Rowe Price has two no-load funds in its automatic investment plan that allow monthly, bimonthly, quarterly, semi-annual, and annual automatic payments. Minimum payments can be as little as $25.

Mutual Funds: Companies and Funds

In this section of the directory, I list mutual fund companies that manage many mutual funds. Purchasing a mutual fund from a company that manages many mutual funds has some advantages. One such advantage is that some mutual fund companies allow you to swap your investment in one of their funds for another of their mutual funds at no charge.

Fidelity

www.fid-inv.com

Fidelity is the largest mutual funds house around, with 35 percent of the total market. This Web site has news about Fidelity investments, a mutual fund library and online prospectuses, online investment and retirement planning advice, and more.

Invesco

www.invesco.com

If you're a beginning investor, you'll appreciate Invesco's useful advice. This Web site includes online prospectuses, charts to compare rates of return, and a list of the firm's financial services.

Janus

www.janus.com

Janus has a family of no-load funds. The site provides account access, brief overviews of fund performance, application forms, investor chats, and articles.

T. Rowe Price

www.troweprice.com

T. Rowe Price provides daily mutual fund prices, brief updates of fund performance, and more. You have the option of downloading a prospectus or having one sent to you by mail.

Vanguard

www.vanguard.com

Vanguard has around 90 funds that do not charge sales fees. Vanguard is one of the largest mutual fund companies. The site includes fund descriptions, downloadable prospectuses, an education center for investors, and more.

Mutual Funds: Information Services

Uncertain about which mutual fund is best for you? The Internet provides lots of mutual fund information sources.

CBS MarketWatch — Super Star Funds

cbs.marketwatch.com

CBS MarketWatch provides articles, news, market data, fund research, links to fund sites, mutual fund tutorials for new investors, market data, portfolios, and a stock chat room.

Mutual Fund Magazine

www.mfmag.com

Mutual Fund magazine requires your free registration at this Web site, but it's worth the effort. The online magazine has a wide variety of features, departments, screens, reports, online calculators, and tools to assist you in making your mutual fund selections.

Mutual Funds Interactive

www.fundsinteractive.com/
   profiles.html

Mutual Funds Interactive has fund manager profiles and outlines of their strategies for using funds to meet your investment goals.

News Tracker Mutual Funds

Nt.excite.com

Excite provides free mutual fund and business news articles. Additionally, News Tracker has links to the Excite Business and Investing channel, investing newslinks, mutual funds online, and NET worth mutual fund manager.

The Mutual Fund Channel

www.mutual-fundchannel.com

The Mutual Fund Channel uses BackWeb to bring you one-stop mutual fund shopping. Using push technology, the Mutual Fund Channel delivers quotes, valuations, market and business news, fund profiles, historical data, and market analyses for more than 5,400 funds.

Other Stuff to Check Out

www.amgdata.com
www.fundalarm.com
www.fundfinder.com
www.mfea.com
nestegg.iddis.com/tradeline
www.stocksmart.com

Mutual Funds: Performance

Check out how your mutual fund stacks up against the competition with these Internet sources.

InvestorSquare

www.investorsquare.com

InvestorSquare ranks more than 9,500 funds on 100 different variables. This Web site also includes a detailed profile of each fund.

The Street.com

www.thestreet.com/
   mutualfundprofiles/funds.asp

The Street provides fund profiles and scorecards. You can search free and fee-based areas. One free area is Lipper Analytical's latest top performers for the week.

Other Stuff to Check Out

nestegg.iddis.com/mutfund
www.investorama.com

Mutual Funds: Prospectuses

The first rule in purchasing mutual funds is to read the prospectus before you buy any shares. Here are a few great online sources for mutual fund prospectuses.

EDGAR for Mutual Funds

edgar.stern.nyu.edu/mutual.html

EDGAR for Mutual Funds is a Web site that provides prospectuses for more than 7,000 mutual funds. If you know the name of the fund you are interested in, you can investigate the fund's activities at this site.

Mutual Fund Resource Center

www.fundmaster.com

The Mutual Fund Resource Center provides free information, prospectuses, and applications for more than 75 mutual funds.

Mutual Funds: Screens

Out of the 9,500 available mutual funds, which one meets your financial objectives? Use a mutual fund screen to help you find likely candidates. Mutual fund screens are on the Internet, easy to use, and often free.

Investor Square

www.InvestorSquare.com

The Investor Square mutual fund screen is particularly useful for beginning investors. The screen is designed to help you find the best 25 performers by category, detailed objective, and specific category (such as short-term or long-term bond fund).

Microsoft Investor

investor.msn.com/home.asp

$

Microsoft Investor charges $9.95 per month for a full package of features that include mutual fund and stock screens. The site offers a 30-day free trial period. The mutual fund screen is easy to use, and you can copy the results to your spreadsheet.

Morningstar

www.morningstar.net

Morningstar uses a few sensible preselected variables in its mutual fund stock screen.

Quicken.com

www.quicken.com

Quicken provides its mutual fund screen free of charge. The screen's values are updated on a monthly basis.

Other Stuff to Check Out

www.researchmag.com
www.thomsoninvest.net

Newsgroups

Newsgroups contain discussions about different subject areas. The content of these discussions ranges from the ridiculous to the sublime. By using the search engines I list in this section, you may find a newsgroup that is a good source for opinions on different investments.

Deja News

www.dejanews.com

You can use this site to search more than 25,000 Usenet newsgroups for the investor information you are seeking. Searches can be by group, author, subject, or dates.

Usenet Info Center Launch Pad

sunsite.unc.edu/usenet-i

Usenet Info Center Launch Pad uses an excellent search engine that can help you find the right newsgroup. Additional information includes statistics about the number of messages posted per month and the percentage of Usenet sites that carry the group.

Robot Wisdom Newsgroup Finder

www.mcs.net/~jorn/html/finder/
    finder.html

Robot Wisdom Newsgroup Finder allows you to search by historical period, numbers of articles, and country or state locations. The site's interface uses clickable maps of the U.S and the world. Responses include the newsgroup name, address, description, charter, and sometimes FAQs (if they are available).

Newsletters

If you subscribe to an online newsletter, you may receive issues several times a day, daily, weekly, bi-weekly, monthly, or even quarterly. Investor newsletters may be free or costly, and they may have hard facts and breaking news or chatty items about the market's latest events.

Holt Stock Report

metro.turnpike.net/holt

The Holt Stock Report can be delivered to your e-mailbox daily. This newsletter provides all the market statistics you may need for your investment decision making.

InvestorGuide Weekly

www.investorguide.com/weekly.htm

InvestorGuide Weekly is designed to keep you informed of new Web-related developments in the areas of investing and personal finance. It includes links to articles on how to use the Internet for investing, new and improved Web sites, investing in Internet companies, and electronic commerce.

Kiplinger Online

www.kiplinger.com

Kiplinger Online provides news of the day, business forecasts, personal finance, stock quotes, lists of top funds, online calculators, retirement advice, listings of great Internet sites, and financial FAQs.

Online Money

www.pathfinder.com

Online Money is designed for online investors and individuals interested in personal finance. One of the newsletter's best features is how it is organized. It starts with the headlines of top stories and personal finance hot links and then provides the news summaries.

Research on Demand
www.gsnews.com

 $

Research on Demand is a high-end service from Goldman Sachs. Research on Demand offers *Research Headlines,* a daily update of rating and estimate changes, and *U.S. Research Viewpoint,* a weekly review of the impact of earnings and rating changes.

Newspapers

Get the news in quick summaries and then read the full story at your leisure, all online. Many online newspapers let you customize your paper so you get just the news that interests you.

Ecola's 24-hour Newsstand
www.ecola.com/news

Ecola's 24-hour Newsstand contains links to more than 1,500 Web sites for published material from local and specialty papers, magazines, and major news services. Titles can be searched for keywords.

Individual NewsPage
www.newspage.com

 $

Individual NewsPage provides free and fee-based information. You can set a personal profile that makes this online newspaper your personal clipping service. Its home page provides breaking news, company links, news searches, and quotes.

InfoBeat
www.infobeat.com

 $

InfoBeat enables you to select user profiles that highlight finance, news, weather, sports, entertainment, or snow. To subscribe, just go to the Web site and enroll.

Newspaper Association of America
www.naa.org/hotlinks/all.html

The Newspaper Association of America offers comprehensive indexes to the online versions of major newspapers.

Other Stuff to Check Out

> www.nyt.com
> www.sjm.com
> www.wsj.com

Online Brokerages

Electronic brokerages often charge the lowest commissions available. Each commercial enterprise charges a different fee and has its own unique features. Online brokerages are generally as accurate as their full-service counterparts.

Ameritrade (Formerly Aufhauser, Ceres, and eBroker)
www.ameritrade.com

$ 🕾

Ameritrade features equity and option trading, retirement accounts, and trading on margin.

Donaldson, Lufkin, & Jenrette (Formerly PC Financial Network)

www.dljdirect.com

Known as DLJ Direct, this New York firm offers a wide variety of brokerage services, downloadable software, and investment information.

E*Trade

www.etrade.com

\$ 📠

E*Trade charges a flat rate for online trades and is based in Palo Alto, California.

National Discount Brokers

www.ndb.com

\$ 📠

National Discount Brokers is a Chicago-based firm that charges a flat fee for basic transactions. The firm offers portfolio accounting, technical analysis, and more.

Schwab

www.schwab.com

\$ 📠 ↘

Schwab (sometimes called eSchwab) offers downloadable trading software, online trading, account information, quotes, and more.

Other Stuff to Check Out

www.computel.com
www.datek.com
www.fidelity.com
www.lombard.com
www.ndb.com
www.jboxford.com
www.protrade.com
www.quick-reilly.com
www.msiebert.com
www.waterhouse.com

Online Calculators

If you have a hard time with the math of personal finance, the Internet can help you. The Net provides many online financial calculators that can do all the math you require.

Altamira Resource Center Net Worth Calculator

www.altamira.com/icat/toolbox/ netcalc.html

The Altamira Resource Center suggests that one of the primary financial goals in life is to increase net worth. Therefore, this site provides an online calculator that is designed to help you determine your current net worth.

Bank of American Investment Services

www.bankamerica.com/tools/ sri_assetall.html

This page from the Bank of America Web site provides a survey of 12 questions. Enter your answers and the online calculator will suggest an investment allocation strategy that suits your current needs and situation.

FinanCenter

www.financenter.com

The FinanCenter provides many online calculators that can help you with your personal finances and investment decision making. Just click on an icon (budget, investments, retirement, and so on) and select the appropriate calculator.

Merrill Lynch's Net Worth Calculator

**www.merrill-lynch.ml.com/investor/
worthform.html**

Merrill Lynch suggests that, before you begin planning for the future, it is important to review your current financial position. This page at the Merrill Lynch site has a net worth calculator to help you get started.

Star Strategic Asset Allocation

www.io.org/~nobid/star.html

Answer the questions, and the online calculator suggests the types of investments that are good matches to your risk-tolerance level.

Portfolio Management: Online Tools

Many online portfolio management programs exist that can monitor your investments, track their performance, and send you end-of-the-day messages to notify you of large changes. This section of the directory lists a few examples.

Stockpoint Portfolio Management

www.stockpoint.com

Stockpoint provides a free personal portfolio tracking program. Other Web site offerings include quotes, analysis, stock news, and end-of-the-day e-mail portfolio updates. You can also download this information to your Quicken personal finance program.

Money Talks

www.talks.com

Money Talks is a free personal investment magazine that has expanded to the Internet. The electronic magazine has a section called Money Manager. Money Manager provides a quote server, a ticker symbol lookup service, and a portfolio tracker. Portfolio information can be sent to your e-mailbox as frequently as twice a day.

Thomson Investors Network

www.thomsoninvest.net

Thomson Investors Network provides free and fee-based services. Subscribers and registered guests can use the Web site's portfolio tracking services (which include end-of-the-day quotes sent to your e-mailbox).

Yahoo!

edit.my.yahoo.com/config

Yahoo! has a personalized portfolio program. To create portfolios, just enter a portfolio name and then add the ticker symbols of your investments separated by commas.

Other Stuff to Check Out

www.moneynet.com
www.wsj.com

Push Technology: Investing

In the past, you had to laboriously search the Internet for that one vital piece of missing investment information. Now you can use push technology to bring that needed information directly to your desktop computer.

BackWeb

www.backweb.com

BackWeb flashes the news you select across your screen when you're not using your computer. BackWeb has a total of 50 channels to select from. It is free and downloadable.

Marimba

www.marimba.com

Marimba can distribute software updates and corporate information directly to your computer. When Marimba detects new or updated information that you are interested in, it retrieves the data and saves it on your hard disk. You can see it at your leisure. The program is free and downloadable.

PointCast

www.pointcast.com

PointCast delivers the information you select to your computer. The company's smart screen acts like a screen saver. You can customize the program so the latest prices of your investments scroll across the screen. The PointCast program has more than 200 information "channels." About 40 are money and investment topics. The program is free and downloadable.

Quote Servers

The Internet provides many quote servers that provide real-time and delayed stock, mutual fund, bond, option, and Treasury security prices. Here are a few examples of online quote services and their features.

Briefing.Com

www.briefing.com

Briefing.Com provides a free introductory service that includes market comments, quotes, charts, portfolio tracking, sector ratings, and an economic calendar.

Data Broadcasting Online

www.dbc.com

Data Broadcasting Online retrieves up to seven ticker symbols at one time. Quotes include last price, change, currency, percent change, opening price, today's low, today's high, previous day's closing price, and volume.

Interquote

www.interquote.com

Interquote provides real-time, continuously updated quotes.

PC Quote

www.pcquote.com

PC Quote offers many free services and five levels of fee-based service. Free services include ticker symbol lookup, current stock prices, portfolio tracker, company profiles, and Zacks Investment Research broker recommendations.

Other Stuff to Check Out

quote.pathfinder.com/money/quote/qc
quotes.quicken.com
www.cnnfn.com
www.stocksmart.com
www.stocktools.com
www.thomsoninvest.net

Retirement Planning

Can you retire early? Check out the helpful guidance the Internet offers, and maybe you can say good-bye to your day job earlier than you think.

Deloitte Touche LLP

www.dtonline.com/promises/cover.htm

Deloitte Touche LLP provides help interpreting the IRS tax language with a summary of new tax laws and Individual Retirement Accounts (IRAs). Following each tax law change, this site offers suggested action steps that you may want to consider.

Ernst & Young

www.ey.com/tax/tips.htm

This Ernst & Young site provides many tips for taxpayers. The suggestions include IRA advice, information about common errors, deductions you may not have included, and strategies to help you reduce your tax liability.

Independence Life and Annuity Company FAQ

www.websaver.com/WSfaq.html

Independence Life and Annuity Company answers the most frequently asked questions about annuities, costs, and income options.

Kiplinger's Retirement Zone

www.bookpage.com/kiplinger/ index.html

Kiplinger's Retirement Zone provides online tutorials, worksheets, and other tools to assist you in planning a comfortable, worry-free retirement.

Other Stuff to Check Out

www.usba.com
www.websaver.com/WSfaq.html

Retirement Planning: Online Worksheets

Need to do a few calculations for your retirement planning? The following Web sites can do the math for you.

Retirement Planning Calculator

personal.fidelity.com/toolbox

Click on the toolbox icon and go to a page with lots of links to online calculators. One of these calculators is for retirement planning. Use the calculator to determine the value of your nest egg at retirement, estimated savings surplus or shortfall, and estimated additional annual savings needed.

Retirement Planning Calculator

www.bygpub.com/finance/ RetirementCalc.htm

This retirement planning calculator can assist you in determining what sort of lifestyle you can expect during retirement by showing your 401(k) account balance before and after retirement. You can experiment with different savings amounts so that you can see the effect they will have on your retirement lifestyle.

Other Stuff to Check Out

www.troweprice.com/retirement/retire.html
www.waddell.com

Savings Bonds

Savings bonds can be purchased at banks, thrifts, or credit unions. Also, many employers offer payroll deduction plans that allow you to purchase savings bonds. For many people, purchasing savings bonds is the only way they can save money.

Market Analysis of Savings Bonds

www.bondinformer.com

One expert provides a market analysis of short- and long-term interest rates for savings bonds.

The Bureau of Public Debt

www.publicdebt.treas.gov/sav/ savbene.htm

The Bureau of Public Debt provides information on the benefits of savings bonds and covers interest rates and maturity periods. You can either purchase (for the cost of the shipping and handling) or download Bond Wizard, a software program that calculates the value of your savings bonds.

Stocks: Historical Prices

As part of your investment research of equities, you'll likely want to know the historical stock prices. This information is valuable for your forecasts of future stock prices.

Quote.Com

www.quote.com

Quote.Com provides historical data files as an additional service ($1.95) for current subscribers.

Dow Jones Retrieval

www.business-line.com/dowjones/ quotes.html

This site offers current and historical quotes for commodities and financial futures traded on major North American exchanges, plus daily values for more than 100 selected indexes. You can also find historical Dow Jones Averages (1982 to the present), and 12-day trading period summaries for the past year.

Other Stuff to Check Out

Biz.swcp.com/stocks
www.prophetdata.com
www.stockwiz.com/stockwiz.html

Stock Screens: Online

Stock screens can help you whittle down your list of investment candidates. Your creative searches can reveal stocks that have just the characteristics you're looking for.

Market Guide's NetScreen

netscreen.marketguide.com

$

Market Guide's NetScreen allows you to screen for stocks using any of 20 variables. The database is updated weekly.

MSN Investor

investor.msn.com

$

MSN Investor has a stock screen called Investment Finder that searches 8,000 companies to find securities that meet your specific criteria. The program uses dozens of variable combinations.

ResearchMag

www.researchmag.com

  $

The stock screen has 12 basic variables that screen more than 9,000 stocks. To use the advanced stock screen, you must be a subscriber. Subscriptions are based on the number of reports you use per year.

Stock Screens: Prebuilt

Online prebuilt stock screens can assist you in finding the stocks that are worthy of your additional analysis. (Remember, the best prebuilt screen is the one that screens for the things that you believe are important.)

Market Player

www.marketplayer.com

Market Player provides a relatively advanced stock screening engine. Instructions about how to use the engine are easy to understand, but you should allow some time for learning the program. Market Player has many prebuilt screens that you may find useful.

The Motley Fool

www.fool.com

Motley Fool offers a weekly discussion of its stock screens. Motley Fool provides screen results that pick out companies that missed or beat analysts' consensus estimates by 9 percent or more. Stocks are listed alphabetically as well as by descending percentages.

Wall Street Voice

www.wsvoice.com

 $

Wall Street Voice provides easy-to-use, prebuilt stock screens with only two variables. The first variable is the stock's beta. *Beta* is a measure of the sensitivity of an investment's return compared to the market. The second variable is rank, as determined by Standard & Poor's analysts. The database of 1,100 stocks in 103 industry groups is updated weekly.

Tax Preparation and Online Assistance

If you're struggling with your taxes, the Internet can help you complete your tax return and file it electronically.

Income Tax Preparation Online

taxreturns-online.netgate.net

$

Income Tax Preparation Online provides fast, accurate, low-priced services. This site includes a *Tax Organizer* to help you gather all the information you need to complete your income tax report.

Secure Tax

www.securetax.com

$

Secure Tax provides reliable and comprehensive on-screen tax preparation and electronic filing services. The audit alert feature checks for omissions, errors, and mathematical mistakes.

Tax Systems

www.taxsys.com/1040ez.htm

$

Tax Systems will assist you in completing 1040EZ, 1040A, and 1040 forms online and filing your return electronically.

U.S. Tax Code Online

www.fourmilab.ch/ustax/ustax.html

This Web site enables you to access the complete text of the United States Internal Revenue Code. It has a powerful search engine that will save you hours of time.

Other Stuff to Check Out

www.1040.com
www.dtonline.com/promises/cover.htm
www.ey.com/pfc/summary.htm
www.hrblock.com
www.irs.ustreas.gov
www.netcpa.com/forms/orglinks.htm
www.quicken.com/taxes/articles/
    878683196_19075
www.scubed.com/tax
www.tax.org/TodaysTaxNews
www.taxsites.com/federal.html
www.taxweb.com

Chapter 15

Looking for the Next Big Thing

● ●

In This Chapter

▶ Evaluating initial public offerings (IPOs)

▶ Getting in early with direct public offerings (DPOs)

▶ Bypassing broker fees to buy shares directly from the company

▶ Using dividend reinvestment plans (DRIPs) to increase your personal wealth

● ●

*E*veryone has heard stories about someone who got rich because he or she purchased the right stock at the right time. Looking back at these stories, the type of stock these individuals usually purchased was an initial public offering — called an IPO for short. In this chapter, I show how you can evaluate these types of stocks, determine what their limitations are, locate online sources of IPO news and research, and know which brokers specialize in IPOs or the mutual funds that include this type of financial asset.

An even grander opportunity is a direct public offering, or DPO. Even more speculative than IPOs, shares in these companies are comparable to investments by venture capitalists. This chapter explains the limitations of DPOs, how to purchase DPOs, and where to find online DPO research and information.

Many online investors want to avoid paying commissions to brokers. In this chapter, I describe a variety of ways that you can purchase your shares directly from the company.

I also show you how to participate in dividend reinvestment plans (DRIPs). You can examine the differences between company plans and find out how to purchase your first share.

Looking for Investment Opportunities: IPOs

When a company sells stock that trades publicly for the first time, that event is called an *initial public offering* (IPO). These IPO company issuers sell shares to an underwriter. The underwriter, in turn, resells shares to investors at a prearranged offering price. Generally, shares begin trading immediately on a stock exchange or "over the counter" through the NASDAQ stock market.

Every year, development companies and companies just starting to generate revenues seek additional capital for business expansions. Investors purchase shares so that they can reap the short-term rewards of price swings or share in the long-term prosperity of being in early for a new investment opportunity.

The investment in an IPO is speculative. These companies often have no proven strategies for success and no track record of marketing success or corporate earnings. Many of these companies crash and burn, and only a few endure to become big-time financial success stories. Keep in mind that for every Intel or Microsoft, 50 companies go bankrupt. In other words, the success rate of IPOs is one out of every 50.

Understanding the basics of IPOs, performing fundamental research, and knowing how to be an early shareholder can increase your chances of success. Figure 15-1 shows Dun & Bradstreet's CompaniesOnline at www.companiesonline.com. CompaniesOnline and other reporting agencies can assist you in checking the financial backgrounds and disclosures of the companies you're researching. The site requires your free registration and charges $20 for each company's Background Business Report.

Getting the scoop on IPOs

The following guidelines may help you select a winner out of the thousands of companies that have initial public offerings each year:

1. **Read the prospectus.**

   Read the preliminary prospectus *(red herring)* to find out about the company's expected growth. The red herring (a preliminary prospectus that provides information but is not an offer to sell the security and does not include any offering prices) includes a description of the issuer's business, the names and addresses of key corporate officers,

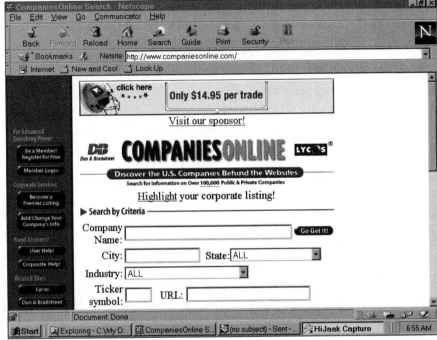

Figure 15-1:
Dun &
Bradstreet's
Companies-
Online can
assist you
in checking
out an
investment
candidate.

the ownership amounts of the key officers, any litigation problems, the company's current capitalization, and how the company plans to use the new funds from the offering.

2. Perform fundamental analysis.

Evaluate the company's financial performance by using fundamental analysis, just like you would for any other stock. (Fundamental analysis is a form of security valuation that seeks to determine the intrinsic value of a stock based on the stock's underlying economics. You then compare the intrinsic value to the asking price. For more details about how to perform a fundamental analysis, see Chapter 8.)

3. Check out the company's management.

Examine the backgrounds of the firm's management. What is their executive management experience and education? Do they have work experience in their current jobs?

4. Read the mission statement.

Investigate the firm's strategy. Is it realistic? How large is the company's market? Who is the competition? If the company plans to gain less than 25 percent of the total market, the firm may not be a long-term success.

5. **Investigate the planned use of funds.**

   Determine why raising a certain amount of capital is so critical to the company's success. If the money is used to pay down debt, the company may be headed for problems. A positive sign is using the money for expansion.

6. **Compare IPO prices.**

   Compare expected IPO prices in the red herring to the final prospectus. If the price is higher in the later prospectus, the underwriters are enthusiastic about the offering. Lower prices indicate a lack of interest by the investment community.

7. **Determine whether it's your kind of company.**

   Decide whether you want to own stock in the company you're researching. Maybe it's a great financial opportunity, but you have reservations about the product or service. (For example, do you really want to be part owner in a company that kills frogs?)

8. **Estimate your planned holding period.**

   Decide how long you plan to keep the shares. Generally, IPOs are better long-term investments rather than short-term investments because their stock prices tend to move up or down with the stock market.

Understanding the limitations of IPOs

If your goal is to create massive wealth or enjoy a comfortable lifestyle, making the most of your money takes time and vigilance. You always need to be on the lookout for new opportunities and new ways to invest your savings. To many online investors, an IPO may seem like the perfect investment. However, IPOs have several limitations:

- ✔ Many IPOs lose much of their value after the first day of trading.

- ✔ Many positive-looking IPOs are offered only to the "best" clients of large brokerage firms, pension plans, and institutions.

  However, you can always gain access to an IPO when it starts trading on the secondary market. (The stock begins trading on the secondary market when an investor purchases it from the investment-banking firm in the primary market and begins to sell it on a stock exchange.) The performances of these stocks are similar to the performances of small cap stocks and are very volatile.

- ✔ After three to six months, IPOs may underperform some small cap stocks. The source of this problem may be employees selling their shares and forcing the stock price to decline.

- ✔ After three to six months, the popularity of a strong IPO often fades.

Before you invest in an IPO, take the time to find out about the regulations governing an IPO. Figure 15-2 shows a useful page titled "Everything about IPOs" (www.moneypages.com/syndicate/stocks/ipo.html), which is part of The Syndicate Web site.

Finding IPO news and research on the Internet

You can access various sources for IPO-related news and information on the Internet. A few of these sources follow companies from the initial filing to their performance after the issue becomes public. Many of these sites provide news, commentary, and quotes. Other information includes Securities and Exchange Commission (SEC) recent filings, scheduled pricing, and registration information. Additionally, some sites include statistics on aftermarket performance, IPO ratings, and company performance data.

The following Internet sites track IPOs:

✔ **Alert-IPO!** (www.ostman.com/alert-ipo) provides complete IPO information. Its system searches the SEC's EDGAR database for new issues. The site includes data on more than 1,664 IPO filings and 1,364 underwriters.

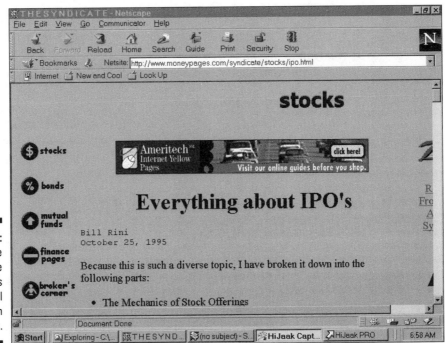

Figure 15-2:
The
Syndicate
provides
useful
information
about IPOs.

- ✔ **IPO Central** (`www.ipocentral.com`) provides the most recent IPO filings, weekly pricing, commentary, and informative articles.

- ✔ **IPO Daily Report** (`cbs.marketwatch.com/news/current/IPO_rep.htx`) offers daily IPO news from CBS MarketWatch.

- ✔ **IPO Data Systems** (`www.ipodata.com`) is a subscription service that includes an IPO calendar, company profiles, listings of top performers, IPOs by underwriter, and online information on IPOs. Fees are $15 per month or $150 per year.

- ✔ **IPO Focus** (`www.bloomberg.com/fun/bbco/ipofocus/ipofocus1.html`) is IPO news from the Bloomberg news service.

- ✔ **IPO Intelligence Online** (`www.ipo-fund.com`), provided by Renaissance Capital, includes an IPO calendar, company profiles, and news.

- ✔ **IPO Interactive** (`www.fedfil.com/ipo/index.html`) shows Federal Filings Business News reports. These reports contain information on all IPOs that exceed $10 million in net proceeds. The reports include actual and pro forma financial results, operational histories, liquidity, and company backgrounds.

- ✔ **IPO Maven** (`www.IPOmaven.com`) is a great source for IPO news, information, and commentary.

- ✔ **IPO Monitor** (`www.ipomonitor.com`) is a fee-based notification service for information and events associated with IPOs. Subscriptions are $29 per month or $290 per year.

- ✔ **TechInvestor** (`www.techweb.com/investor/ipowatch/iposwatch.html`) lists technology-oriented IPOs and pending registrations.

- ✔ **The Online Investor** (`www.investhelp.com`) provides educational information and investing data. Updated daily, this site has weekly articles and special sections on stock splits, IPOs, stock buybacks, analysts' upgrades and downgrades, and more.

- ✔ **Yahoo! IPO News** (`biz.yahoo.com/reports/ipo.html`) is IPO news from Yahoo! (Yahoo! started as a type of topic-specific search engine, and has expanded into different areas such as the IPO News.)

Finding online brokers that specialize in IPOs

After researching IPOs, you may decide that you want a broker who specializes in this type of security. The Internet can assist you in locating the right broker. Here are a few examples:

✔ **InvestIN.com Securities Corporation** (investinIPOs.com) is an online brokerage that specializes in IPOs.

✔ **Schwab** (www.schwab.com) provides its best customers with offerings underwritten by Credit Suisse, First Boston, Hambrecht & Ouist, and J.P. Morgan Securities, Inc.

✔ **Wit Capital** (www.witcapital.com) provides offerings to customers on a first-come, first-served basis.

Including IPOs in mutual funds

Several large mutual funds include IPOs. However, participation in IPOs shouldn't be the only reason you purchase a mutual fund. Before making your investment decision, you still need to carefully read the fund's prospectus and compare it to other mutual funds and your overall financial objectives.

Here are a few examples of mutual funds that include IPOs:

✔ Govett Smaller Companies (GSCQX)

✔ Janus Olympus (JAOLX)

✔ PBHG Emerging Growth (PBEGX)

✔ USAA Aggressive Growth (USAUX)

✔ Warburg Pincus Post-Venture (WPVCX)

For more details, use the ticker symbol lookup feature at Morningstar (www.morningstar.net).

Be Your Own Broker with Direct Public Offerings (DPOs)

Historically, small companies have had a difficult time finding capital to expand their businesses. Traditional lenders are frequently unwilling to take risks with untried companies, venture capitalists negotiate tough deals that often force company founders out of key management roles, and traditional IPOs require a minimum of $15 million in annual revenue.

If you take an initial public offering (IPO) and cut out the underwriter, what you have left is a direct public offering (DPO). DPOs have been around for more than 20 years. For example, Ben & Jerry's used a DPO to raise capital for the ice cream company. However, the offering was limited to its home state of Vermont.

In October 1995, the SEC fueled DPOs with a ruling that makes electronic delivery of a prospectus okay. Consequently, companies can raise needed capital by selling their shares directly to the public via the Internet. These DPOs have the following advantages for small companies:

- **Cost and time savings:** The company saves thousands of dollars in underwriting expenses.

- **Regulation of Internet IPOs:** Issuers can file faster, turnaround times are quicker, filing is less expensive, fewer restrictions exist on the sales process, and issuers can announce planned offerings.

- **Management remains focused:** Management isn't drawn away from the company's day-to-day business needs and customers.

- **Investors can get in really early:** Investors have access to venture capital-types of investments.

- **No broker commissions:** Investors don't have to pay high broker commissions.

Recognizing the limitations of DPOs

Many companies are offering a DPO instead of an initial public offering (IPO). For many online investors, a DPO is the best way to get in on the ground floor and share in a company's success. Investors can purchase shares directly from the companies that they want to be part owners of. However, DPOs have some limitations:

- **Blue sky laws:** Issuing companies must be registered with the SEC and the states where they offer securities, but new legislation allows companies to use the Internet to present initial public offerings. This new legislation is inconsistent with regulations passed in 1911. The 1911 rule requires that issuers register in the states where they offer stocks, but the Internet has no boundaries and thus offers worldwide distribution of stock offerings. Does this mean that issuers don't have to register in each state that uses the Internet? Some issuers register in all 50 states before offering shares. However, one state, Pennsylvania, only requires companies to clearly indicate where they are registered and who may purchase securities.

- **Fraud and abuse:** Stock issues are highly regulated, but the Internet is an unregulated environment. The enforcement of registration issues on the Internet is keeping the SEC more than busy. The result may be fraudulent solicitations on the Internet.

Buying DPOs

DPO issues often open in a blaze of glory due to strong public interest. Then the share prices settle down to a consistent trading range. During the stock's initial period of volatility, the stock price may double or triple. Cashing in at this point can be very profitable and may compensate you for many of your earlier investment mistakes.

DPOs are speculative and definitely for aggressive investors. In other words, if you can't afford to lose all your investment, then you shouldn't be in this market. That said, even the most aggressive investors should only invest between 5 and 10 percent of their total portfolio in this type of financial asset.

To purchase shares, obtain a subscription agreement for the DPO. The subscription agreements are usually included in the last page of the prospectus. If you can't find the form, request one by e-mail or through the U.S. mail. Send the completed agreement and a check for the appropriate amount to the company. The company sends a confirmation letter within five days and the stock certificate within 30 days. (I suggest making a duplicate copy of your check and subscription agreement for your records and sending the originals by registered mail.)

Here are some online sources for DPOs:

- ✔ **Direct IPO** (www.directipo.com) provides investor resources, information about traditional IPOs and DPOs, an industry spotlight, an IPO contest, a newsroom, and more.

- ✔ **Internet Capital Exchange** (www.inetcapital.com) is designed to bring companies and investors together to generate funding capital and investment opportunities. Companies that are already public can allow their stock to be traded by investors using an interactive trading system.

- ✔ **SCOR-NET** (www.direct-stock-market.com) is a site for DPOs, quarterly filings, and trading.

- ✔ **The Direct Public Offering Council** (www.dpo-council.org) is a not-for-profit organization that hosts a forum for people to share information and knowledge about DPOs.

- ✔ **The Direct Stock Market** (www.dsm.com), shown in Figure 15-3, provides a central online location from which companies that are issuing DPOs can distribute their prospectuses and documents. This opportunity is ideal for companies that may not have many buyers and sellers actively trading their shares. The site is subject to regulatory approval.

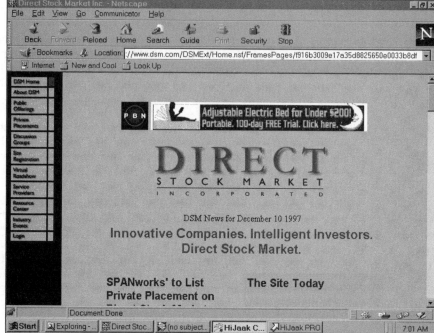

(Reprinted with the permission of Direct Stock Market.)

Figure 15-3:
The Direct
Stock
Market
provides
information
about
DPOs.

✔ **Virtual Wall Street** (www.virtualwallstreet.com) provides information about DPOs, financial links, and more.

✔ **WebIPO** (www.webipo.com) provides information for companies that want to go public via the Internet. The site provides articles about the components of an IPO, a database of recent IPOs, articles on personal finance, and more.

The investment analysis of a direct public offering is a challenge. Matthew Harris, at www.goharris.com/matt/dpo.htm, provides one way to analyze a DPO.

Figure 15-4 shows Netstock Direct (www.netstock.com), one of the best DPO sites on the Internet. Netstock Direct is an online source for direct investing, statistics, and materials related to direct stock plans. Netstock's search functions can assist you in creating a short list of DPO investment candidates.

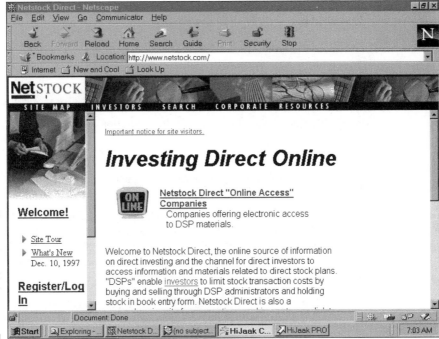

Figure 15-4:
Netstock
Direct is a
great
source for
DPOs and
information.

Buying Stocks Direct

The Securities and Exchange Commission eased regulations in 1994 so that companies can comfortably offer their shares directly to the public. This change has caused a small boom in the number of companies that allow investors to buy shares directly.

Sometimes direct purchase plans (DPPs) are called *no-load* stock plans. These plans allow you to join their dividend reinvestment plan without first purchasing a share through a broker. Some corporations with DPPs sell shares only to corporate customers, and others are open to all investors.

In the past, utilities were the main companies that had DPPs. In 1996, 150 companies sold their stock directly to the public. In 1997, more than 300 companies offered DPPs. In the coming years, as many as 1,500 companies may sell their stock directly to the public.

About one million individuals purchase their stocks directly. Minimum investments can be as small as $50 a month for IBM shares. Some of the DPPs include dividend reinvestment plans (DRIPs), tax-deferred IRA investments, and loans against stock holdings. A few companies even sell shares below market price. Currently, you can't purchase shares over the Internet, but that's expected to change soon.

The Internet provides many sources for DPP information and education. Here are a few examples:

- ✔ **Direct Purchase Plans** (cnnfn.com/yourmoney/9707/15/ yomo_direct) is an article from CNNfn about direct purchase plans.
- ✔ **Direct Stock Buying** (www.businessweek.com/1997/24/ b3531156.htm) is an excellent article on direct stock purchases.
- ✔ **Mike's Page** (mk.ml.org/noload) provides a list of 183 no-load stocks.

Buying that First DPP Share

Ford, IBM, British Telecommunications, and many other companies have direct purchase plans (DPPs). All you have to do is contact the firm via the Internet, telephone, or U.S. mail. Direct your request to the Investor Relations Department and ask whether they have a direct purchase plan and an application.

Complete the application form and include a check for your initial investment. Make a copy of these items for your records. Send the signed application and check to the company by registered mail.

In more than half of the DPPs, the minimum investment is $250 or less, and as little as $10 thereafter. The plans are designed for long-term investors who plan to hold their shares for at least three to five years. Processing your order is slower than going through a broker; it usually takes about a week. You can make subsequent stock purchases with cash payments and reinvested dividends.

However, purchasing DPPs is proof that there's no such thing as a free lunch, because these so-called no-load stocks are not cost-free. You still have to pay a few fees. You often pay a one-time enrollment fee of $5 to $15, a per-transaction fee of up to $10 plus $0.01 to $0.10 per share, and higher fees when you sell. Some plans charge an annual account management fee. To reinvest your dividend, you may have to pay up to $5 per quarter.

When comparing the fees of some DPPs to the low rates that online brokers charge (between $10 and $30 per transaction), you don't appear to be saving much by buying shares directly from the company. However, the SEC is continuing to relax its regulations about DPPs. Soon companies will be able to advertise their programs at their Web sites. As the market for DPPs heats up, fees are likely to decrease, and you may be able to charge your DPP purchase to your credit card via the Internet.

Profiting with Dividend Reinvestment Plans

Dividend reinvestment plans (DRIPs) are sometimes called *shareholder investment programs* (SIPs). These plans are an easy, low-cost way to purchase stocks and reinvest your dividend income. About 1,000 companies and closed-end funds sponsor DRIPs.

Most plans require you to purchase your first share through a broker, the National Association of Investors Corporation (NAIC), or some other method. A share purchased in a DRIP is like any other stock share. You have voting rights and stock splits, and dividends are taxed when you sell your shares.

Shares must be registered in your name. You can purchase subsequent shares directly from the company, often at discounted prices and with no broker commissions. Most plans allow investors to make voluntary payments to the DRIP to purchase more shares. In other words, the advantages of DRIPs include:

- No brokerage commissions and few fees for purchasing stock through the DRIP.

- Frequent discounts of 3 to 5 percent off the current stock price.

- Optional cash payment plans (OCPs). These plans are often part of DRIPs. Usually after the first dividend has been reinvested, the investor can send voluntary cash payments directly to the company to purchase more shares. Amounts can be as small as $10 to $25. (This option allows investors to own fractions of stocks.) For example, General Electric allows OCPs of $10 to $10,000 every month.

Many of the nation's premier corporations have DRIPs, including most of the companies in the Dow Jones Industrial Averages. Figure 15-5 shows InvestorGuide's page on DRIPs and DPPs (www.investorguide.com). This Web site has a public directory with links to the corporate home pages of many companies that have dividend reinvestment plans. For more information, contact each company you're interested in and ask for a DRIP prospectus. At the corporate home page, you can e-mail your request. If the company doesn't have a Web site, use Stock Smart, at www.stocksmart.com, to locate the corporation's address and telephone number.

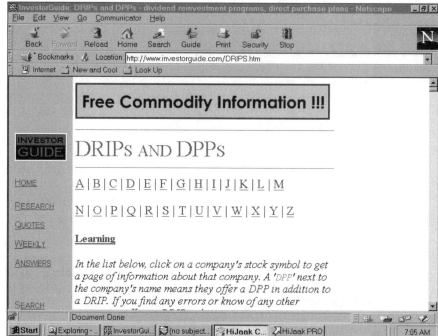

(Copyright © 1998 Web Finance, Inc.)

Figure 15-5: Investor Guide has a lengthy list of companies that offer DRIPs.

Additional features of DRIPs

One of the benefits of DRIPs is their (often free) certificate safekeeping service. This service eliminates the need for paying for a safe-deposit box and the possibility of your stock certificates becoming lost or stolen.

DRIPs often have gift-giving programs. For example, Texaco enables you to open an investor services plan in another person's name, and the company provides you with a gift certificate to give to the recipient.

Not all DRIPs are alike

Each company has its own plan. With some firms, you can pay for additional shares with cash; some allow partial redemption of shares; and some have termination fees. However, the plan may only purchase shares once a month, and if you want to sell your shares, completing the transaction may take five to ten days.

Some plans allow you to buy shares one at a time. However, some companies have a minimum purchase amount. For example, Bristol-Myers Squibb requires a minimum purchase of 50 shares. Bristol-Myers Squibb also charges a fee of 4 percent of the dollar amount of dividends being reinvested (a maximum of $5 per share).

In general, plans differ from one another in the following ways:

✔ Some companies allow (and some companies don't allow) the reinvestment of preferred dividends for common shares.

✔ Some companies allow partial reinvestment of dividends.

✔ The amount of optional cash payments (OCPs) varies from company to company.

✔ Fees for participating in the DRIP vary from company to company.

How to get your first DRIP share

Sometimes, getting started is the hardest part of investing. Many ways exist to go about getting your first share for a DRIP. Here are five different approaches — one of these methods may be right for you:

✔ **Find a brokerage that charges special rates for single shares:** Several brokerages charge special commission rates to current accountholders for the purchase of single shares. A.G. Edwards charges a flat 16 percent of the share price. Dean Witter charges a flat 10 percent of the share price.

✔ **Join a special investment club:** First Share Buying Club can assist you in getting your first share so that you can participate in a DRIP. Annual membership is $18 a year ($30 for two years). Members receive a handbook about DPPs and DRIPs, transferring shares, and the registration of shares.

For individuals who don't want to join the club, you can buy one share in one company for a flat fee of $20. If you want to purchase more than one share, becoming a member is more cost-effective. You can request any number of shares in any number of companies. For more information, call 800-683-0743.

✔ **Share the cost with a friend:** You can use a buddy system to reduce the cost of purchasing your first share. You and a friend pay the brokerage to purchase two shares. Have both shares registered to one person and join the company's DRIP. After you've joined, transfer one share to your friend and split the cost of the fees.

✔ **Join the NAIC:** The National Association of Investors Corporation (NAIC) enrolls people in any of more than 100 DRIPs via its Low Cost Investment Plan. The NAIC enrolls its members in a company for a $7 per company fee. Membership in the NAIC is $39 for individuals and $35 for an investment club plus $14 per member of the club. See the NAIC Web site at `www.better-investing.org` or telephone 801-583-6242 for details.

✔ **Use a deep-discount online broker:** Sometimes, the simplest way to purchase your first share is to go through a deep-discount broker. Online brokerage costs vary from free to $40. To participate in the DRIP, you need the stock registered in your name. To get the stock registered in your name (rather than in the brokerage's default street name), you may have to pay an additional fee.

Selecting the right DRIP

DRIPs have many advantages, but you shouldn't let one characteristic be your sole criterion for purchasing the stock. Regardless of how attractive the DRIP program is, you still need to make certain that the stock fits in with your overall investment strategy. In other words, don't select a stock just because it has a DRIP.

Here are two online resources for finding out more about dividend reinvestment plans:

✔ **DRIP Investor** (`www.dripinvestor.com`) is a guide to buying stocks without a broker by using dividend reinvestment plans.

✔ **Kiplinger Magazine** features an article titled "32 Stocks for Buy and Hold Investors" (`www.kiplinger.com/magazine/nov96/lifetab.html`). This article lists 32 companies that have dividend reinvestment plans. These companies have an additional benefit: They allow you to purchase shares directly from the firm. Buying direct means that you can see profits sooner because you don't have to pay brokerage fees.

Part IV
Making More Money on the Internet

The 5th Wave   By Rich Tennant

"I don't see it as a chart of a poorly performing stock as much as a sign to invest in lava lamps and portable televisions."

In this part . . .

The chapters in this part of the book show you how to monitor, buy, and sell securities online to increase your returns. You discover how electronic brokerages work and how you can open an account. You examine the differences between a full-service broker, a discount broker, and a deep-discount broker, and you find out how the right trading strategies can increase your profits. This part of the book also shows you how to use online and PC-based portfolio management programs to track your investments and how to get daily updates sent to your e-mailbox free of charge.

Chapter 16

Deep-Discount Brokers and Online Trading

. . . .

In This Chapter

▶ Checking out online brokerages

▶ Finding the type of brokerage that meets your needs

▶ Opening your electronic brokerage account

▶ Increasing your profits by choosing the right trading techniques

. . . .

*I*n this chapter, I show you how to save money on trades, gain unlimited control over your investments, and enter trades from your computer 24 hours a day, seven days a week. You just need to understand a few online trading basics and the risks that any investor faces.

This chapter describes three types of brokers: full-service, discount, and deep-discount. Each type of broker offers a different range of services. Internet deep-discount brokers are generally the least expensive, but they offer bare-bones services. However, not all brokers are alike. Occasionally, an inexpensive broker will cost you more money. For example, if you require real-time stock quotes and subscribe to an online service, the cost is about $30 per month. If you select a broker who may have a commission rate that is higher than some others but includes free online securities quotes, you may save money. This chapter describes some of the additional features of brokerages. This information can help you decide which brokerage is right for you.

Online trading accounts require you to complete an application form and to open and maintain a minimum cash account balance. While your electronic brokerage is processing your account (which takes two to three weeks), you can turn to this chapter to find out where you can practice trading online and how to increase your profits by using the right trading strategies.

Finding a Brokerage Firm

For each trade, you pay commissions ranging from a few dollars to hundreds of dollars per order. Commissions can take a large bite out of your profits. For example, assume that you invest $2,000 and pay a $200 commission to a full-service broker. Your securities must increase to $2,200 for you to break even. One way to avoid high commissions is to use a discount broker or a deep-discount broker.

A full-service broker researches many companies and securities, helps you organize your goals, and gives you advice on specific securities that match your financial goals. These firms often use a *commission grid* to calculate the fees they charge their customers. For example, if you purchase 10 shares of a stock that costs $47 per share, the commission may be $47 (a commission rate of 10 percent). If you purchase two shares of a stock that costs $75 per share, the commission may be $35 (a commission rate of about 23 percent).

All brokers physically handle your securities, maintain a history of your transactions, and calculate your gains (or losses). Additionally, they track how many shares you own, when the stock splits, and when dividends are paid.

Full-service brokers inform you of initial public offerings (IPOs), insider trading, and legal concerns about your investments. If you own stock in a firm that is a takeover target, a full-service broker notifies you and provides you with any relevant information regarding offers to buy your stock.

A discount broker offers no advice and conducts no research. The discount broker receives your telephone order and relays it to the firm's floor broker, who in turn contacts the individual who executes your order. The discount broker then confirms that your order has been completed.

Deep-discount brokers are electronic brokerages in every sense of the word; contact with a human broker is rare and may cost you more money. Deep-discount brokerages often start as subdivisions of discount or full-service brokerages. They may offer lower prices by automatically accepting touch-tone telephone orders. With the convenience and the popularity of the World Wide Web, many deep-discount brokers have expanded their services to accept Internet-based stock orders.

You can locate a broker via the World Wide Web. For a complete alphabetical list of licensed brokers, see the Web site at www.brokerlinks.com/brokers.html

Checking Out Prospective Brokers

The Securities Investor Protection Corporation (SIPC) insures brokerage accounts in a way that is similar to how the Federal Deposit Insurance Corporation (FDIC) insures bank accounts. Each customer's account is insured to $500,000, and some brokerages have additional insurance. If your brokerage firm goes belly-up, you're covered. However, if you make poor investment selections, you can lose all your money.

As an investor, you're wise to look into the background of a brokerage firm before investing. The Central Registration Depository (CRD) — a registration and licensing database used by regulators throughout the securities industry to collect data about securities firms and their brokers — is available at your state securities agency or the National Association of Securities Dealers (www.nasdr.com/2000.htm). Additionally, each month the New York Stock Exchange releases a disciplinary action list at www.nyse.com.

Your state securities regulator can tell you whether the broker you're considering is registered, and some state securities commissions provide cautionary lists at their Web sites. Good examples are at the Oklahoma Securities Commission site at www.state.ok.us/~osc and at the Illinois Secretary of State's Office at www.sos.state.il.us/pubs/securities/invguide/invguide.html.

Getting the Best Online Trading Services for Less

As I mention at the beginning of this chapter, no two brokerages are alike. Furthermore, individual brokerages may change their services and fees to keep pace with their competitors. To find the online broker that best meets your needs, you must investigate the prices, services, and features that various brokers offer.

Ameritrade is a good example of how quickly things change on the Internet. Until recently, Ameritrade didn't exist. This online brokerage came into being as a result of the merger of three former online brokers — Aufhauser, Ceres, and eBroker.

Trading online for $20 or less

Before 1975, the only type of stockbroker available was a full-service broker. All brokerages charged the same fees and commissions. Regulatory changes in 1975 allowed brokerage firms to start competing with one another on the basis of price, and the discount broker was born. Discount brokers' commissions were typically 50 to 75 percent lower than those of full-service brokers. This change helped make Fidelity, Charles Schwab, and Waterhouse Securities the leading discount brokers they are today.

The rapid growth of the Internet and more brokerage evolution has led to the deep-discount brokers. Generally, all Internet brokers can handle any type of basic transaction with a minimum of human contact. This evolution has lowered the cost of doing business and fueled a fierce price war. Many reputable online brokerages can complete your trade for $20 or less. Table 16-1 lists several examples of these deep-discount brokerages.

Table 16-1	You Can Trade Online for $20 or Less	
Brokerage Name	*Web Address*	*Commission Structure*
Ameritrade	www.ameritrade.com	$8 flat rate + $5 for limit orders
Burke, Christensen & Lewis	www.bclnet.com	$18 to 1,000 shares, + $0.02 thereafter; $13 market order to 1,000, + $0.02 thereafter
CompuTEL Securities	www.computel.com	$9 market orders of 1,000 to 5,000 shares; $14 market orders of less than 1,000; $19 limit orders; + $2.50 postage and handling
Datek Securities	www.datek.com	$9.99 to 5,000 shares
DLJDirect (Formerly PCFN)	www.dljdirect.com	$20 to 1,000 shares + $0.02 thereafter
Empire Financial Group	www.lowfees.com	$0 on at least 1,000 @$5; $15 on market orders less than 1,000 @$5; $20 on limit orders for NASDAQ, less than 5,000; $20 + $0.01 for limit orders over 5,000 shares
E*Trade	www.etrade.com	$14.95 market trades to 5,000, + $0.01 thereafter; $19.95 limit orders to 5,000, + $0.01 thereafter
Farsight Financial Services	www.farsight.com	$10 flat rate

Brokerage Name	Web Address	Commission Structure
Fidelity Investments	personal.fidelity.com	$14.95 for active traders to 5,000 shares + $0.03 thereafter; $19.95 for online traders to 1,000 shares, + $0.03 to 5,000 shares, over 5,000 shares + $0.02
ForbesNET	www.forbesnet.com	$12.95 for up to 5,000, + $0.01 thereafter
Freedom Investments	www.freedominvestments.com	$15 flat rate
Investex	www.investexpress.com	$13.95 market orders; $17.95 limit orders; $17.95 for up to 5,000, + $0.05 thereafter
Investrade Discount	www.investrade.com	$13.95 flat rate
J.B. Oxford & Company	www.jboxford.com	$15.00 up to 3,000 shares, + $0.01 thereafter
Pacific Brokerage Services	www.tradepbs.com	$15 flat rate (all market and limit orders)
ProTrade	www.protrade.com	$5 for 1,000 shares or more, market orders; $12 for less than 1,000 shares and limit orders
Quick & Reilly	www.quick-reilly.com	$14.95 market orders; $19.95 limit orders; + $0.02 for over 1,000 shares
Scottsdale Securities	www.scottrade.com	$9.00 flat rate
Stocks4Less	www.stocks4less.com	$10 market orders; $15 limit orders; + $2.50 postage and handling
SureTrade.com	www.suretrade.com	$7.95 flat rate
Trade Fast	www.tradefast.com	$15 minimum for market or limit orders + $0.03 per share
Trading Direct	www.tradingdirect.com	$9.95 for up to 5,000 shares, + $0.01 thereafter
Waterhouse Web Broker	www.webbroker.com	$12 for up to 5,000 shares, + $0.01 thereafter

Note: The brokerage commission structures listed in this table use notations like the following example: 0 on at least 1,000 @$5; $15 on market orders less than 1,000 @$5; $20 on limit orders for NASDAQ, less than 5,000; $20 + $0.01 for limit orders over 5,000 shares. Here's what this notation means:

✔ The commission fee is $0 on a minimum order of 1,000 shares that are priced at $5 or more. (Total cost $0.)

✔ The commission fee is $15 on *market orders* (instructions for the broker to immediately buy or sell a security for the best available price) of 1,000 shares that are priced at $5 or more. (Total cost $15.)

✔ The commission fee is $20 on *limit orders* (trading orders that specify a certain price at which the broker is to execute the order) for the NASDAQ (an automated nationwide communications network operated by the National Association of Securities Dealers that connects brokers and dealers in the over-the-counter market) of less than 5,000 shares. (Total cost $40.)

✔ The commission fee is $20 plus $0.01 (a penny) for limit orders of 5,000 shares or more. For example, if you want a limit order for 6,000 shares, the fee is $20 for 5,000 shares plus $10 for the quantity over 5,000 ($0.01 × 1,000) for a total cost of $30.

Finding online brokers with no or low initial account minimums

One of the things that many investors may find prohibitive about online trading is the initial minimum deposit required for opening a cash account. This requirement means that the broker already has your money when you request a trade. However, this requirement is changing, just like everything else on the Internet. Table 16-2 lists several online brokerages that offer cash accounts with no minimum deposit or a low minimum deposit.

Table 16-2   Minimum Amounts to Open Trading Accounts with Online Brokers

Online Brokerage	Web Address	Account Minimum
Burke, Christensen & Lewis	www.bclnet.com	$0
CompassWeb Brokerage	broker.compassweb.com	$0
DLJDirect (Formerly PCFN)	www.dljdirect.com	$0
Empire Financial Group	www.lowfees.com	$0
Investex	www.investexpress.com	$0

Online Brokerage	Web Address	Account Minimum
Muriel Siebert & Company	www.msiebert.com	$0
Quick & Reilly	www.quick-reilly.com	$0
SureTrade.com	www.suretrade.com	$0
Trade Fast	www.tradefast.com	$0
E*Trade	www.etrade.com	$1,000
American Express Financial Direct	www.americanexpress.com/direct	$2,000
Ameritrade	www.ameritrade.com	$2,000
Datek Securities	www.datek.com	$2,000
Investrade Discount	www.investrade.com	$2,000
ProTrade	www.protrade.com	$2,000
Waterhouse Web Broker	www.webbroker.com	$2,000

Checking Out Online Broker Special Features

Commission structures change radically from firm to firm. One reason for this wide range is that some Internet brokers include special or additional features. When deciding which broker is best for you, factoring in some or all of the features that I list in this section is wise.

First, consider whether each broker offers the following features in your cash account:

✔ Low minimum amount required to open an account

✔ Low monthly fees with minimum equity balance

✔ No additional charges for postage and handling

✔ A summary of cash balances

✔ A summary of order status

✔ A summary of your portfolio's value

✔ Confirmation of trades (via e-mail, phone, or U.S. mail)

✔ A historical review of your trading activities

✔ No charges for retirement account maintenance

✔ Consolidation of your money market, investments, checking, and savings accounts

When comparing brokers, consider whether each broker offers the following account features:

- ✔ Unlimited check-writing privileges
- ✔ Dividend collection and reinvestment
- ✔ Debit cards for ATM access
- ✔ Interest earned on cash balances
- ✔ Wire transfers accepted
- ✔ No IRA inactivity fees

You should ascertain which of the following types of investments the broker enables you to trade:

- ✔ Stocks (foreign or domestic)
- ✔ Options
- ✔ Bonds (corporate or agency)
- ✔ Treasury securities
- ✔ Zero coupon bonds
- ✔ Certificates of deposit
- ✔ Precious metals
- ✔ Mutual funds
- ✔ Investment trusts

Finally, you need to determine whether the brokerage offers the following analytical and research features:

- ✔ Real-time online quotes
- ✔ Reports on insider trading
- ✔ Economic forecasts
- ✔ Company profiles and breaking news
- ✔ Earnings forecasts
- ✔ End-of-the-day prices automatically sent to you

One feature that is of interest to frequent traders is real-time quotes. Some brokerage firms offer real-time quotes for free, other firms offer a limited number for free when you open an account or make a trade, and several firms charge $30 a month for nonprofessional, real-time quotes.

Table 16-3 shows a few examples of the features that online brokers offer. These additional benefits change regularly, so check at the online broker's Web site before you open an account.

Table 16-3 Additional Features That Online Brokers Offer

Online Brokerage	Web Address	Additional Benefits
Accutrade	www.accutrade.com	Market news, daily earnings, price charts, top performers, industry reports, and mutual fund news. Thomson MarketEdge Reports, delayed stock quotes, and real-time quotes for a low monthly fee. Free dividend reinvestment.
American Express Financial Direct	www.americanexpress.com/direct	Unlimited quotes, charts, news, S&P reports, and Zacks estimates.
CompassWeb Brokerage	broker.compassweb.com	Free investment services for visitors and members: delayed quotes, stock charts, research reports, market indexes, news, and more. For members: real-time quotes, company news, S&P research, Lipper Reports, Zacks Research.
CompuTEL Securities	www.computel.com	Research from Reuters, Inc., portfolio tracker, personalized market snapshot, charting, company news, historical company data, and delayed quotes.
Datek Securities	www.datek.com	Free unlimited real-time quotes, free news and charts, no commission on orders not executed in 60 seconds, free trade on your birthday (valid for one month following your birthday).
DLJDirect (Formerly PCFN)	www.dljdirect.com	Stock screens, fund screens, DLJ research, S&P research, Lipper Reports, Zacks Research, DLJ IPOs research.

(continued)

Table 16-3 *(continued)*

Online Brokerage	Web Address	Additional Benefits
E*Trade	www.etrade.com	Check-writing privileges, investing game, news, delayed quotes.
Fidelity Investments	personal.fidelity.com	News, quotes, research, interactive investment tools, and calculators. Can use Quicken to trade online.
Muriel Siebert & Company	www.msiebert.com	Free check-writing, no per check fees, free trades for referring customers, customized commission for active traders, $100 million account insurance, free dividend reinvestment.
Quick & Reilly	www.quick-reilly.com	$300 worth of research for free, database searches, stock screening, reports, real-time quotes, news, charts, and portfolio tracker.
Charles Schwab	www.eschwab.com	Free downloadable stock trading software, 100 free real-time quotes when you open an account, 100 free real-time quotes for each trade. Bonus offer: One company report at no charge, 60 minutes access to S&P Market Scope (Windows users only), one month Reuters Money Network Reports (Macintosh users only).
Stocks4Less	www.stocks4less.com	50 real-time quotes when you open an account, 50 free real-time quotes when you trade, unlimited historical charts and delayed quotes.
Waterhouse Web Broker	www.webbroker.com	Free check writing, ATM card, free dividend reinvestment, research, real-time quotes, news and charts, portfolio tracking, Zacks earnings estimates, and S&P stock reports.

Ratings of online brokers

Gomez Advisors (www.gomezadvisors.com) is a Boston-based independent rating agency that specializes in online investing. This firm has developed a quarterly Internet Broker Scorecard to help investors select the online broker that's right for them.

Online brokerage rankings are based on ease of use, customer confidence, on-site resources, relationship services, and overall cost. According to the Internet Broker Scorecard, the top five online brokerages are

1. PC Financial (www.pcfn.com), which is now called DLJ Direct (www.dljdirect.com)

2. eSchwab (www.eschwab.com)

3. E*Trade (www.etrade.com)

4. Datek (www.datek.com)

5. CompuTEL (www.computel.com)

Deep-discount brokers offer investors more power over their portfolios and lower transaction fees. Limitations of online brokerages are that your broker may not protect you from speculating with your life savings. You must take responsibility for analyzing your financial goals, creating a plan to achieve those goals, and building (as risk-free and diversified as possible) a portfolio to reach those goals. You have to be disciplined and able to take responsibility for your own trading successes and mistakes.

How to Open Your Online Brokerage Account

Internet brokerage firms are basically cash-and-carry enterprises. They all require investors to open an account before trading, a process that takes from two to three weeks to complete. Account minimums vary from $1,000 to $10,000.

When you place an order, your Internet broker withdraws money from your cash account to cover your trade. If you sell stock or receive a dividend, the Internet broker adds money to your cash account. If you develop a good history, your Internet broker may allow you to place trades without funds in your cash account if you settle within three days.

Is online trading accurate?

Over the last several years, Internet brokerages have maintained a good record of placing and confirming orders. That is, about the same number of online orders are lost or traded incorrectly as are telephone orders.

All Internet brokers require that you complete an application form that includes your name, address, social security number, work history, and a certified check or money order for the minimum amount needed to open an account. Some brokers accept wire transfers or securities of equal value. All brokerages are required by law to have your signature on file. Figure 16-1 shows the online application form for CompuTEL Securities (www.computel.com).

To speed up the application process, you can complete application forms online or fax them to the Internet broker. You must then follow up by sending the completed, written, and signed forms via U.S. mail within 15 days, or the account is canceled.

The Internet broker then verifies all the information on the form and opens your account. Investors receive a personal identification number (PIN) by mail. After you receive your PIN, you're ready to begin trading.

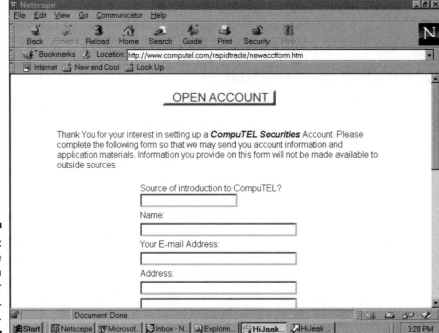

Figure 16-1:
The online application form for CompuTEL Securities.

(Reprinted with permission of Thomas F. White & Co., Inc.)

Practicing Online Before You Begin Trading

When you trade online, you basically do the same work your stockbroker does after you place a telephone order. The EduStock Web site at `portia.advanced.org/3088/simulation/simulation.html` provides a stock trading simulation to help you understand how to place an online trade. The site also includes a research center with a company symbol lookup to verify the stock market symbol of the company you're trading. You can also obtain delayed (20-minute) stock quotes, P/E ratios, and other investor-related information.

EduStock can assist you in discovering how to execute trades online. The program is valuable because you can make mistakes without losing money.

When practicing with the EduStock simulation, you need to create an account and login name. To purchase stocks, select the stock symbols from the symbol lookup list. Enter the number of shares you want to purchase in the *Number of Stocks* field. Click on Buy, and if you have enough funds in your hypothetical cash account, the transaction is successful. If you don't have enough funds, an error message appears.

To sell stocks, select the stock symbol from the drop-down menu. Enter the number of shares you want to sell in the *Number of Shares* field and then click on Sell.

Increasing Profits with Simple Order Specification Techniques

In the past, brokers recommended the order specifications for your stock transactions and confirmed that your transaction was completed. Specifying security execution orders was one of the expert services that brokers used to justify their fees. Order specifications define how your request is completed. One type of order specification is called a *day order*. Day orders are good only on the day you place the order.

Another type of order is the Good Till Canceled (GTC) order. The investor decides when the order expires but is uncertain about the order being executed. In other words, if no one in the market takes the order within the specified time (which can be anywhere from several hours to several days), the order is canceled. For example, an investor wants to buy a certain company's shares, but not until the shares a few dollars cheaper. The investor specifies a GTC order and determines when the order will expire. If the company's shares reach the predetermined limit (today, tomorrow, or next year), the order is filled.

Figure 16-2 shows an online order form from SureTrade.com (`www.suretrade.com/QRS/homeOUT.html`). Trading online means that you are now in charge of specifying your stock order. Knowing how to designate the terms of your order can increase your profits.

For example, using a *limit order* when purchasing or selling *odd lots* (less than 100 shares of any one stock) can increase your profits. Odd lots rarely get the best price because they must be bundled with other orders. The following example shows how you can get, if not the best price, at least a better price by using a limit order.

Assume that the stock you want is offered by the specialist (someone who specializes in selling a certain firm's stock) at $25.60 (the asking price), and the bid price is $25. You should place a *limit order* of $25.25 so that you have a chance of paying less than the market order price of $25.60.

Someone other than the specialist is likely to take this order ($25.25) because it's more than the specialist's bid price of $25. (They get a better deal.)

Figure 16-2: SureTrade.com online order form.

Note: This strategy only works if a $0.25 or greater spread exists between the bid and asking price.

Here are the four most popular ways to specify your stock order:

- ✔ **Limit orders:** Any order in which the buyer or seller specifies the top price he or she is willing to pay. For sell orders, the "limit" specified is the minimum price at which the investor is willing to sell. For buy orders, the limit is the maximum price the investor is willing to pay.

- ✔ **Market orders:** Any order (buy or sell) to be executed immediately at the "best effort" price available. In other words, the investor wants to buy or sell a stated number of shares at the best price at the time the order is placed.

- ✔ **Stop:** After a security reaches the price set by the investor, the order becomes active. When the order is activated, that investor is guaranteed that the order will be executed. However, the investor isn't guaranteed the execution price.

- ✔ **Stop-limit orders:** After a security reaches the investor's predetermined price, the order is activated. The order can only be executed at the set price or better, so the order may not be completed.

Chapter 17

Online Portfolio Tracking

. . . .

In This Chapter

▶ Using Web-based tools to track your investments

▶ Understanding the advantages of using special PC software to track your investments

▶ Letting your online broker update your portfolio

▶ Automatically receiving end-of-the-day stock prices and alerts

. . . .

*P*ortfolio management may sound like busywork, but knowing how much you own in cash, stocks, bonds, and other investments is important. Without portfolio management, how can you determine whether your returns are meeting your financial requirements? Are you missing opportunities by not buying or selling securities at the right time?

In this chapter, I offer an overview of the reasons why portfolio management is important to your financial future. I also outline the data you should use to determine the performance of your investments. I introduce you to three types of portfolio management programs: Web-based programs, PC-based programs, and portfolio management programs with your electronic broker.

I also discuss the next big thing: performing your online banking, managing your portfolio, and trading online without changing software programs. It's quick, it's easy, and you can get started today. Some banks and brokerages enable you to perform these tasks using Microsoft Money or Quicken, making it easier than ever before to create and maximize wealth via the Internet.

Why Manage Your Investments?

You may select the best investments, but if you don't have a way to track your gains and losses, you can lose time and money. Good record-keeping is invaluable for calculating your taxes, preparing for retirement or estate planning, and taking advantage of opportunities to increase your personal wealth.

Sources on the Internet can assist you in keeping careful records of every stock, mutual fund, bond, and money market security you own. Setup time can be as little as ten minutes. You can update and monitor your portfolio once a week or once a month. Your investments can be in one portfolio (for example, your retirement fund) or many (say, your retirement fund, an emergency fund, and your children's college fund). You can also track investments that you wish you owned or that you're considering for investment.

The Internet offers programs that automatically update your portfolio with daily price changes and then re-tally your portfolio's value. To sum up, many portfolio management programs can perform the following tasks:

✔ Help you determine how much you own in cash, stocks, and bonds

✔ Show you how these investments line up with your asset allocation targets

✔ Indicate what returns (capital gains or losses) you're receiving

✔ Compare returns to your financial requirements

✔ Alert you that securities are at the prices at which you want to buy (or sell)

How often do you need to monitor your investments? Once every two or three days is a little aggressive, once a week is average, and some investments only require monitoring once a month.

Tracking the Right Information

If you own more than one investment, you probably want to compare their performance. The more investments you have, the harder this task is. Many novice investors find it difficult to determine whether they're making money, losing money, or just breaking even. To determine how your investments are performing, you need to look at the following data:

✔ **52 week high and low:** The highest and lowest selling price in the previous 365 days

✔ **Dividend:** The annual per-share amount of cash payments made to stockholders of the corporations

✔ **Dividend yield percent:** The total amount of the dividend paid in the last 12 months divided by the closing price (the price at which the last trade of the day was made)

✔ **Growth rate:** How much the dividend increases from one fiscal year to the next

✔ **P/E ratio:** The ratio of the closing price to the last 12 months' earnings per share

✔ **Volume:** The number of shares traded in one day

✔ **High, low, close:** Highest selling price of the day, lowest selling price of the day, and closing selling price

✔ **Net change:** The difference between the day's closing price and the previous day's closing price

You can compare these amounts and ratios to the performance of your other investments, the firm's previous performance, the industry, and the market indexes (for example, the S&P 500).

If you own several securities, how do you keep track of all this data? Once again, the Internet provides an answer. The Internet has hundreds of Web- and PC-based portfolio management programs that are just waiting to assist you. Some of them are free, others are fee-based, and some are automatically set up for you by your online broker.

Your Portfolio Management Options

The Internet offers three types of portfolio management programs:

✔ **Web-based portfolio management programs:** Online portfolio management programs are generally sponsored by investor compilation sites such as Thomson Investors Network (www.thomsoninvest.net). These programs usually don't require any software downloading, and they constantly update your portfolio. Limitations of these programs are that they don't offer many features, such as customized graphs or charts, fundamental analysis, or tax planning tools.

✔ **PC-based portfolio management programs:** You generally perform PC-based portfolio management with software programs downloaded from the Internet. These programs usually have more choices and functions than Web-based portfolio management programs. A good example of a PC-based portfolio management program is StockTracker Lite, which you can find at www.stockcenter.com. Limitations of this approach are that you must download the proprietary software and you may have to *import* (transfer data from one source to another) stock quotes.

> ✔ **Portfolio management with your online broker:** Portfolio management with your online trader is automatic. Your online broker knows what you traded, so the brokerage can automatically update your portfolio. A good example of an online brokerage with portfolio management features is CompuTEL at `www.computel.com`. The advantages of using your broker's portfolio management system are that you don't have to manually add transactions and your portfolio always reflects the current value of your investments.

In the following sections, I offer examples that detail the features and functions of these three types of portfolio management programs.

Using Web-Based Portfolio Management Programs

Many Web sites provide online portfolio management services. Web-based portfolio managers offer tools that can help you make better investment decisions and thus increase your capital gains. Each Web-based portfolio management program offers something different. In the following sections, I describe just a few examples.

Don't let the fascination of having your portfolio online tempt you into over-trading (buying or selling) your investments.

Thomson Investors Network

Thomson Investors Network (`www.thomsoninvest.net`) provides free and fee-based services. Registered guests can use the site's free quote server. You can also use portfolio-tracking services with end-of-the-day quotes sent to your e-mailbox, and you can have limited access to other site services. Guests can purchase company and mutual fund reports on a pay-per-view basis ($2.50 for a company report and $1.50 for a mutual fund report) or a pay-per-day basis.

The Web site is a subsidiary of Thomson Financial Services and includes a wide variety of high-quality investment research, screening tools, and news services (S&P Comstock, CDA/Wiesenberger, First Call, Institutional Shareholder Services, and more).

Figure 17-1 shows the Thomson MarketEdge Portfolio Tracker, which allows up to ten securities in one portfolio. The portfolio starts with "Today's Market Performance," which includes the last traded price (delayed 20 minutes), today's change, high and low prices, volume, and news and alerts.

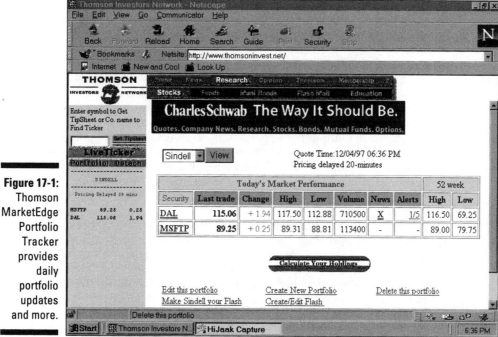

(Copyright © 1998 Thomson Investors Network.)

Figure 17-1: Thomson MarketEdge Portfolio Tracker provides daily portfolio updates and more.

An X in the news box next to a security means that breaking news exists about your investment. Click on the X, and the news page appears. Articles include company news, changes in credit ratings, and other pertinent information about your investment.

The alert box next to your security shows the number of changes your investment has recently undergone. Click on the alert box, and the next page shows the date, the name of the security and its ticker symbol, and the alert type. Alerts include notices about earnings, institutional holdings, price changes, insider trading, ratio changes, and SEC filings. Alerts for mutual funds include risk and standard deviation changes, as well as asset allocation, fee, and management changes.

Annual information includes each security's 52-week high and low selling price. The section marked "Your Holdings" shows the number of shares you own, your purchase price (the amounts you entered when you set up the portfolio), and the current value of your holdings. This program provides the following key portfolio management information:

✔ Capital gains (or losses) and percentage of return

✔ Your portfolio's original and current values

✔ The total dollar value and percentage of your portfolio's return

Thomson MarketEdge Portfolio Tracker allows you to edit your portfolio, create a new portfolio, or delete the portfolio. If you decide to edit your portfolio, you can add new securities or edit the values for shares and your purchase price.

Membership is $9.95 per month or $89.95 per year for unlimited access. This access includes a "live ticker" that you can detach and use on your computer's desktop for real-time indexes and delayed stock quotes. Other membership services include flash mail (reports sent directly to your e-mailbox), 25 mutual fund reports and 25 company reports per month, company and mutual fund screening tools, and intraday updates of market news and analyses. Municipal bond news, bulletin boards, chats with experts, and an education center are also included. Additional company reports are $2.50, and additional mutual fund reports are $1.50.

One limitation of the Thomson MarketEdge Portfolio Tracker is that you can't download portfolio data to a spreadsheet or to the Quicken software program for additional analyses. (I discuss Quicken in Chapter 5 and later in this chapter, in the section "Using Quicken to Manage Your Portfolio.") Moreover, the program doesn't provide any fundamental analysis or graphing features, and you have to add all stock splits manually.

Stockpoint Portfolio Management

Stockpoint Portfolio Management (www.stockpoint.com) provides a personal portfolio, stock news, and end-of-the-day e-mail portfolio updates. The portfolio management program requires your free registration. Stockpoint Portfolio Management allows you to download current share options in a Quicken software format and handles up to 50 U.S. and Canadian stocks, mutual funds, and stock indexes (so that you can compare the performance of your investment selections). To access the portfolio management Web page from the Stockpoint home page, click on Portfolio.

As shown in Figure 17-2, this portfolio management program includes last traded price, each day's price changes, the percentage of each day's price changes, and the current value of each holding. It calculates the capital gains and losses and the percentage of capital gains and losses from the initial purchase price that you entered when you set up the portfolio. The program provides information about volume and moving averages of several securities at once. You can click on the Export button to download all the portfolio information to Quicken software for additional analysis.

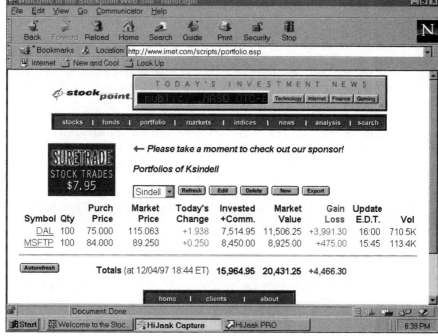

Figure 17-2:
Stockpoint's
portfolio
management
program
allows you
to easily
track your
investments.

(Reprinted with permission of Stockpoint.)

Limitations of Stockpoint's portfolio management program are that it doesn't provide any fundamental analysis or graphing and you must add all stock splits manually.

Money Talks Portfolio Tracker

Money Talks (www.talks.com) is a personal investment magazine that has expanded to the Internet. The electronic magazine has a section called Money Manager and requires your free registration. Money Manager provides free access to many Internet tools and databases. Money Talks includes historical quotes, graphs, market information, statistics, and indexes. One special feature is the IPO (initial public offering) database, which provides access to in-depth IPO information, company calendars of the latest filings, registrations, pricing, and withdrawals or postponements. Additional information in the "What's New" section offers access to daily company, industry, and sector analyses.

The Money Talks Portfolio Tracker program is designed to keep you on top of your investments. At the Money Talks home page, click on Portfolio Tracker.

Figure 17-3 shows the free Portfolio Tracker program, which can help you track as many as ten personalized portfolios with up to 30 securities in each. Enter the symbols of the stocks, mutual funds, and options you want to track and how many shares you own. You can connect to Portfolio Tracker whenever you want for your latest portfolio update (quotes are delayed at least 20 minutes). If you want more information about how your portfolio is faring, the program delivers statistics about your portfolio to your e-mailbox up to twice a day.

The Wall Street Journal Interactive Edition

The Wall Street Journal Interactive Edition (`www.wsj.com`) offers easy access to your portfolio. Click on the top-right corner of almost any page of the Interactive Edition to access the portfolio program. You can establish five portfolios with as many as 30 securities in each one. Delayed stock prices constantly update the portfolio, which also shows percentage change and gain/loss information.

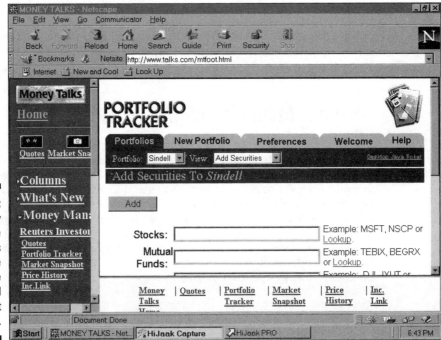

Figure 17-3: The Money Talks site makes its magazine interactive and helpful to Internet users.

The grid displays an issue-by-issue breakdown of your investments. Total value (along with your portfolio's current gain/loss and percentage of change) is included at the top of the grid, along with the current value of the Dow Jones Industrial Average. You can download investment information to your favorite spreadsheet program.

If news is available for any company in your portfolio, a flag appears next to the company's name. To access the news, click on the flag. Links to detailed quotes and mutual fund snapshots are also available. These links provide additional performance and background information.

You can download the portfolio by using either comma-delimited text or plain text. To import data to your spreadsheet program, use the comma-delimited format. Use your browser to save the file with .cvs as the file's extension — for example, Stocks.cvs. You can open the file by using any spreadsheet program. If you want to paste the portfolio information into a word-processing file, download it as a plain text (.txt) file — for example, Stocks.txt. The plain text format is best used with a fixed-width font, such as Courier.

Like many Web-based portfolio management programs, this program doesn't provide any graphs or charts of your portfolio. However, you can perform fundamental analysis by using a spreadsheet program, downloaded portfolio data, and additional information.

Yahoo! Portfolio Management

Yahoo! now has a personalized portfolio program (edit.my.yahoo.com/config). To create portfolios, just enter a portfolio name and then add the ticker symbols of your investments, separated by commas. You can also enter indexes like the S&P 500 (SPX) for comparison purposes. You can use the same ticker symbol to record separate purchases. You can enter or edit the number of shares or purchase prices by clicking on the "Enter More Info" button at the bottom of the page.

Figure 17-4 shows the portfolio management program. Quotes are delayed by 15 minutes for NASDAQ and 20 minutes for other exchanges. Portfolio management information includes company ticker symbol, price at the last trade, change, volume, number of shares held, the total value of the issue, dollar and percentage of change between the purchase price and the current value, amount paid per share, and dollar and percentage of capital gain or loss.

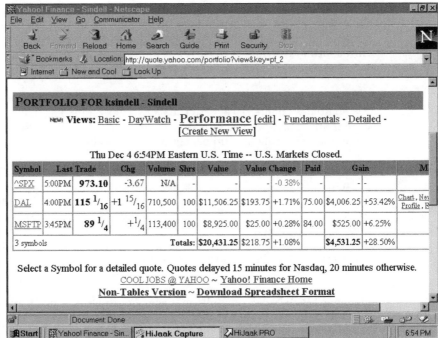

Figure 17-4:
Your Yahoo!
provides
portfolio
management
with charts
and data
you can
download
to your
spreadsheet.

The program provides charts, news, research, SEC filings data, and related information. Recent headlines that link to news stories about your portfolio investments are at the bottom of the page. You can get your information by signing in on any computer (and use the sign-out feature to make certain that others can't pry).

You can select a non-table version of the portfolio's data, choose to have all portfolio data downloaded to a spreadsheet, and retrieve detailed quotes for each investment. You can customize the portfolio by deciding to sort information alphabetically, use a small font, or display the portfolio by using detailed quote information rather than basic quote data.

Detailed quote information includes last trade (date and time), change (dollars and percent), previous closing price, volume, the day's price range, 52-week range, and bid, ask, and open prices. Also included are ex-dividend dates, earnings per share, P/E (price-earnings ratio), last dividend per share amount, and yield. Charts of the security's price for the last three months, year, two years, five years, and maximum number of years are available.

Other Online Portfolio Tracking Programs

Moneynet (www.moneynet.com) is a Reuters-sponsored investment supersite that has a free, easy-to-use, Web-based portfolio management program called Portfolio Tracker. This program can create up to ten customized portfolios for as many as 30 stocks, mutual funds, and options in each portfolio. The easy-to-read grid includes security symbol, company name, price or NAV (Net Asset Value of a mutual fund), volume, high, low, and date/time stamp.

At the Reuters Moneynet home page, click on Portfolio Tracker. To create a portfolio, click on Add Securities, enter a portfolio name or multiple portfolio names, and then add investments and the number of shares (optional). After you build a portfolio, the program automatically monitors the market for you.

Alerts include e-mails about current market value and market information. You can select notifications for up to twice a day, weekly, monthly, or quarterly. Click on the investment name, and a Quote Detail Report appears that includes 52-week high/low, P/E ratio, EPS (earnings per share) information, and more.

Money Online's Portfolio Tracker (cgi.pathfinder.com) offers a service that allows you to maintain your investment portfolio online and to track your holdings in any 30 U.S.-traded stocks or mutual funds. Current prices are continuously updated. Click on Build My Own Portfolio to create your portfolio. Money Online's Portfolio Tracker is divided into columns that show the ticker symbol, company name, shares owned, current price, purchase price, current value, the net gain or loss of each issue, and the total value of the portfolio.

Philadelphia Online is the Web site of *The Philadelphia Inquirer* and *Philadelphia Daily News* (business.phillynews.com/portfolio). In addition to a portfolio tracker, the site provides daily news updates; a searchable database of the 300 largest publicly traded corporations; quotes; charts; and breaking news for stocks, bonds, and mutual funds provided by Data Broadcasting Corporation. This site also includes daily rates on auto loans, mortgages, consumer loans, certificates of deposit (CDs), and money market accounts.

The Washington Post offers a free personal portfolio when you access its Web page at www.washingtonpost.com/wp-srv/business/longterm/stocks/stocks.htm. This portfolio management program allows you to track from one to four portfolios with up to ten stocks or mutual funds in each. To create a portfolio, just click on Edit Portfolio, and a form appears. Enter the name of the portfolio, each investment's ticker symbol, purchase price, number of shares, purchase date, and broker's commission (in dollars and cents, without the dollar sign). Space is available for you to make notes to yourself (sell price, sell date, or other targets). To complete the process, save your changes.

The portfolio is updated continuously. To check how your investments have changed, click on the Calculate Value or Current Price buttons. Click on Edit Portfolio to make additions or deletions. Data Broadcasting Corporation provides stock and market data.

To ensure your privacy, all data is stored on your hard drive and updated when you log on. A limitation of this approach is that you can't get information about your portfolio if you log on from another computer.

The site provides a portfolio FAQ (frequently asked questions) page for additional information. This page is helpful if you're uncertain about the meaning of any of the column headings and the format used (for example, how to enter the number of shares if you're selling short).

Using PC-Based Portfolio Management Software

If you want more analysis, including graphs of your investments' performance, tax data, and price and volume alerts, you may want to consider a PC-based portfolio manager (a software program that operates on your PC). For example, you can select Money 98 or Quicken (which you may already use for your online banking), shareware, or free Internet programs. In the following sections, I describe a few examples of PC-based portfolio management programs.

StockTracker

StockTracker is free, downloadable software available at www.stockcenter.com. You need to register and download the software (downloading takes about five minutes). Figure 17-5 shows the download site of this program at www.stockcenter.com/download.htm.

StockTracker automatically updates securities prices, values the portfolio, and provides price alerts that you predetermine. The program is connected to the Internet and has access to all the principal U.S. and Canadian markets. You can create up to 12 portfolios. You can also save intraday pricing data and build charts while the program constantly updates your portfolio.

A severe limitation of StockTracker is that users need to open a Wall Street Access Account, with which the firm trades stocks, options, and bonds. The minimum to open an account is $10,000. Placing an order with a trader averages $45. Trades placed electronically average $25.

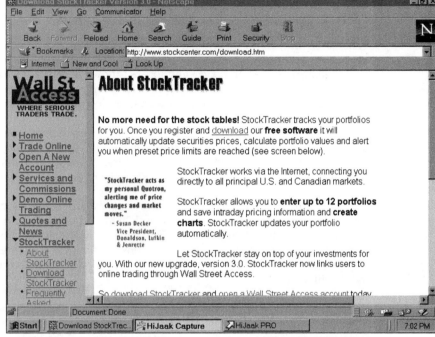

(Reprinted with permission of Wall Street Access.)

Figure 17-5:
StockTracker
portfolio
management
software
provides
continuous
updates of
your
investments.

Inside Track Lite

MicroQuest develops investment tracking and analysis software. Downloadable "Lite" editions are available free but require a subscription to one of MicroQuest's data providers. The Lite edition of MicroQuest's Inside Track software can track up to 100 securities (stocks, bonds, or mutual funds) and up to 50 market indexes.

Figure 17-6 shows the download site for Inside Track Lite (www.quote.com/info/microquest/liteinst.html). Inside Track Lite is an offline application that requires a subscription to PC Quote to obtain late-breaking market information via the Internet. Security for your investments is ensured because all information stays on your hard drive, not a server.

The program connects to the Internet by using PC Quote's free MarketSmart with your user ID and password (which you receive with your free registration). All price quotes are delayed 15 minutes. For real-time stock quotes, you need to subscribe to PC Quote for around $11.95 per month.

You can use the program's Quick Pick page to specify which securities you want to track. Start by using the Quick Pick page to enter a security. Enter the ticker symbol and company description. Click on the Get It button, and a page appears with the latest pricing data; the last 30 days' high, low, and close; and volume data displayed on a chart, as well as the latest news published on the security. If you want to add more securities, just click on the Add button.

Quick View allows you to sort Quick Pick data in 16 different ways. The largest gainers (shown in black) and losers (shown in red) show the dollar and percentage of change. If articles or wire service news is available on the company, you see a news icon. Click on a news icon for the entire story.

Double-clicking on a security in Quick View brings up a detail page that shows the latest pricing data (change, high/ask, low/bid, current volume, share earnings, 52-week high and low, volatility, P/E ratio, and an intraday trading chart).

Clicking on the History button shows the security's high, low, close, and volume for the last 30 days, 30 weeks, and 30 months. The Get Price History option instantly downloads one year's worth of historical data. You can also compare the investment performance to one of 50 indexes. Dividend information and dates, average trading volume, and total shares outstanding data are also included.

The Market Value feature calculates the value of your portfolio based on the latest prices. You can determine how well you did last month, last year, year to date, or any date range. The percentage of gain and the total dollar amount are automatically calculated.

Breakpoints show when you've reached your predetermined objectives. Breakpoints can be for low price or low percentage, high price or high percentage, and trading volume.

MarketSmart provides a ticker symbol lookup. You can also look up companies that have changed their names or ticker symbols, companies that have declared stock splits, new initial public offerings, the top ten best performing stocks, the ten worst performing stocks, and a glossary.

PointCast

Figure 17-7 shows the guided tour and download page for PointCast, a free, downloadable, real-time stock and news service. (The PointCast home page is at www.pointcast.com.) When your desktop computer isn't in use, the screen saver function brings up the PointCast program. You can customize the screen to view news and weather topics that interest you. More important, you can personalize the program so that you see real-time stock quotes for the investments in your portfolio. PointCast requires an Internet connection and plenty of memory. (The program is large, about 1MB.)

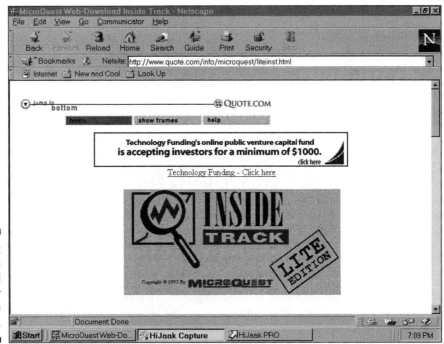

Figure 17-6:
The download site for Inside Track Lite.

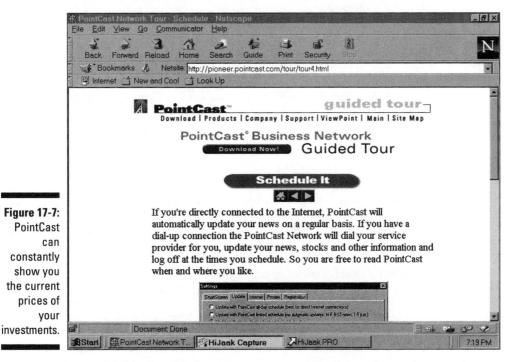

Figure 17-7:
PointCast can constantly show you the current prices of your investments.

PointCast also offers a free evaluation copy of a downloadable portfolio management program called IIDBS Portfolio Excel Spreadsheet and DLL (`iidbs.com/portfolio`). The portfolio management program requires a PC running the Windows 95 or NT operating systems, a connection to the Internet, and the Office 97 version of Microsoft Excel. The program pulls portfolio values directly from the Internet.

Using Online Brokerage-Based Portfolio Management Tools

You have to manually update Web-based portfolio management programs when you make a trade. You must account for what you bought, what you sold, and any commissions you paid. For active traders, this task can be time-consuming.

Some online brokers provide portfolio management services for their clients and guests. For example, Salomon Smith Barney (`www.smithbarney.com`) provides a free Watch List so that guests can monitor their investments. Prices and other data are delayed for at least 20 minutes (while U.S. securities markets are open) for stocks only. All other prices and NAVs (net asset values of mutual funds) reflect the previous day's closing prices. (It warns that all data is for informational purposes only and should not be used to make a decision to buy or sell a security or mutual fund.)

The Salomon Smith Barney Watch List requires your free registration. At its home page, click on the link watch list. The Watch List program allows you to create a list of up to 20 securities that you want to monitor. Enter the ticker symbol and the quantity you own (or wish you owned). The program provides a symbol lookup if you're uncertain about the ticker symbol. You can sort the investments by name, value, or latest news. Click on the Save Changes icon at the bottom of the page when you are done.

Figure 17-8 shows the Watch List program, which includes the ticker symbol of the investment, the company name, quantity owned, current price, dollar amount of change, date of change, and the current value of your holdings. If icons appear next to the security, you can access pricing charts, company news, and Salomon Smith Barney Research. The bottom of the portfolio grid shows the total value of the Watch List.

The Pricing Chart shows the closing price and volume of the security for the last year. Other charts show the monthly pricing over the last 36 months and the monthly volume of the security. Company data includes closing price and net change, day high and low, volume and average volume, 52-week high plus the date of that high, 52-week low plus the date of that low, last dividend and date paid, the industry's average dividend and yield, 12-month EPS and date, P/E ratio and beta factor, number of shares

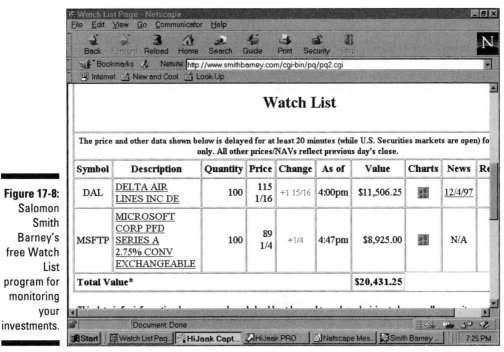

Figure 17-8:
Salomon
Smith
Barney's
free Watch
List
program for
monitoring
your
investments.

(Courtesy of Salomon Smith Barney.)

outstanding, market value of the shares, percentage of institutional holdings, number of institutions, and primary market (for example, NYSE). The
pricing chart also indicates whether the security is a component of an index
(for example, the Dow Jones Industrial Average).

News Headlines indicates the date, source, and nature of the most recent
company news. Complete articles are available with Salomon Smith Barney's
premium service.

Research includes analyst evaluations, Fact Sheets, information about
management changes, and earnings estimates. Research reports are available with Salomon Smith Barney's premium service. Premium service has a
60-day free trial and is $8.95 per month.

Using Quicken to Manage Your Portfolio

Quicken Deluxe 98 for Windows has a new feature called Online Investment
Tracking. This feature connects investors to brokerage and mutual fund
account information provided by participating electronic brokers and
financial institutions.

The portfolio management program uses the Open Financial Exchange Server software, which was developed by Microsoft, Intuit, and CheckFree. Currently Open Financial Exchange supports a wide range of consumer and small business needs with electronic bill paying, banking, bill presentment, and investments, including stocks, bonds, and mutual funds. Figure 17-9 shows Quicken 98's home page (`www.intuit.com/quicken98`). This Web site shows the benefits of online investment tracking.

Quicken Deluxe 98 with Online Investment Tracking currently has nine participating brokerages and financial institutions. Table 17-1 lists the names and Internet addresses of these firms. Quicken's management expects other financial institutions that use the Open Financial Exchange Server to join this new online portfolio tracking program.

Table 17-1	Firms That Support Quicken Online Tracking
Brokerage or Financial Institution	*Internet Address*
Accutrade	`www.accutrade.com`
American Century Investments	`www.americancentury.com`
Ameritrade	`www.ameritrade.com`
Charles Schwab & Co.	`www.eschwab.com`
DLJdirect, Inc.	`www.dljdirect.com`
E*Trade Securities, Inc.	`www.etrade.com`
Fidelity Investments	`www.fidelity.com`
Smith Barney	`www.smithbarney.com`
Waterhouse Securities	`www.webbroker.com`

The service delivers financial information directly from the Internet into Quicken Deluxe 98. You can retrieve current balances, transactions, and holdings from your investment accounts (which may be the ultimate in portfolio tracking). Additionally, this program allows financial institutions to offer you the capability to place trades via links to their Web sites through Quicken Deluxe 98.

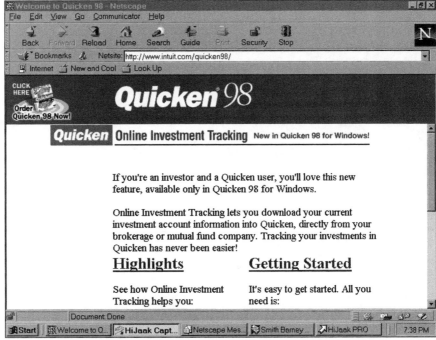

Figure 17-9:
The
Quicken 98
home page
shows the
benefits of
Online
Investment
Tracking
and
describes
how to get
started.

(Copyright © 1997 Intuit Inc. Used with permission.)

Part V
The Part of Tens

The 5th Wave — By Rich Tennant

"All of our financial Web site booths are taken; however, I do have a table with a lovely view of a current events Web site."

In this part . . .

In The Part of Tens, you discover the ten prerequisites for online investing. Determine whether you're ready to become an online investor and see what you have to do (if anything) to get your financial house in order. Discover how you can use the Internet to help you plan for a cozy retirement and find out about all the online resources that exist for seniors. You can also check out ten cybertax tips that can help you reduce your tax burden. Interested in preparing and filing your taxes online? You can find out how in this part of the book.

Chapter 18

Almost Ten Prerequisites for Online Investing

● ●

In This Chapter

▶ Getting your ducks in a row before investing

▶ Calculating your net worth, how much you spend, and how much you need to earn

▶ Determining your financial objectives and setting a ten-year goal

▶ Setting aside emergency funds

▶ Planning and maximizing your wealth

▶ Determining your risk-tolerance level

▶ Finding Internet investing starting points

● ●

*Y*ou may not have a formal investment plan, but you probably do some financial planning, even if it's only noting the bills that need to be paid on the back of your paycheck envelope. However, if you want to be a successful online investor, you need to do a little more homework to get your financial ducks in a row.

In this chapter, I show you what you need to do before you begin investing, as well as how the Internet can help you get started. I explain how you can use an online worksheet to determine your starting point and use an online calculator to compute your personal net worth. I show you how to determine your investment objectives and understand how much you need to earn to meet those goals. I provide guidelines for setting a ten-year goal and setting aside emergency funds. I also show you where to go online for financial planning resources, how to determine your risk-tolerance level, and how to start maximizing your personal wealth now.

Settling Your Personal Finances

The beginning of personal wealth is the accumulation of capital that you can use for investing. This capital often begins with savings and expands into other types of more profitable investments.

Saving and investing are different, although savings are often the source of funds for investing. *Savings* are a set level of funds that you put aside, usually at a low interest rate. They are readily accessible and often insured by a financial institution.

Investment funds are the funds that you don't have earmarked for the rent, groceries, taxes, and so on. You place these funds in securities that can increase or decrease in value. They may earn interest or dividends, but you have no guarantee of increased value or future income. (Investment funds should be free of any obligations. Good examples of investment fund sources are inheritances, gifts, and disposable income.)

If you want to start investing but are having trouble making ends meet, you may be due for a financial health checkup. You can test your financial fitness by visiting the Quicken site at www.quicken.com/saving/checkup. Answer a series of questions covering key areas like investments, debt management, and retirement planning. After you complete the questionnaire, you get a summary based on your financial objectives along with a set of suggestions and remedies.

Calculating Your Net Worth

The first step in getting to where you want to go is to figure out where you are now. One prerequisite to online investing is taking the time to calculate your net worth. I know that calculating your net worth doesn't sound exciting, but consider this exercise the creation of a starting line for your online investment program. Later, you can compare your increased net worth to this starting line.

Credit-card debt and investing online

If you use a credit card to pay for everyday expenses but you don't pay off the card balance at the end of the month, you aren't ready to be an investor. You need to change your spending habits and pay off those credit cards before you begin investing.

Interest rates on credit-card debt are often between 16 and 21 percent. Over the last 50 years, the average annual return on stocks is 13 percent. Even if your investments beat the market, you'll still have a difficult time covering your credit-card interest expenses.

One of the things that makes calculating net worth difficult is finding the sources for the data entries. Here are some suggestions about sources for the categories you use to calculate your net worth:

- ✔ **Liquid assets:** To find the value of your investments, refer to your most recent bank and brokerage statements.

- ✔ **Property assets:** For real estate assets, use your most recent property appraisal or check with a realtor who knows your neighborhood.

- ✔ **Vehicles:** Remember to deduct depreciation from the original cost.

- ✔ **Jewelry, art, and collectibles:** Use your insurer's appraised value or your best estimate.

- ✔ **Other assets:** Use your best estimate of each asset's resale value.

Many professional financial planners tell you that most people don't know their net worth and that when potential customers make a ballpark guess, they usually aren't even close. The Internet provides many online calculators that can assist you in determining your exact net worth. These calculators do much of the work for you. Here are two examples:

- ✔ **Merrill Lynch's Net Worth Calculator** (www.merrill-lynch.ml.com/ investor/worthform.html) suggests that you review your current financial position before you begin planning for the future.

- ✔ **Altamira Resource Center Net Worth Calculator** (www.altamira.com/ icat/toolbox/netcalc.html) suggests that as you go through life, one of the primary financial goals is to increase your net worth. This calculator is designed to help you determine your current net worth and track the change over time.

Using Online Calculators to Determine How Much You're Spending

Whatever your personal situation dictates, you can find investments that are tailor-made for your requirements. Determining how much money to invest (or whether you have any money to invest) is a big step in the right direction.

Use the following online calculators to determine your *net cash flow* — that is, the amount of money that comes into your household each year and the amount of money you spend:

✔ **Understanding and Controlling Your Finances** (`www.bygpub.com/finance/CashFlowCalc.htm`) provides an online calculator that shows your income and expenses and determines whether you're living within your means.

✔ **FinanCenter** (`www.financenter.com`) offers a "How Much Am I Spending?" calculator, which you access by clicking on the Budget icon. This calculator shows your income, how much you're spending, and the amount available for investment. The online calculator even derives the future value of your investments if invested for ten years. With this feature, you know exactly what the benefits are of changing your spending habits.

A *surplus* means that you have excess funds — that is, money that may be available for investment. A *shortfall* means that you're living beyond your means and may need some assistance with debt management. If you spend more than you make, you may need to make some lifestyle corrections. Here are a few examples of Internet sources that can help you with this problem:

✔ **The Sensible Saver** (`www.sensiblesaver.com`) is a commonsense guide to saving and investing that includes a newsletter, savings tips, and links to related sites.

✔ **Ohio State University Extension** (`www.ag.ohio-state.edu/%7eohioline/home/money`) offers a tutorial about managing your money. The tutorial includes six lessons: Where do I begin, Where does your money go, Stop spending leaks, Developing a spending plan, How much credit can you afford, and Keeping records in order.

Determining Your Personal Investment Objectives

Many people want to jump into investing before they know where they are and where they're going. Investing is always a risk, and you need to understand how this risk relates to your financial base.

Figure 18-1 shows a diagram of your financial base that uses information from the North Dakota State University, NDSU Extension Service (`www.ext.nodak.edu/extpubs`). The first level is your budget, setting up a savings plan for an emergency fund, acquiring insurance, and developing a home ownership plan. The second level is developing a savings plan that meets your short-, intermediate-, and long-term financial goals. The third level is having six months of take-home pay ready for emergencies. The fourth level is keeping your contributions to your individual retirement plan on track.

Stocks, bonds, real estate, collectibles, and other investments			
Mutual funds			
Qualified retirement plan			
Half-year's income in low risk investments			
Systematic savings plan to meet short-, intermediate-, and long term goals			
Budget	Emergency fund	Insurance	Home mortgage

Figure 18-1: Diagram of an investor's financial base.

Source: *North Dakota State University, NDSU Extension Service*

After you have this financial foundation set in place, you're ready to invest in mutual funds and then in stocks, bonds, real estate, and collectibles.

How Much Do You Need to Earn?

Your income level doesn't determine whether you'll be financially successful. Financial success means not having to stretch to pay the monthly bills, living a comfortable lifestyle, and having the resources necessary for your family and retirement.

How much you earn today impacts your investment decision making in the following ways:

- ✔ Do you need more income now?
- ✔ How much time do you have to meet your financial goals?
- ✔ Do you require a stable rate of capital appreciation or are you willing to speculate?

Can you pass a Debt Repayment Test? Many lenders use a 36 percent rule. That is, if your monthly debt is greater than 36 percent of your income, they may not approve your loan application. For example, if your gross monthly income is $6,000, your combined expenses can't exceed $2,160 ($6,000 × 0.36 = $2,160). Individuals with higher debt-to-income ratios have a hard time qualifying for a loan and aren't likely to have any funds available for investing.

Setting a ten-year goal

Determining how much you need to earn requires having a clear understanding of where you are and where you expect to be in the coming years. Here's an example of the factors you need to consider in setting a ten-year goal. Assume that you're married, both you and your spouse have relatively well-paying jobs, you own a home (with a hefty 30-year mortgage), you have $5,000 in an IRA, and you're vested in your employer's pension. You have two children, one is six years old and the other is seven. You expect that both children will want to go to college.

Your financial objectives for the next ten years are pretty clear: You need to raise the cash to send your children to college and still cover your other obligations. What about the next ten years after that? Do you want to retire early? How much cash will you need for a comfortable retirement? Will your investment strategies get you to your financial objectives? How much of your income should you invest?

Strategic financial goals can be stated in broad terms, such as, "I want to retire early." *Tactical* goals are specific and short-term — for example, "I want to save $20,000 by 2001." In other words, your goals and objectives are the finishing line, and how you get there is by creating and implementing your investment program. To start your online investment program, write down what you want:

- ✔ **An emergency fund:** For most people, the first thing on their list should be their emergency fund, which exists to protect them from unexpected situations. Unexpected expenses can include uninsured medical costs, property losses, and unemployment. (A recent survey indicated that only 17 percent of 1,000 respondents had a sufficient emergency fund, and one out of every five respondents didn't even have an emergency fund.)

- ✔ **Adequate insurance:** You need insurance to cover disability, health, life, automobiles, and property.

- ✔ **The ability to pay the monthly bills without stretching:** For many people, the goal is to pay the monthly bills without relying on future cash sources (that year-end bonus you were promised) or credit cards. For other people, the goal is to pay their children's college tuition, take care of their parents, or help their children with the down payment for their first car or home. Some goals include taking an ocean cruise, purchasing a vacation home, making home improvements, or purchasing a new home. Whatever your goals, make certain that they don't prevent you from covering your monthly bills.

- ✔ **Early or comfortable retirement:** Most people want to maintain their same standard of living during their retirement years.

- ✔ **Maximizing your personal wealth:** Some individuals want to start their own businesses (with their own money) or engage in philanthropy.

Want to be a millionaire? Go to FinanCenter at www.financenter.com. Click on the Savings icon and then click on the calculator titled "What will it take to become a millionaire?" Enter the required data and then click on Calculate. The results show how much you need to invest today to be a millionaire in the future.

Rainy days and emergency funds

Savings are the beginning of your capital accumulation. Families need a regular savings program that is between 5 and 10 percent of take-home pay per month. Some people even manage to put away 15 percent. Getting into a regular rhythm with saving is important.

Additionally, individuals and families need emergency funds. Folks with fluctuating income, few job benefits, and little job security may need to have a larger emergency fund. Families with two wage-earners may need a smaller emergency fund.

A general rule is to have three to six months of take-home pay in a savings account for emergencies. If you don't have an emergency fund, you need to increase your savings. Payroll deduction plans into a savings account or money market fund are often the most painless way to achieve the best results. On the other hand, if you've been saving a surplus, you may want to consider using these funds for investing.

Tables 18-1 and 18-2 provide examples of how much you need to save each month to reach a specific financial goal. For example, assume that you need $10,000 for your emergency fund. If you save $147.05 per month for five years at a 5 percent rate of return, you have the money you need.

Table 18-1 Monthly Savings Needed to Reach Your Financial Goal

Dollars Needed	Years to Achieve Goal at a 5% Rate of Return		
	5 Years	10 Years	20 Years
$5,000	$73.52	$32.20	$12.16
$10,000	$147.05	$64.40	$24.33
$20,000	$294.09	$128.80	$48.66
$50,000	$735.23	$321.99	$121.64
$300,000	$4,411.37	$1,931.97	$729.87

Table 18-2 Monthly Savings Needed to Reach Your Financial Goal			
Dollars Needed	*Years to Achieve Goal at a 7% Rate of Return*		
	5 Years	*10 Years*	*20 Years*
$5,000	$69.84	$28.89	$9.60
$10,000	$139.68	$57.78	$19.20
$20,000	$279.36	$115.56	$38.40
$50,000	$698.40	$288.90	$96.00
$300,000	$4,190.40	$1,733.40	$576.00

The Internet provides several online calculators to assist you in determining exactly how much you need to save for your emergency fund. FinanCenter (www.financenter.com) provides one such calculator. At the FinanCenter home page, click on the Budget icon and then select the "How Much Should I Set Aside for Emergencies" calculator. Enter the data where requested and then click on Calculate. The calculator indicates how much you need for covering emergencies, losses, and unemployment that may occur during the next year. It also tells you when you'll have an adequate emergency fund if you save a specific amount per month and add it to your current savings.

How Much Risk Can You Take?

Your investment decisions should take into consideration your attitudes about risk. The amount of risk you can tolerate often depends on your knowledge of investments, your experience, and your personality. Each person has his or her own style and needs. Knowing exactly what your risk-tolerance level is can help you select investments that offer the highest return for the investment's level of risk.

The Internet provides many personal investment profiles. Here are two examples.

- ✔ **Bank of America Investment Services** (www.bankamerica.com/tools/sri_assetall.html) offers a survey of 12 questions. Enter your answers, and the online calculator suggests an investment allocation strategy that suits your current needs and situation.

- ✔ **Vanguard** (majestic1.vanguard.com/RRC/DA/0.1.32) provides a risk-tolerance questionnaire. Answer the questions, and the online calculator suggests the level of risk you can accept.

Online Investing Starting Points

How you choose to invest your capital (in mutual funds, stocks, bonds, Treasury securities, money market funds, and other types of investments) depends on a number of considerations:

- ✔ Your required rate of return
- ✔ How much risk you can tolerate
- ✔ How long you can invest your capital
- ✔ Your personal tax liability
- ✔ Your need for quick access to your cash

When you have factored these elements into your online investment plan, you can start researching the appropriate securities. The Internet provides many resources for assisting investors. Here are some of the best Internet investment starting points:

- ✔ **Invest-O-Rama** (www.investorama.com) includes more than 2,000 investor-related links sorted into categories and commonsense advice. The site has a directory that covers bonds, brokerages, dividend reinvestment plans, futures, mutual funds, and more.

- ✔ **Investorguide** (www.investorguide.com) is a well-organized guide with links to thousands of investor-related sites. It includes site reviews, summaries, and an extensive section on initial public offerings (IPOs).

- ✔ **Morningstar** (www.morningstar.net) is a Chicago-based independent rating company that specializes in mutual funds. The site includes information about stocks and mutual funds, easy-to-use screening tools, and research sources.

- ✔ **The Syndicate** (www.moneypages.com/syndicate) offers informative articles on investor topics, more than 2,000 links to related investor sites, information on brokers, bonds, and more.

- ✔ **Wall Street Research Net** (www.wsrn.com) focuses on stock market research. The site offers more than 65,000 links to company information, the economy, market news, investor reports, quotes, mutual fund indexes, and more.

Chapter 19

Ten Ways to Plan a Comfortable Retirement Online

In This Chapter

▶ Understanding how the Internet can assist you in planning your retirement

▶ Using the Internet to determine your retirement benefits

▶ Locating online calculators that can do your retirement planning for you

▶ Understanding and taking advantage of retirement tax benefits

▶ Finding free and nearly free downloadable software for retirement planning

*C*onventional wisdom says that the elderly need less money to live on than the young do. This notion is true only if you lower your standard of living when you retire. As a general rule, expenses for the elderly are *more* than those for young people. After all, in your retirement years, don't you plan an active life? A life filled with sport activities, entertainment, and travel?

In this chapter, I show you how the Internet can assist you in mapping out a comfortable retirement. With careful planning, you can reduce the risk of outliving the money you set aside for your easy-living retirement years. Careful planning and the Internet can make certain that you celebrate your 110th year in peace and free of money worries.

Can You Retire Early?

Some experts say that determining your retirement needs is more art than science. You need to consider many elements when you estimate how much money you need to retire — for example:

✔ Your life expectancy

✔ Your future earnings between now and your desired retirement date

- ✔ Your prediction of the actual inflation rate
- ✔ The amount of taxes you will have to pay in coming years

The Internet provides a wide variety of software products, online calculators, and worksheets that can assist you in determining how much you need to save. Here are a few examples:

- ✔ **Retirement Planning Online Worksheet** (www.corestates.com) can assist you in projecting your annual retirement expenses.

- ✔ **Retirement Planning Worksheet** (www.troweprice.com/retirement/retire.html) is a set of worksheets for estimating the percentage of your salary you need to save each year to accumulate enough assets for retirement.

- ✔ **The Worry-Free Retirement Worksheet** (www.bookpage.com/kiplinger/rene.html) can help you understand your retirement needs.

Calculating Your Retirement Benefits

The Social Security Administration can't help you with your financial planning, but it can tell you what benefits you can expect. Benefits are based on your date of birth and complete work history. Pension insurance amounts are calculated on your earnings during a lifetime of work under the social security system. Years of high earnings increase the amount of the benefit. Each person's number of work years and wages is unique, which means that each person's *primary insurance* amount varies (unless it's at the maximum benefit amount).

The Social Security Administration Web site at www.ssa.gov can assist you in determining the exact amount of your benefits. Just print the request form for your Personal Earnings and Benefit Statement. Complete the form and mail it to the Social Security Administration. You receive your completed Personal Earnings and Benefit Statement in about two weeks.

Kiplinger's Retirement Zone (www.bookpage.com/kiplinger/index.html) provides online tutorials, worksheets, and other tools to assist you in planning a comfortable, worry-free retirement. Online tools include a worksheet to help you understand your retirement needs, a table to help you plan your savings, a tutorial for forty-somethings and retirement, and a checklist to guide you to your retirement date.

Why You Need to Understand Your Employer's Pension Plan

Employer-sponsored plans can be qualified or nonqualified. The *qualified* plans have contributions in pretax dollars and are tax-deductible in the year they are made. Interest, dividends, and income made by the investments of the qualified plan are not taxable while held in the plan. In contrast, *nonqualified* plans do not meet IRS standards for tax-deductibility, so contributions must be in after-tax dollars.

Table 19-1 shows the difference between a qualified and a nonqualified employer-sponsored pension plan. The amounts shown are for an initial investment of $10,000 and a 7 percent annual return on fully taxable and tax-deferred retirement investments. After 10 years, the advantage of the qualified plan (with its tax deferrals) is only $536; in 20 years, the advantage is $6,157; and in 30 years, the advantage is a significant $22,895. In other words, if you and your neighbor put the same amount of money into employer-sponsored pension plans, but your neighbor's plan is qualified and yours is not, your neighbor receives $22,895 more than you do in 30 years.

Table 19-1	The Tax Impact of Nonqualified Plans		
	Tax Types		
	Tax-Deferred	**Fully Taxable**	**Difference**
Tax rate	30%	30%	0%
After-tax values after 10 years			
	$16,770	$16,134	$536
Pretax return	7.0%	7.0%	0.0%
After-tax return	5.3%	4.9%	0.4%
After-tax values after 20 years			
	$32,989	$26,832	$6,157
Pretax return	7.0%	7.0%	0.0%
After-tax return	6.1%	4.9%	1.2%
After-tax values after 30 years			
	$64,896	$42,001	$22,895
Pretax return	7.0%	7.0%	0.0%
After-tax return	6.4%	4.9%	1.5%

Source: John Wilkinson, "Mistakes in Retirement Planning" (1997)

How Large a Nest Egg?

Statistics from the Social Security Administration (1994) indicate that income for households headed by adults 65 years or older usually consists of social security benefits (42 percent), pensions and annuities (19 percent), asset income (18 percent), earnings (18 percent), and other income (3 percent). If this statistic is true, then how big a retirement nest egg do you need?

How large a nest egg you need depends on your retirement expenses less the amount of your social security benefits and your employer's pension plans. The difference, which is usually a shortfall, is how large a nest egg you require at the time of your retirement.

After you determine how much you need, start saving as soon as possible. This is one way to battle the retiree's biggest threat — inflation. At a 3 percent inflation rate, a dollar is worth only $0.55 in 20 years. Individuals need an income of $36,000 in 20 years to have the same purchasing power as $20,000 today. Social security benefits are tied to inflation and increase at the rate of inflation, but most employer-sponsored pension plans don't have this characteristic. In other words, you probably need savings to make up the shortfall.

Here are a few online calculators that can help you crunch the numbers:

- ✔ **How Big A Nest Egg You Need to Cover an Income Gap** (`www.bookpage.com/kiplinger/nestegg.html`) is a helpful graph about the savings needed to permit monthly withdrawals of $1,000 at each rate of return.

- ✔ **Retirement Funding Calculator** (`www.waddell.com`) determines how much you should be saving for your retirement years.

- ✔ **Retirement Planning Calculator** (`www.bygpub.com/finance/RetirementCalc.htm`) can assist you in determining what sort of lifestyle you can expect during retirement by showing your 401(k) account balance before and after retirement. You can experiment with different savings amounts so that you can see the effect those amounts have on your retirement lifestyle.

- ✔ **Retirement Planning Calculator** (`personal.fidelity.com/toolbox`) is a handy set of tools to calculate your estimated savings goals. Use the calculator to determine the value of your nest egg at retirement, estimated savings surplus or shortfall, and estimated additional annual savings needed.

- ✔ **Retirement Savings Calculator** (`www.1sttech.com`) can help you find out how much you need to save to maintain your standard of living.

Don't Miss Those Tax Benefits

The Taxpayer's Relief Act offers reductions in long-term capital gains tax rates and other benefits. With the new tax laws beginning in 1998, now is the time to re-evaluate your investment strategies and retirement planning. You don't want to miss any of the new tax benefits. Here are a few examples:

- Roth IRAs are contributions to a retirement fund using after-tax dollars. Qualified withdrawals from the fund's income are generally tax-free.

- You may want to invest your retirement funds in stocks that you plan to hold for the long-term. Taxes on ultra long-term capital gains can be as low as 18 percent for investments held for more than 60 months.

- Spouses, regardless of earnings, who don't participate in an employer-sponsored retirement plan can make tax-deductible contributions of up to $2,000 to a traditional IRA. (The deductibility phases out for married taxpayers with an adjusted gross income of between $150,000 and $160,000.)

Three Retirement Plan Favorites

In the following sections, I offer brief descriptions of the three most popular retirement plans used in the U.S. today:

- Individual retirement accounts (IRAs)

- 401(k) plans

- Keogh plans

Each plan has its own advantages and disadvantages. The Internet provides additional information, online calculators, and other tools for your retirement planning. These tools can assist you in determining which plan or combination of plans meets your retirement objectives.

IRA plans

Individual retirement accounts (IRAs) are available for any employed person. The two most popular types of IRAs are the traditional IRA and the Roth IRA. Traditional IRAs allow individuals to deposit up to $2,000 annually in an IRA, and another $2,000 can be deposited for a nonworking spouse. In other words, $4,000 per year in pretax dollars can be contributed to the family's IRA. Taxes are payable on the contribution and the income on tax savings at the time of withdrawal.

The second type of IRA account is a Roth IRA. Roth IRAs follow the same general income guidelines as traditional IRAs. The big difference is that income from a Roth IRA is often tax free and, under certain conditions, can be borrowed before retirement without penalty.

The plan that is best for you depends on your tax bracket when you retire. If you'll pay lower taxes when you retire, the traditional IRA may be best. If you'll pay the same amount of taxes, the Roth IRA may be better. For online calculators, see the IRA Deductibility Tool at www.bankamerica.com/tools/ret_deduct.html and the online calculator at the IRA Corner, located at www.frontier-news.com/retire/home.htm.

For IRA planning questions and information on the new IRA rules effective December 31, 1997, see T. Rowe Price's article "New IRA Rules" at www.troweprice.com/retirement/newira.html, and use the online calculator at this site to determine which retirement plan is best for you.

401(k) retirement plans

Cash or deferred arrangements (CODAs) — usually called 401(k) plans — allow workers to voluntarily place a certain amount of their paychecks in a qualified retirement savings plan. (Some employers match all or some of this amount.) Workers can contribute up to $9,500 per year. The maximum contribution is the lesser of 25 percent of your salary or $30,000, including the employer's matching funds.

One benefit of a 401(k) plan is that it reduces your tax liability, usually by reducing the amount of taxes you pay. All contributions to 401(k) plans are made with pretax dollars, and returns are tax deferred as long as they stay in the plan. (Retirees often pay less taxes than when they were in their high-income-producing years.) The American Association of Retired Persons (AARP) provides additional information about the tax advantages and penalties of 401(k) plans at www.aarp.org/finance/retire.htm.

Understanding and Controlling Your Finances (www.bygpub.com/finance/CompoundingCalc.htm) can assist you in determining how much money you can accumulate by making monthly contributions to your 401(k) account. Enter the amount you plan to add to your account each month and the expected interest rate. The online calculator indicates how much money you can accumulate over different time spans.

Keogh (HR-10) retirement plans

Keoghs (HR-10) are qualified retirement plans designed for business owners (small corporations, partnerships, and sole proprietorships) and the self-employed (sole-practitioner consultants, independent contractors, authors, and so on). Two types of plans exist. The first is a *money purchase plan* that designates an annual contribution. The maximum is $30,000, and you're allowed to save up to 20 percent of self-employment income. The second plan is a *profit sharing plan* that changes if company profits increase or decrease.

If an employer sets up a Keogh plan for him- or herself, a comparable plan must exist for the employees. Contributions are with pretax dollars, and earnings are tax deferred until funds are paid out to account holders. Individuals who are self-employed on a part-time basis and have a full-time employer-sponsored plan can still qualify for a Keogh Plan.

The Fidelity Retirement Plan Worksheet (`personal.fidelity.com/toolbox`) is an online worksheet and calculator that can help you determine your Keogh contributions for a money purchase plan or a single profit sharing plan.

Free Downloadable Retirement Planners

The Internet provides many downloadable retirement planning software programs. Here are two of the best:

- ✔ **The 401K Calculator** is an Excel spreadsheet that compares a 401(k) investment plan with tax strategies. The program is easy to use. The evaluation shareware is free and downloadable. If you decide to keep the program, the developers would like you to send them $10. It's available from the ZNET Software Library at `www6.zdnet.com/cgi-bin/texis/swlib/hotfiles/info.html?fcode=000HKA`.

- ✔ **Torrid Technologies** (`www.torrid-tech.com`) provides a free, downloadable, evaluation copy of an interactive program that calculates the amount of 401(k) savings you need for retirement, how those savings are depleted over your retirement, and investment tips if your current plan has a shortfall.

Nearly Free Retirement Planning Software

If you're looking for a comprehensive retirement planning software package, the Internet provides many options. Here are a few examples of retirement planning software programs that you can download from the Internet for a small price:

- **Quicken Financial Planner** (www.quicken.com) is an all-purpose tool for retirement, insurance, tuition, and other big-ticket items. The online version is free and helpful, but you can't print any of the results. ($40)

- **Retirement Manager** (www.vanguard.com/catalog/manager5_5_5. html#instructions) enables you to track the progress of your investments and make certain that your retirement program remains on track. ($20)

- **RetireReady from Individual Software** (www.individualsoftware. com) is designed for both retirees and people planning their retirement. RetireReady Deluxe offers three tools: an interactive retirement planning calculator that helps you assess your current and future financial situation; an educational multimedia workshop; and an extensive list of related resources with addresses, phone numbers, and Web URLs. ($50)

More Links to Retirement Planning Sites

Many retirees depend on *annuities* (insurance company-sponsored plans) to pay for their monthly living expenses. Annuities are agreements between a buyer and the insurance company to pay a lump sum (or installment payments) to the buyer at some future time. Two types of annuities exist: *fixed* annuities, which guarantee a specific rate of return, and *variable* annuities, which have no guarantee of a specific return — that is, the value of the annuity changes. Some insurance companies offer a hybrid, which is a combination of the two types of annuities.

Payout options include monthly benefit checks that start at a certain time and continue for life, benefit checks for a certain time period, benefit checks until a buyer's death, and a certain number of benefit checks to a designated party if the buyer dies.

Here are some interesting online annuity sites:

- ✔ **Uniformed Services Benefit Association** (`www.usba.com`) offers whole-life insurance products for active-duty military, military veterans, federal employees, and their families.

- ✔ **Independence Life and Annuity Company FAQ** (`www.websaver.com/WSfaq.html`) explains annuities, costs, and income options.

- ✔ **The Consumer Information Center** sponsored by the GSA (`www.pueblo.gsa.gov/press/nfcpubs/annuity.tx`) and provides basic information about annuity types.

FinanCenter (`www.financenter.com`) has an excellent collection of online retirement planning calculators. Go to the FinanCenter home page and click on Retirement. Next, click on the pull-down menu for calculators. To go to the online calculator of your choice, just click on the title and then click on Go To Calculator. Here are my four favorite online calculators:

- ✔ Am I saving enough? What can I change?

- ✔ What will my income be after I retire?

- ✔ What will my expenses be after I retire?

- ✔ How much will social security provide?

It's Never Too Late to Begin Saving

It's best to start saving when you're young, but it's never too late to start saving for your retirement. This chapter details a variety of investments that can help you realize your retirement goals, whatever your time horizon may be. Even some new federal tax laws can help you retire comfortably. For example, businesses with 100 or fewer employees can offer SIMPLE (savings incentive match plans for employees) IRA plans or SIMPLE 401(k) plans. Under these plans, employers can match employee contributions dollar-for-dollar up to 3 percent of the employee's compensation. For additional information about these plans, see the following sites:

- ✔ **BizMonthly** (`www.bizmonthly.com/april/paniculam.shtml`) details savings incentive match plans for employees in an article titled "A SIMPLE Answer for Small Business Retirement Plans."

- ✔ **T. Rowe Price** (`www.troweprice.com/retirement/25emps.html`) provides a brief description of retirement plans for small businesses. Click on the links that let you compare several types of retirement plans.

Chapter 20
Ten Cybertax Tips

*T*axes have always been troublesome for investors. In this chapter, I provide ten cybertax tips that can assist you in reducing your taxable investor income. I explain how you can use the Internet to help reduce your tax bill, and I provide you with year-round tax savings strategies. I discuss how you can use the Internet to receive top-of-the-line advice from major tax accounting firms, as well as how the Internet can provide you with helpful tips to trim your tax bill.

As I demonstrate in this chapter, not only can the Internet help you in preparing this year's income tax return, but it also provides several tax organizers to help you streamline the process for next year. It can also keep you current with changes in the tax laws.

This chapter also shows how taxpayers can save time and money by using the Internet. For example, as I discuss in the following sections, you can have your taxes prepared online, and many online tax preparers offer same-day service. You can also reduce the likelihood of getting your tax return returned because of simple mistakes.

If your income taxes are complex, you may want a professional tax preparer to assist you. The Internet provides information about many independent certified public accounting firms. For example, The University of Iowa publishes a list of eligible tax preparers called the *Directory of CPA Firms* (www.biz.uiowa.edu/misc/links/acct_tax.html). This directory lists more than 600 CPA firms that have Internet addresses. All you have to do is click on the state you desire, and a linked list of company names and addresses appears.

Preparing Your Tax Return Online

Several companies provide online tax preparation. Costs for the online service average $35 for an itemized Form 1040. (Itemized elements can include rental income, self-employment, capital gains, pensions, alimony, moving expenses, and selling a home.)

What do you have to do? Just enter your tax information online. The online tax preparation service fills out both federal and state tax returns. If any information is incomplete, the tax preparation service contacts you via e-mail or telephone to gather the needed information.

Tax returns can be completed in one day. The tax preparation service sends you a summary of the finished forms by e-mail. At the same time, the company sends you the tax return via overnight mail so that you can attach the related documentation. Just sign the forms and send the return to the appropriate agencies.

Having your income taxes prepared online offers the following benefits:

- ✔ No time away from work to meet with your tax preparer
- ✔ Same-day completion of your income tax return and e-mailed summary of your income tax return
- ✔ A conscientious effort to obtain the best tax refund allowed for you

Examples of online tax preparation services

You may want to consider using one of the following online tax preparation services:

- ✔ **Income Tax Preparation Online** (taxreturns-online.netgate.net) provides fast, accurate, low-priced services. This site includes a Tax Organizer to help you gather all the information you need to complete your income tax return.
- ✔ **Tax Filer** (www.taxfiler.com) was formerly Net-Fax. Tax Filer allows you to open an account online, and it provides links to related sites, tax tips, and instructions to guide you through the process of submitting information and signing up for its service. Tax Filer includes a helpful tool to estimate your total income tax and the proper amount of your

withholding taxes. Click on Tools to check it out. Tax Filer guarantees its work and has your completed tax return signed by a CPA. Tax Filer charges $69 for basic returns and an additional $29 for returns that include IRA distributions and more complex issues.

✔ **Secure Tax** (`www.securetax.com`) provides reliable, comprehensive on-screen tax preparation and filing. Complete the online forms free of charge. Make certain that all your calculations are correct. For $9.95, you can print unlimited copies of your return directly from the site. For an additional $4.95, Secure Tax files your tax return electronically. For $1.00, Secure Tax provides access to its Audit Alert, which helps you find errors and omissions.

✔ **Electronic Filing Service** (EFS), at `www.efs.com`, offers a free downloadable program, PREP 1040 Personal, which includes more than 50 forms and schedules. For $29.95, the company provides electronic filing of your tax return.

For additional online tax preparation assistance

The following online sources are useful for answering questions about preparing your income tax return:

✔ **Internal Revenue Service (IRS)** site at `ustreas.gov/prod/cover.html` offers official guidance on preparing your tax return.

✔ **Taxing Times** (`www.scubed.com/tax`) is an electronic compendium of information related to the task of filling out and filing your income tax returns. This site includes federal tax information, forms for downloading, instructions about how to complete specific schedules, telephone numbers of IRS offices, and toll-free help telephone numbers.

✔ **U.S. Tax Code Online** (`www.fourmilab.ch/ustax/ustax.html`) allows you to access the complete text of the United States Internal Revenue Code. This site has a powerful search engine that can save you hours of time.

Are you eligible for a tax refund? You can find out by using H&R Block's (`www.hrblock.com`) online refund calculator. Just enter your filing status, standardized deduction preferences, number of exemptions, gross income, and taxes paid. The calculator reports how big a refund you can expect.

Using Online Tax Organizers

The Internet provides income tax organizers that can assist you in organizing the data needed for your income tax returns. Online organizers are designed to help you plan to prepare your own tax return or have someone else prepare it. Here are a few examples of online tax organizers:

- ✔ **Fredriksen & Com** (www.fredriksen.com/taxorg5.html) invites you to print all five sections of this online tax organizer. It can help you organize your tax information so that you don't miss any important tax deductions. This site also includes an online questionnaire. If you complete the online questionnaire, the company provides you with a quote for preparing your taxes and gives you a 10 percent discount.

- ✔ **The NET CPA** (www.netcpa.com/forms) provides a tax organizer that can assist you in preparing your taxes. It provides helpful tips about checking for mistakes, not overlooking deductions, how to select a tax preparer, and more.

- ✔ **The Tax Return Service** (tax-returns-online.netage.net/ organzr.htm) has a tax organizer that is divided into seven sections. The first section is for taxpayer information. The second section is for child care, moving expenses, and other adjustments. The third section is about income, interest, dividends, and IRAs. The fourth section is about capital gains and the sale of your home. The fifth section covers itemized deductions. The sixth section is for the self-employed and includes company profits and losses. The seventh section covers rental income and expenses.

Using the Internet to Stay Current with New Tax Laws

The Internet provides several directories, indexes, discussion groups, and tax news services to assist you in keeping current with the latest changes in the tax laws. Here are a few examples:

- ✔ **Drake Software** makes filing help available at 1040.com (www.1040.com). The Web site has a tax preparer's database available.

- ✔ **Ernst & Young** at www.ey.com/pfc/summary.htm provides a summary that includes an overview of the Tax Relief Act. It covers child tax credits, new educational IRAs, retirement IRAs, home sales, estate planning, capital gains, and other tax breaks.

✔ **Excite/Quicken Tax Discussion** is available at `boards.excite.com/goweb?13@-d^62419eeeca058`. If you're looking for hot discussions of the new tax laws, this site is the place to go.

✔ **Federal Tax Law** (`www.taxsites.com/federal.html`) offers links to summaries of new tax legislation, the tax code, regulations, court decisions, tax rates, payroll taxes, and U.S. tax treaties.

✔ **Tax Sites Directory** (`www.uni.edu/schmidt/sites.html`) is a guide to tax resources on the Internet.

✔ **Tax Web** (`www.taxweb.com`) is a consumer-oriented source for federal, state, and local tax-related news and questions. This site includes links to current federal and state-sponsored tax sites.

✔ **Taxpayer Help & Ed** (`www.irs.ustreas.gov`) is an IRS-sponsored site that includes extensive Frequently Asked Questions listings.

✔ **The IRS *Digital Daily*** (`www.irs.ustreas.gov`) provides tax news, taxpayer information, and explanations of federal regulations. (They promise to use plain English to explain the income tax code, but is that possible?) Additional features include what's hot in tax forms, getting the tax facts with fax on demand, and downloading all the tax regulations issued since August 1, 1995.

✔ **Today's Tax News** (`www.tax.org/Today'sTaxNews`) is continuously updated, features highlights of the latest tax news, and offers summaries of documents from the U.S. and around the world.

Calculate the impact of the latest changes on your tax bill at `msnbc.com/modules/budget/tcalculator.aasp`. You can find out whether you will save money on federal taxes under the key tax-cutting provisions.

Filing Your Taxes Electronically or Using an Online Service

Electronic filing simply involves the transmission of data on your return from the computer of a tax preparer to an IRS computer. Here are the requirements for electronic filing:

✔ You must use an authorized service. Many tax preparers now offer this service.

✔ You must complete a form that authorizes the electronic transmission of your tax return.

✔ If you report salary income, you must attach your W-2 Forms to Form 8453, which you mail to the IRS.

✔ Even electronically filed IRS reports must have the signatures of the taxpayers.

✔ If you file electronically and owe taxes, you must pay by mail. In this case, you send your payment with Form 1040V (Payment Voucher) before April 15.

The IRS acknowledges receipt of your return within two working days from the time of transmission. Electronic filers often receive faster refunds — a check mailed within three weeks or a direct deposit to your bank account. (To authorize direct deposits, complete the bank information on Form 8453.)

The following online services will file your income tax return electronically:

✔ **Tax Filer** (`www.taxfiler.com`) was formerly Net-Fax. Tax Filer files your tax return electronically and guarantees their work. All tax returns are signed by a CPA.

✔ **TaxLogic** (`www.taxlogic.com`) uses a secure network to deliver your electronically prepared tax return via the Internet. This service minimizes the hassles of tax preparation. Additionally, the site includes a summary of the new tax laws in plain English, an advisory forum for your specific tax questions, news and information, Web resources, and Frequently Asked Questions.

Online Mutual Fund Tax-Saving Strategies

Mutual funds are investment trusts that distribute capital gains, interest, and dividend income to the fund's shareholders. Investors are responsible for the taxes on their share of the fund's distributions. Several ways exist for reducing your tax liability on these distributions:

✔ **Timing:** If you want additional shares, make your purchase after the fund makes its annual distribution to shareholders (for details, see Ernst & Young's Web site at `www.ey.com/pfc/mutual.htm`).

✔ **Buy tax-exempt mutual funds:** Explore tax-exempt mutual funds and compare their yields to similar taxable investments (for suggestions, see American Express at `www.americanexpress.com/advisors/ info/products/mutfund/Cmutfund.html`).

✔ **Understand the taxation of your mutual fund distributions:** Don't pay more taxes than you need to because you don't understand the tax code. If you're struggling over how to compute your mutual fund tax liability, read the IRS Publication 564 at www.irs.ustreas.gov/basic/tax_edu/teletax/tc404.html.

For more mutual fund tax strategies, see the following online sources:

✔ **Mosaic Funds** (www.fitfund.com/taxtips.htm): "Nine Tax Tips for Mutual Fund Investors" provides many suggestions that can help you reduce your taxes.

✔ **Personal Finance** (detnews.com/menu/stories/39404.htm): "Personal Finance: Deduct Cost From Mutual Fund Gain at Tax Time" is an informative article that can assist you in keeping as much of your mutual fund returns as possible.

How Tax-Exempt Are Those Bonds Anyway?

Tax-exempt municipal bonds are debt instruments issued by states, cities, counties, and other government entities to raise money for public projects. In some situations, bonds are totally tax-free. For example, interest on state and municipal bonds isn't subject to federal taxes because the government doesn't want to tax what it borrows. Income from state and municipal bonds, therefore, is tax-exempt, and investors keep more of what they earn.

In the past, Alaska, Florida, Indiana, Nebraska, Nevada, New Mexico, South Dakota, Texas, Utah, Vermont, Washington, Wyoming, and Washington, D.C. have exempted interest from bonds issued by other states, as well as their own bonds, from their income tax. For details, see State Taxation of Municipal Bonds for Individuals at www.pas.com.

In some situations, you have to pay taxes on your state and municipal bonds. For example, you may generate capital gains on a tax-exempt security if you sell it at a profit in the secondary market (NYSE, NASDAQ, and so on) before it matures. The maximum tax rate is 28 percent. If you sell the bond at a loss (less than your original purchase price), you can claim up to $3,000 in net capital losses per year. If your losses exceed $3,000, the IRS allows you to carry them over to subsequent tax years. Check with your broker for details.

For additional online sources of nontaxable or partly taxable income, see the Quicken Web site at www.intuit.com/turbotax/taxcenter/perguide/checknon.html. This site provides a checklist of nontaxable income.

Tax Savings, Education, and Savings Bonds

You can purchase savings bonds by mail from your local Federal Reserve Bank, at savings institutions, or through your employer's payroll deduction plan. Treasury securities are risk-free because they're obligations of the federal government.

Savings bonds are good intermediate- to long-term investments. The return on savings bonds is generally higher than the return on savings accounts. You can cash the bonds at any bank in the U.S., but the return is higher if you hold the bonds until maturity.

Income from savings bonds is exempt from state and local taxes if you use the bond to pay for higher education. However, to qualify for this exemption, the bond must be in the taxpayer's name, and the taxpayer's adjusted gross income (which must include the interest earned on redeemed savings bonds) must be under certain limits in the year the bonds are redeemed.

For additional information, see the Department of Public Debt at www.publicdebt.treas.gov/sav/saveduca.htm.

Finding Online Information about Capital Gains Taxes

A *capital gain* is when you sell a security for a profit. Specifically, it's the difference between the net sales price of a security and its net cost (or original price). If you sell a stock below cost, the difference is a *capital loss*. The capital gains tax rates are based on your personal tax bracket and how long you hold an asset before you sell it. The holding period of the asset falls into one of the following categories:

✔ **Short-term:** Less than 12 months

✔ **Medium term:** More than 12 months and less than 18 months

> ✔ **Long-term:** More than 18 months and less than 60 months
>
> ✔ **Ultra-long-term:** More than 60 months

Table 20-1 illustrates the interrelationship between your personal tax bracket and the holding period of the asset.

Table 20-1 Your Personal Tax Bracket, Time, and Your Tax Liability				
Personal Tax Bracket	Short-Term Rate	Medium-Term Rate	Long-Term Rate	Ultra-Long-Term Rate
15%	15%	15%	10%	8%
28%	28%	28%	20%	18%
31%	31%	28%	20%	18%
36%	36%	28%	20%	18%
39.6%	39.6%	28%	20%	18%

Table 20-1 shows the many factors that are used to calculate your capital gains tax. For example, for most people with long-term investments (assets that you hold for at least 18 months), the maximum capital gains tax rate is 20 percent (it was 28 percent). If you sell your asset before that time, the tax rate is higher. For people in the 15 percent tax bracket, the capital gains tax rate is 10 percent. These rates are effective for all sales (including installment payments) made after May 6, 1997.

Here are some helpful online sources for information about the capital gains tax laws:

> ✔ **American Association of Individual Investors** (www.aaii.org/promos/hpa971124.shtml) has information about the ramifications of the new capital gains tax laws.
>
> ✔ **Deloitte & Touche LLP** (www.dtonline.com/promises/cover.htm) has tips and strategies for capital gains planning.
>
> ✔ **Excite Quicken Com Message Boards** (boards.excite.com/go.webx/13@-d^62419@eeca058) has a forum to discuss capital gains on rental property and other issues related to changes in the tax code.
>
> ✔ **H&R Block** (www.handrblock.com/tax/tip/capgain.html) provides some online tips about the new capital gains laws.
>
> ✔ **MSN Money Insider** (moneyinsider.msn.com/content/takingcharge/taxes/TaxS8.htm) has additional information on the new capital gains tax laws.
>
> ✔ **Quicken.com Taxes** (www.quicken.com/taxes/articles/878683196_19075) provides answers to frequently asked questions about the new capital gains tax laws.

Which Type of IRA Is Best for You?

New IRA tax laws went into effect on December 31, 1997. These laws permit greater flexibility in traditional IRAs as well as higher income limits. The new Roth IRA provides some additional benefits. The following Internet sources offer IRA information:

- **Deloitte & Touch LLP** (www.dtonline.com/promises.cover.htm) provides help interpreting the IRS tax language with a summary of the new tax laws. The summary is illustrated with charts and graphs. Suggested action steps that you may want to consider follow each tax law change.

- **Ernst & Young** provides many tax tips for taxpayers at www.ey.com/tax/tips.htm. The suggestions include common errors to avoid, deductions you may not have included, and strategies to help you reduce your tax liability.

- **Essential Links** (www.elinks.com) provides online resources for taxpayer tips and information on income tax preparation assistance, rules, tax codes, financial planners, tax preparers, forms (from W-2 to Form 1040), publications, instructions, deductions, and more.

- **Frank McNeil's Web Site** (www2.best.com/%7eftnexpat/html/tazsites.html) can assist you in completing your income tax return correctly. This site offers links to news, articles, newsletters, government agencies, accountants, software providers, and more.

Finding Internet Sources for Information on Tax-Sheltered Investments

A *tax shelter* is designed to reduce or avoid federal income taxes. Tax shelters are often sold to high-income investors. Use of a tax shelter can often offset the purchase price of the tax shelter by many times. Here are a few examples of legal tax shelters:

- **Real estate:** If the project breaks even or loses money, you may still be ahead because the depreciation reduces your taxable income.

- **Equipment leasing programs:** These programs often offer tax savings by accelerating the depreciation of the equipment.

- **Oil and gas:** With oil and gas, you can frequently deduct the cost of capital expenditures for intangible drilling and development costs.

- **Cattle feeding and breeding programs:** These programs can offer tax savings by accelerating the deductions.

For more online information about legal tax shelters, check out the following resources:

- ✔ **Quicken's Legal Tax Shelters** (`www.intuit.com/turbotax/ taxcenter/perguide/taxshelt.html`) can help you understand legal tax shelters. You can start at Intuit's home page (`www.intuit.com`), click on the Turbo Tax icon, and then click on Tax Center. The tax center includes many informative articles on tax shelters.

- ✔ **The Tax Library: 101 Perfectly Legal Tax Wise Strategies** (`www.cyberhaven.com/taxtips`) provides asset protection plans, tax tips for your investments, and more.

- ✔ **MSN's Money Insider** (`www.moneyinsider.msn.com/content/ takingcharge/taxes/index.htm`) provides helpful advice about the benefits of tax shelters and the questionable usefulness of unprofitable tax shelters.

For more expert advice on tax shelters and an online tax guide, try *J.K. Lasser's Your Income Tax* at `mcp.com/mgr.lasser`. This guide has timely, expert advice that you may find invaluable. You can view the book online chapter by chapter by using Adobe Acrobat Reader.

Appendix

About the CD

H ere's what you can find on the *Investing Online For Dummies* CD-ROM:

- An easy-to-navigate, electronic version of the book's Internet Directory so that you can quickly jump to the Internet sites that offer the tools you need for selecting, buying, selling, and tracking your investments online
- Shareware and freeware programs for financial planning and analysis, portfolio management, and other essential investor tasks
- Demonstration versions of invaluable software tools for online investors

System Requirements

Make sure your computer meets the following minimum system requirements:

- A PC with a 486 or faster processor, or a Mac OS computer with a 68030 or faster processor.
- Microsoft Windows 3.1 or later, or Mac OS system software 7.5 or later.
- At least 8MB of total RAM. For best performance, Windows 95-equipped PCs and Mac OS computers with PowerPC processors should have at least 16MB of RAM installed.
- At least 100MB of hard drive space available to install all the software from this CD. (You need less space if you don't install every program.)
- A CD-ROM drive — double-speed (2x) or faster.
- A sound card for PCs. (Mac OS computers have built-in sound support.)
- A monitor capable of displaying at least 256 colors or grayscale.
- A modem with a speed of at least 14.4 Kbps (28.8 Kbps preferred).

If your computer doesn't match up to most of these requirements, you may have problems in using the contents of the CD.

If you need more information on the basics, check out *PCs For Dummies,* 5th Edition, by Dan Gookin; *Macs For Dummies,* 5th Edition by David Pogue; *Windows 95 For Dummies,* 2nd Edition, by Andy Rathbone; or *Windows 3.11 For Dummies,* 4th Edition, by Andy Rathbone (all published by IDG Books Worldwide, Inc.).

How to Use the CD Using Microsoft Windows

To install the items from the CD to your hard drive, follow these steps:

1. **Insert the CD into your computer's CD-ROM drive.**

2. **Windows 3.1 or 3.11 users: From Program Manager, choose File⇨Run.**

   Windows 95 users: Click the Start button and click Run.

3. **In the dialog box that appears, type** D:\SETUP.EXE.

   Note: In the preceding command, substitute the appropriate letter if your CD-ROM drive letter differs from D:.

4. **Click OK.**

   A license agreement window appears.

5. **Read through the license agreement, nod your head, and then click the Accept button.**

   After you click Accept, you'll never be bothered by the License Agreement window again. The CD interface appears. This little program shows you what's on the CD and coordinates installing the programs and running the demos. The CD interface lets you click a button or two to make things happen. The first screen you see is the Welcome screen.

6. **Click anywhere on this screen to enter the CD interface.**

   Now you're getting to the action. The next screen lists categories for the software on the CD.

7. **To view the items within a category, just click on the category's name.**

   A list of programs in the category appears.

8. **For more information about a program, click on the program's name.**

   Be sure to read the information that's displayed. Some programs may require you to do a few tricks on your computer first, and this screen tells you where to go for that information, if necessary.

9. **To install the program, click on the appropriate Install button. If you don't want to install the program, click on the Go Back button to return to the previous screen.**

   You can always return to the previous screen by clicking on the Go Back button. You can browse the different categories and products and decide what you want to install.

   After you click on an Install button, the CD interface drops to the background while the CD begins installation of the program you chose.

10. **To install other items, repeat Steps 7, 8, and 9.**

11. **When you're done installing programs, click on the Quit button to close the interface.**

    You can eject the CD now. Carefully place it back in the plastic jacket of the book for safekeeping.

To run some of the programs, you may need to keep the CD inside your CD-ROM drive. This is a Good Thing. Otherwise, the installed program would have required you to install a very large chunk of the program to your hard drive space, which may keep you from installing other software.

How to Use the CD Using the Mac OS

To install the items from the CD to your hard drive, follow these steps:

1. **Insert the CD into your computer's CD-ROM drive.**

   An icon representing the CD appears on your Mac desktop. Chances are, the icon looks like a CD-ROM.

2. **Double-click on the CD icon to show the CD's contents.**

3. **Double-click on the Read Me First icon.**

   This text file contains information about the CD's programs and any last-minute instructions you need to know about installing the programs on the CD that I don't cover in this appendix.

4. **To install the software on this CD, just drag the program's folder from the CD window and drop it on your hard drive icon.**

   After you install the programs that you want, you can eject the CD. Carefully place it back in the plastic jacket of the book for safekeeping.

What You'll Find

Here's a summary of the software on this book's companion CD. If you use Windows, the CD interface helps you install software easily. (If you have no idea what I'm talking about when I say "CD interface," flip back a page or two to find the section, "How to Use the CD Using Microsoft Windows.") If you use a Mac OS computer, you can enjoy the ease of the Mac interface to quickly install the programs.

Shareware and freeware investor programs

The Internet provides many downloadable shareware and freeware financial programs for PC and Macintosh computers. Here's a quick rundown on the shareware and freeware investor programs you can find on the *Investing Online For Dummies* companion CD-ROM (along with the addresses of the Web sites for these programs):

- ✔ **Tradex:** Tradex is a Macintosh demo program for technical analysis and portfolio management. (www.ilanga.com/ilanga/index.html)

- ✔ **Financial Authority for Windows:** A program that tracks loans, annuities, your retirement savings, Series EEE bond appreciation, mutual fund performance, and more. (www.halcyon.com/cbutton/welcome)

- ✔ **Market Watcher for Windows:** An Internet-based, interactive program for tracking your portfolio. (www.marketwatcher.com)

- ✔ **NetStock:** A fast, easy way to keep track of your stocks and mutual fund investments via the Internet. (www.splitcycle.com/pages/netstock.html)

- ✔ **Personal Stock Monitor:** A portfolio management program that retrieves stock quotes from various free online quote servers. (www.personaltools.com)

- ✔ **Stock Smart:** If you want research investment information, this is the program for you. This program is actually a set of HTML pages that demonstrate how you can use the Stock Smart Web site to update stock info. **Windows 3.1 users:** The HTML files all have long filenames; therefore, you won't be able to access the pages from the CD. But you can certainly check out the Stock Smart Web site on the Web. (www.stocksmart.com)

- ✔ **StockTracker:** Portfolio management program that helps you stay on top of your investments by linking you to online trading through Wall Street Access. (www.stockcenter.com)

✔ **The Wall Street Analyst SE:** Beginning investor's freeware version of a more advanced investment analysis program. *Note:* When you run Wall Street Analyst SE for the first time, you need to call Omega Research (800-422-8587) to get an access code to unlock the program. (www.omegaresearch.com)

Investor demonstration programs

The Internet provides many downloadable demonstration programs for PC and Macintosh computers. These demonstration programs are often just like the full editions but they have a limited life. You can find the following demo programs on the *Investing Online For Dummies* companion CD-ROM:

✔ **Capital Gainz for Windows:** A terrific program for handling stocks, bonds, and mutual funds. Record your purchases, sales, dividends, capital gains, and other transactions. Calculate your gains or losses, and print reports and tax forms. (www.quoteline.com)

✔ **First Finance:** Software for financial planning and financial management calculations. (www.what.com/firstfin)

✔ **Fund Manager:** Portfolio management program that's useful for stocks but is especially well suited for managing your mutual funds portfolio. (www.aaii.org/dload/archive)

✔ **Investor's Advantage:** Investment analysis software for stocks, commodities, mutual funds, options, and market indexes. This program has a self extractor that places all the setup files onto a default directory on your computer and then runs the setup routine. **Windows 3.1 users:** The default directory for the self extractor may be C:\DOS or C:\WINDOWS. You may want to extract the program files to a folder for temp files rather than allow the files to be placed in a DOS or WINDOWS directory. You can change the destination directory in the Self Extractor dialog box, even directing the self extractor to place the files in a folder that doesn't yet exist. The self extractor will then create the folder and place the files there. (www.sacc.com)

✔ **MetaStock:** Sophisticated investment analysis software. (www.metastock.com)

✔ **StockVue:** Track financial information on the Internet with Stock Vue. (www.stockvue.com)

The Links page

Links.htm is an HTML page that you can open in your Web browser and have point and click access to all of the Web sites listed in the Directory section of this book. To view the Links page, open your Web browser and use the File⇨Open File command to open the Links.htm document from the LINKS folder on the CD-ROM. Click on Go Back to return to the previous screen.

If You've Got Problems (Of the CD Kind)

I tried my best to compile programs that work on most computers with the minimum system requirements. Alas, your computer may differ, and some programs may not work properly for some reason.

The two likeliest problems are that you don't have enough memory (RAM) for the programs you want to use, or you have other programs running that are affecting installation or running of a program. If you get error messages like `Not enough memory` or `Setup cannot continue`, try one or more of these methods and then try using the software again:

- ✔ Turn off any anti-virus software that you have on your computer. Installers sometimes mimic virus activity and may make your computer incorrectly believe that it is being infected by a virus.

- ✔ Close all running programs. The more programs you're running, the less memory is available to other programs. Installers also typically update files and programs. So if you keep other programs running, installation may not work properly.

- ✔ Have your local computer store add more RAM to your computer.

If you still have trouble with installing the items from the CD, please call the IDG Books Worldwide Customer Service phone number: 800-762-2974 (outside the U.S.: 317-596-5430).

Index

• J •

• K •

Notes

Notes

IDG Books Worldwide, Inc., End-User License Agreement

READ THIS. You should carefully read these terms and conditions before opening the software packet(s) included with this book ("Book"). This is a license agreement ("Agreement") between you and IDG Books Worldwide, Inc. ("IDGB"). By opening the accompanying software packet(s), you acknowledge that you have read and accept the following terms and conditions. If you do not agree and do not want to be bound by such terms and conditions, promptly return the Book and the unopened software packet(s) to the place you obtained them for a full refund.

1. **License Grant.** IDGB grants to you (either an individual or entity) a nonexclusive license to use one copy of the enclosed software program(s) (collectively, the "Software") solely for your own personal or business purposes on a single computer (whether a standard computer or a workstation component of a multiuser network). The Software is in use on a computer when it is loaded into temporary memory (RAM) or installed into permanent memory (hard disk, CD-ROM, or other storage device). IDGB reserves all rights not expressly granted herein.

2. **Ownership.** IDGB is the owner of all right, title, and interest, including copyright, in and to the compilation of the Software recorded on the disk(s) or CD-ROM ("Software Media"). Copyright to the individual programs recorded on the Software Media is owned by the author or other authorized copyright owner of each program. Ownership of the Software and all proprietary rights relating thereto remain with IDGB and its licensers.

3. **Restrictions on Use and Transfer.**

   (a) You may only (i) make one copy of the Software for backup or archival purposes, or (ii) transfer the Software to a single hard disk, provided that you keep the original for backup or archival purposes. You may not (i) rent or lease the Software, (ii) copy or reproduce the Software through a LAN or other network system or through any computer subscriber system or bulletin-board system, or (iii) modify, adapt, or create derivative works based on the Software.

   (b) You may not reverse engineer, decompile, or disassemble the Software. You may transfer the Software and user documentation on a permanent basis, provided that the transferee agrees to accept the terms and conditions of this Agreement and you retain no copies. If the Software is an update or has been updated, any transfer must include the most recent update and all prior versions.

4. **Restrictions on Use of Individual Programs.** You must follow the individual requirements and restrictions detailed for each individual program in the "About the CD" appendix of this Book. These limitations are also contained in the individual license agreements recorded on the Software Media. These limitations may include a requirement that after using the program for a specified period of time, the user must pay a registration fee or discontinue use. By opening the Software packet(s), you will be agreeing to abide by the licenses and restrictions for these individual programs that are detailed in the "About the CD" appendix and on the Software Media. None of the material on this Software Media or listed in this Book may ever be redistributed, in original or modified form, for commercial purposes.

5. **Limited Warranty.**

   (a) IDGB warrants that the Software and Software Media are free from defects in materials and workmanship under normal use for a period of sixty (60) days from the date of purchase of this Book. If IDGB receives notification within the warranty period of defects in materials or workmanship, IDGB will replace the defective Software Media.

   (b) **IDGB AND THE AUTHOR OF THE BOOK DISCLAIM ALL OTHER WARRANTIES, EXPRESS OR IMPLIED, INCLUDING WITHOUT LIMITATION IMPLIED WARRANTIES OF MER-CHANTABILITY AND FITNESS FOR A PARTICULAR PURPOSE, WITH RESPECT TO THE SOFTWARE, THE PROGRAMS, THE SOURCE CODE CONTAINED THEREIN, AND/OR THE TECHNIQUES DESCRIBED IN THIS BOOK. IDGB DOES NOT WARRANT THAT THE FUNCTIONS CONTAINED IN THE SOFTWARE WILL MEET YOUR REQUIREMENTS OR THAT THE OPERATION OF THE SOFTWARE WILL BE ERROR FREE.**

   (c) This limited warranty gives you specific legal rights, and you may have other rights that vary from jurisdiction to jurisdiction.

6. **Remedies.**

   (a) IDGB's entire liability and your exclusive remedy for defects in materials and workmanship shall be limited to replacement of the Software Media, which may be returned to IDGB with a copy of your receipt at the following address: Software Media Fulfillment Department, Attn.: *Investing Online For Dummies,* IDG Books Worldwide, Inc., 7260 Shadeland Station, Ste. 100, Indianapolis, IN 46256, or call 800-762-2974. Please allow three to four weeks for delivery. This Limited Warranty is void if failure of the Software Media has resulted from accident, abuse, or misapplication. Any replacement Software Media will be warranted for the remainder of the original warranty period or thirty (30) days, whichever is longer.

   (b) In no event shall IDGB or the author be liable for any damages whatsoever (including without limitation damages for loss of business profits, business interruption, loss of business information, or any other pecuniary loss) arising from the use of or inability to use the Book or the Software, even if IDGB has been advised of the possibility of such damages.

   (c) Because some jurisdictions do not allow the exclusion or limitation of liability for conse-quential or incidental damages, the above limitation or exclusion may not apply to you.

7. **U.S. Government Restricted Rights.** Use, duplication, or disclosure of the Software by the U.S. Government is subject to restrictions stated in paragraph (c)(1)(ii) of the Rights in Technical Data and Computer Software clause of DFARS 252.227-7013, and in subparagraphs (a) through (d) of the Commercial Computer–Restricted Rights clause at FAR 52.227-19, and in similar clauses in the NASA FAR supplement, when applicable.

8. **General.** This Agreement constitutes the entire understanding of the parties and revokes and supersedes all prior agreements, oral or written, between them and may not be modified or amended except in a writing signed by both parties hereto that specifically refers to this Agreement. This Agreement shall take precedence over any other documents that may be in conflict herewith. If any one or more provisions contained in this Agreement are held by any court or tribunal to be invalid, illegal, or otherwise unenforceable, each and every other provision shall remain in full force and effect.

Installation Instructions

* *

*T*he *Investing Online For Dummies* CD-ROM contains some of the most useful Internet investment software tools available for investors. Here's a quick overview of the tools you can install from the book's companion CD-ROM:

- ✔ An electronic version of the book's Internet Directory
- ✔ Shareware and freeware programs for financial planning and analysis, portfolio management, and other investor tasks
- ✔ Demonstration versions of software tools for online investors

For details about the contents of the CD-ROM and instructions for installing the software from the CD-ROM, see the "About the CD" appendix in this book.

WWW.DUMMIES.COM

Discover Dummies Online!

The Dummies Web Site is your fun and friendly online resource for the latest information about ...*For Dummies*® books and your favorite topics. The Web site is the place to communicate with us, exchange ideas with other ...*For Dummies* readers, chat with authors, and have fun!

Ten Fun and Useful Things You Can Do at www.dummies.com

1. Win free ...*For Dummies* books and more!
2. Register your book and be entered in a prize drawing.
3. Meet your favorite authors through the IDG Books Author Chat Series.
4. Exchange helpful information with other ...*For Dummies* readers.
5. Discover other great ...*For Dummies* books you must have!
6. Purchase Dummieswear™ exclusively from our Web site.
7. Buy ...*For Dummies* books online.
8. Talk to us. Make comments, ask questions, get answers!
9. Download free software.
10. Find additional useful resources from authors.

Link directly to these ten fun and useful things at
http://www.dummies.com/10useful

For other technology titles from IDG Books Worldwide, go to
www.idgbooks.com

Not on the Web yet? It's easy to get started with *Dummies 101*®: *The Internet For Windows*® *95* or *The Internet For Dummies*,® 4th Edition, at local retailers everywhere.

Find other ...*For Dummies* books on these topics:
Business • Career • Databases • Food & Beverage • Games • Gardening • Graphics • Hardware
Health & Fitness • Internet and the World Wide Web • Networking • Office Suites
Operating Systems • Personal Finance • Pets • Programming • Recreation • Sports
Spreadsheets • Teacher Resources • Test Prep • Word Processing

IDG BOOKS WORLDWIDE
BOOK REGISTRATION

Register This Book and Win!

We want to hear from you!

Visit **http://my2cents.dummies.com** to register this book and tell us how you liked it!

- Get entered in our monthly prize giveaway.
- Give us feedback about this book — tell us what you like best, what you like least, or maybe what you'd like to ask the author and us to change!
- Let us know any other *...For Dummies*® topics that interest you.

Your feedback helps us determine what books to publish, tells us what coverage to add as we revise our books, and lets us know whether we're meeting your needs as a *...For Dummies* reader. You're our most valuable resource, and what you have to say is important to us!

Not on the Web yet? It's easy to get started with *Dummies 101*®: *The Internet For Windows*® 95 or *The Internet For Dummies*®, 4th Edition, at local retailers everywhere.

Or let us know what you think by sending us a letter at the following address:

...For Dummies Book Registration
Dummies Press
7260 Shadeland Station, Suite 100
Indianapolis, IN 46256-3945
Fax 317-596-5498

BUSINESS AND
GENERAL
REFERENCE
BOOK SERIES
FROM IDG

COMPUTER
BOOK SERIES
FROM IDG